ACADEMY OF SCIENCES OF THE CZECH REPUBLIC
CHARLES UNIVERSITY, FACULTY OF ARTS, CZECH INSTITUTE OF EGYPTOLOGY

Forgotten Pharaohs, Lost Pyramids

ABUSIR

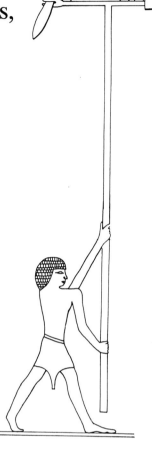

Forgotten Pharaohs,
Lost Pyramids

ABUSIR

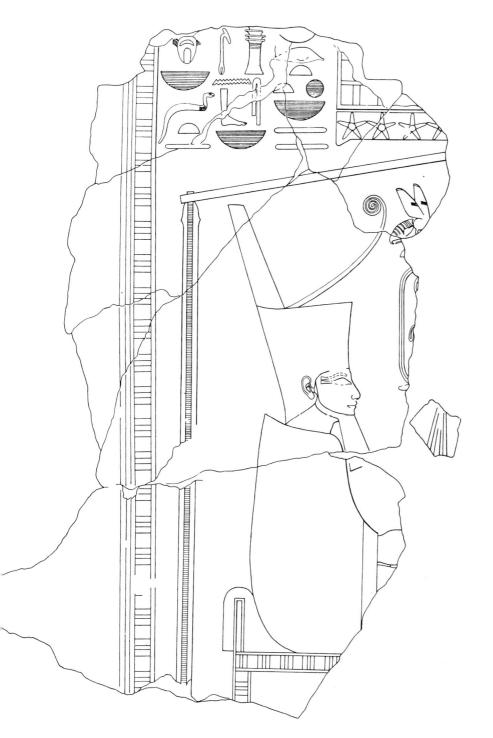

by MIROSLAV VERNER

Photographs by
MILAN ZEMINA

ACADEMIA
ŠKODAEXPORT

PRAHA 1994

© Miroslav Verner, 1994
Photography © Milan Zemina, 1994
Translation © Anna Bryson, Jana Klepetářová, 1994
ISBN 80-200-0022-4

This book, "Forgotten Pharaohs, Lost Pyramids. Abusir", is not intended as a general account of either Egyptian history or the history of Egyptology. It is devoted to only one of Egypt's many archaeological localities — to its once famous monuments and the historical figures associated with them. It is dedicated to Abusir as both an archaeological locality and as one exciting chapter in the history of Egyptian archaeology. The book is arranged in such a way as to present Abusir and its most important monuments in the context of the Memphite necropolis as a whole, and at the same time to lay emphasis on the major archaeological finds of the expedition of the Czech Institute of Egyptology at Charles University. The archaeological antiquities discovered are opening up new and previously unknown chapters of Egyptian history, particularly from the period of the Old Kingdom, while also making valuable contributions to areas of established study and deepening understanding of the broader historical context of knowledge already gained.

The first chapter, "In the Shadow of Memphis", seeks to introduce the reader, on a very general level, to the history and topography of the oldest capital city of Ancient Egypt and the great royal cemeteries with the pyramids that were gradually established on its western margins on the edge of the desert.

The second chapter, "Abusir — the Destiny of One Cemetery", focusses attention on one of these pyramid cemeteries, an area that has until recently received less than its fair share of archaeological interest; this is the pyramid field at Abusir and its most important monuments.

The third chapter, "Under the Sign of the Sun", gives the reader a very general account of the basic conceptual and historical framework of the epoch that saw the greatest flowering of the solar cult, and also of the Abusir cemetery in the course of the 5th Dynasty.

The fourth chapter, "The Royal Mother", concerns the complex historical problem represented by the fall of the 4th Dynasty and rise of the 5th Dynasty; it explores the role played in these events by the royal mother Khentkaus, who bore a title, "Mother of the King of Upper and Lower Egypt (exercising office as) King of Upper and Lower Egypt", which so far seems to have been unique in Egyptian history.

The fifth chapter, "The Secret of the Unfinished Pyramid", describes the circumstances of what has been, up to now, the most important discovery made by the Czech Egyptological expedition during its excavations at Abusir: the discovery of the pyramid complex of the previously almost unknown pharaoh Raneferef.

The sixth chapter, "The Testimony of the Papyrus Archives", discusses the unique discovery of the papyrus archives of the Abusir pyramid temples. These papyri represent the earliest written records of their type yet to have been found in Egypt. Although the papyri are very difficult to read and to interpret, their historical value is immense. They provide us with an opportunity to gain a detailed picture of the organisation of royal mortuary cults and to gain insight into state administration in general in the period of the Old Kingdom. Their relatively detailed testimony concerning the Abusir necropolis and the monuments existing there at the time when the papyrus archives were established, is opening up unexpected and fascinating new possibilities for archaeological research in this locality.

The following chapter, "The Dazzling Career of the Royal Hairdresser", looks at research on the grand tomb of the vizier Ptahshepses, considering both the circumstances of its archaeological excavation and the wider historical context and implications of the finds at this monument to one of the major protagonists in the historical events of the 5th Dynasty.

The penultimate chapter, "The Traitor's Tomb?", concerns the find of a previously unknown cemetery dating from the Saite-Persian period on the south-west edge of the Abusir cemetery; it focusses on the surprise find of the huge shaft tomb of one of the highest state officials of the Egypt of that time — Udjahorresnet, whose name is linked to the end of Egyptian independence and the beginning of Persian domination.

The concluding chapter offers a brief overview of the archaeological researches which have been undertaken at the Abusir Cemetery from the beginning of the nineteenth century up to the present day.

The book is accompanied by a list of the Czech archaeological expeditions to Abusir to date, a select bibliography of publications relating to excavations at Abusir,
a chronological table, list of illustrations and detailed index of proper names, places and subjects.

Preface

In Egypt today there are several dozen villages called Abusir. Only one of them, however, can boast an archaeological site of the first importance: this is the Abusir near which lies the cemetery dominated by the pyramids of the 5th-Dynasty pharaohs. But although situated in the very centre of the renowned pyramid fields of the Memphite Necropolis, which is one of the most important concentrations of antiquities in the world, Abusir has always remained at the periphery of archaeological interest and in the shadow of its more attractive neighbours Saqqara and Giza. This is understandable. It is no disgrace to be overshadowed by the Great Pyramid, one of the Seven Wonders of the World, or by the Great Sphinx at Giza on one side and the Step Pyramid at Saqqara on the other. But what is more surprising than the relative lack of tourist interest, is the low level and especially the unsystematic character of archaeological attention to Abusir, at least until quite recently. One factor that has undoubtedly contributed to this lack of interest is the lamentable state of the major monuments of the Abusir cemetery — the pyramids of the 5th-Dynasty kings. Their casings ripped away, their cores crumbling, and for centuries plundered by thieves searching for treasure or at least for rare kinds of stone, the pyramids of Abusir today resemble uninviting heaps of rubble. The sand still mercifully covers some, at least, of the damage inflicted by man on the pyramids and on the temples and tombs that lie at their feet. Perhaps another factor contributing to the waning of interest in Abusir was the impact of the earlier excavations carried out there in the first years of this century by a German archaeological expedition. The breadth of these excavations and their outstanding quality for the period seemed to pre-empt further efforts. The Germans' brilliant and rapidly published results contributed to the spread of the idea that everything of archaeological importance and interest in the locality had already been thoroughly investigated. All in all, Abusir came to be generally regarded as an archaeologically exhausted and essentially uninteresting site.

Nevertheless, the results of the first Czech Egyptological project at Abusir, which involved excavations in the area of the great tomb of the vizier Ptashepses, were to indicate that the site has not yet yielded up all its secrets. The excavations in the great tomb, led by Zbyněk Žába, continued with some intervals throughout the 1960s and into the early 1970s; they were aimed at throwing light on social and economic conditions in the Egypt of the 5th dynasty. In the mid-1970s, however, when the Czechs gained a major archaeological concession giving them access to what had previously been archaeologically almost untouched territory, including the southern part of the Abusir pyramid field right down to the northern edge of the Saqqara cemetery, the overall conception and character of the excavations at Abusir changed fundamentally. The sheer extent of the concession made it possible and in fact essential to change the working methods and the archaeological research goals as they had been established up to that point. After all, it is at its southern margin that the Abusir cemetery meets the Early Dynastic royal necropolis in North Saqqara, the place where the first lines of the first great chapter of the historic age in Egypt were written. And it is here too that the cemetery touches the places which provided the setting for the no less splendid final chapter of the history of Pharaonic Egypt, in the Late and Ptolemaic Period. This was the era of the flowering of the cults of sacred animals which made North Saqqara, with its cemeteries of divine bulls, baboons, falcons and ibises, the religio-political centre of the Egypt of that period.

The financial resources of the Abusir expedition of the Czech Institute of Egyptology at Charles University were and continue to be very limited. They only allow for excavations of a much less extensive type than those carried out at the start of the century by the German archaeological expedition to Abusir. Moreover, since the beginning of the century there has been a fundamental change, and rightly so, in the conditions laid down by the

Egyptian authorities not only in relation to the conduct of excavations but for the security, restoration, reconstruction, and provision of public access to the antiquities discovered.

From the point of view of the Egyptian Antiquities Law the current Czech archaeological research work at Abusir has the most important status because it consists not only in "surveying" or "cleaning" but in "excavations". The long-term and systematic character of this research project need not be emphasised. It includes surface and geophysical surveying, geodetic measuring and cartographic work, special anthropological investigation, the reconstruction of selected monuments, and various other activities. The ongoing excavations are fundamentally extending and modifying our archaeological picture of Abusir. Previously unknown pyramids, temples, tombs and even entire large cemeteries have been discovered, all dating from different periods of Egyptian history. Newly discovered papyri from the Abusir temple archives have been deposited in the vaults of the Egyptian Museum at Cairo, and the most interesting and valuable archaeological finds from the new Abusir excavations have been exhibited at selected Egyptian museums. Research papers drawing on the newly discovered archaeological and epigraphic sources have been multiplying. This book aims to become one of the pieces which will gradually be put together to reveal the once lost but progressively rediscovered mosaic of the history of the royal cemetery at Abusir.

The book could never have been written without the support of leading representatives of the Egyptian Antiquities Organisation and without the unstinting co-operation of Egyptian colleagues and friends in the Saqqara Antiquities Inspectorate. To all these we offer much-deserved thanks.

* * *

The author is indebted to PhDr. Jiřina Růžová, Dr.Phil. Wolf B. Oerter, Miroslav Bárta, Jaromír Krejčí, Dušan Magdolen, Barbara Patočková and Květa Smoláriková for help in the preparation of this book for publication. The illustrative drawings were prepared in collaboration with Eng. Luděk Wellner, Miroslava Sodomková, Tomáš Kraus, and others.

Prague
10th August 1993

Miroslav Verner

The pharaoh Sahure, wearing the *atef*-crown, brings an offering to the goddess Bastet.
Low relief. Detail from the decoration of the king's mortuary temple at Abusir.

In the Shadow of Memphis

Flooded with sunlight, the landscape of the Nile valley appears as a network of irrigation canals interwoven with a many-coloured mosaic of fields, villages, gardens and palm groves. The area around the village of Mit Rahina, not far from the famous Step Pyramid at Saqqara, is no exception. At first sight there is almost nothing to suggest that it was here, almost within sight of the high-rise buildings of Cairo as they encroach ever further from the north, that Memphis, oldest of Egypt's capital cities, once lay. It was a city of temples, royal residences, palaces, monumental gates, luxurious houses, artisans' workshops, military establishments and storehouses. It was a city which at the height of its prosperity extended over an area of approximately 50 square kilometres, but which then vanished without trace. The efforts of the archaeologists who from the beginning of the last century have been attempting to unearth its secrets in some ways resemble the proverbial drop in the ocean, but they have nevertheless continued to bring us new discoveries and new knowledge. The history of the magnificent city has not been lost forever.

Meni, the legendary unifier of Egypt and founder of the 1st Dynasty, who is credited with the founding of Memphis, could scarcely have chosen a more suitable site on which to build a powerful administrative centre for the

View of Qom el-Fakhry. The older part of the complex of the Temple of Ptah is believed to lie under this hill. Mit Rahina.

View of Qom el-Nawa. Mit
Rahina.

newly established state. He selected a place on the southern bank of the Nile, almost at the point where the Nile valley spreads out into the Nile delta. Only a few kilometres to the north the Nile, whose river bed has shifted 3 kilometres to the east in the course of five thousand years, divides into the branches that create the basic shape of the spreading mouth of the delta. To the east and west the narrow valley with its confining rocky banks, and the widening plain of the delta, are surrounded by the immense desert. The city which Meni founded was called *Ineb-hedj*, "The White Wall", perhaps because of the white colour of its fortification walls, i.e. the ramparts of the stronghold that was at the same time the royal residence. The precise site of this historic centre of Memphis has not yet been located with any certainty although the latest British archaeological researches, using deep-hole drilling, have indicated that it could lie under the present-day village of Mit Rahina. The remains of "the White Wall" and of later Memphis lie under strata of Nile mud several metres deep.

It is believed that in addition to the

stronghold, Meni founded the temple of Ptah, the chief god of the new royal seat. The temple afterwards became one of the greatest in the land and was called *Hutka-ptah*, "the Temple of the Spirit of Ptah", in the later pronunciation, *Hikupta*. In its garbled and Graecized form it was the origin of

Ruins of the Columned Hall of the Temple of the God Ptah. Mit Rahina.

The god Ptah, Lord of Memphis. Detail of a sunken relief from the small Temple of Ptah of Ramesses II. Qom el-Rabiaa, Mit Rahina.

Plan of the parts of ancient
Memphis so far archaeologically investigated.
  1 Northern Enclosure
  2 Palace of Apries
  3 Ptah Enclosure
  4 Pylon and Hypostyle Hall
  5 Embalming House of
    Apis-Bulls
  6 Tombs of High Priests of
    Memphis
  7 Temple of Ramesses II.
  8 Temple of Hathor
  9 Museum with the colos-
    sus of Ramesses II.
 10 Temple of Ramesses II.
 11 Colossal Alabaster
    Sphinx (of Amenophis II.
    ?)
 12 Palace of Merenptah
 13 Water canal

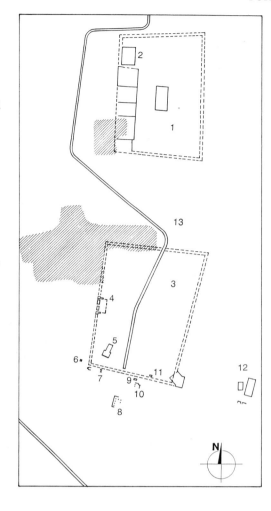

the name Egypt itself. It seems that every
Egyptian ruler considered it an obligation to
extend and augment the Temple of Ptah with
his own buildings, statues, obelisks and other
features. As in the case of the Temple of
Amon in Karnak, so in Memphis there
gradually emerged an enormous temple
complex, of which only a small part has so far
been discovered and archaeologically investigated. For much information about the
Temple of Ptah at Memphis we are indebted
to the Greek historian Herodotus who in the
5th century BC may actually have visited
Egypt. The ancient Egyptians regarded the
god Ptah as the god-creator and the patron
of builders and artisans. Ptah with his wife
the lion goddess Sakhmet and his son Nefer-
tem formed what is called the Divine Triad of
Memphis. There was later to develop a complete Memphite religious doctrine concerning the creation of the world and the Ogdoad
of gods whose basis was Ptah. A major contribution to the development of the Temple
of Ptah was made by Ramesses II, from
whose reign date a number of the parts of the
building which have so far been uncovered.
These include, for example, the hypostyle
hall and the South Gate, at which colossal
statues of the pharaoh once stood, accompanied by other figures. Extension of the
Temple of Ptah was still proceeding in the

Detail of the face of a colossal limestone statue of Ramesses II. The statue, which
once decorated one of the
entrances to the Temple of
Ptah, is now on display in
the small museum in Mit
Rahina.

Alabaster sphinx (Amen-
hotep II ?) which originally
adorned the southern ap-
proach to the Temple of
Ptah. Mit Rahina.

Alabaster embalming table. The so-called Embalming House of the Sacred Bulls of Apis from the reign of Sheshonq I. Mit Rahina.

Detail of a lion head from the decoration of one of the alabaster embalming tables of the sacred bulls of Apis in Mit Rahina.

Greek period under the rule of the Ptolemaic Dynasty. Besides Ptah and his triad other deities were worshipped in Memphis, first place among them being taken by Hathor, the goddess of love and beauty and guardian of the family. There were also non-Egyptian deities, whose cults were practised by the numerous foreigners living in Memphis. One important Memphis deity was the sacred bull Apis, regarded as the earthly incarnation of the god Ptah. His temple has not yet been discovered, but a building in which embalming and mummification ceremonies were carried out on the dead sacred bulls has been found. Enormous alabaster embalming tables decorated with lion figures had been preserved within it. The mummies of the sacred bulls were buried not far away in the underground catacombs of the Serapeum in North Saqqara.

The district of the Temple of Ptah constituted the Southern centre of Memphis. A second centre, lying a few kilometres to the north, was formed by the district of the Palace of Apries. Apries, the Egyptian equivalent of the Greek name being pronounced *Haaibre,* was one of the still relatively powerful pharaohs of the 26th Dynasty. In Memphis he built a fort with a rectangular ground plan and a massive enclosure wall. At the north-east corner of the fort, on a raised platform, he constructed a large palace. The platform and the major part of the other buildings making up the Apries Palace and the fort were built out of mudbricks. It is possible that this building material, which at the time of the destruction of the monuments attracted less interest than did the various kinds of stone, contributed to the survival of the ruins of the Apries Palace up to a height of approximately 10 metres. This means that today they are one of the highest places in

So-called Hathor capital. Temple of the Goddess Hathor built by Ramesses II. Qom el-Rabiaa, Mit Rahina.

Limestone fragments including palm column capitals. Palace of Apries, Mit Rahina.

Memphis. Looking westward from the top of the ruins there is an entirely unique panorama of the Memphite necropolis and the pyramids that dominate it.

From ancient Egyptian written materials we know that Memphis was the capital of Egypt throughout the entire period of the Old Kingdom and up to the 8th century, i.e. perhaps to the end of the third millenium BC. For a short time it also became the capital even under the New Kingdom, in the period after the foundering of Akhnaten's

Ruins of the Palace of Apries from the 26th Dynasty. Mit Rahina.

In the palm groves at Kazruni near Mit Rahina.

experiment in reform. Even in the periods when it was not the capital city it maintained an important status as an administrative and religious centre, especially of the northern and central parts of the country, and it continued to be the biggest city in Egypt. Its fame was only to dwindle definitively in the first centuries AD. The half-crumbled and deserted temples and palaces of Memphis were transformed into a large quarry from which building material could be cheaply obtained. After the occupation of Egypt by the army of Amr Ibn el-Aas in 641, the fortress of Fustat was built out of the ruins of Memphis on the site of the fallen Byzantine stronghold Babylon, a place that was to be the future site of the new capital city Cairo.

Research up to the present day has made it possible to identify more than one hundred archaeological locations in the area covered by ancient Memphis. So far, the oldest antiquities uncovered are the remains of a residential area and artisans' workshops dating from as early as the 1st Intermediate Period and beginning of the Middle Kingdom. They were discovered near the hillock Kom el-Fakhry to the south of what is be-

lieved to have been the southern, and at the period just mentioned also the main gate of the Temple of Ptah. So far, it has not proved possible to find monuments from the third millennium BC although there must once have been a very large number of these. The Old Kingdom, after all, which was the "era of the pyramid-builders", was the age of the greatest flowering of Memphis.

The monuments, undoubtedly very diverse, were located at city sites which were often quite distant from one another. Attached to them were groups of administrative and residential buildings which despite their peripheral position were very important. These grew up in the vicinity of the valley temples of the royal pyramid complexes on the edge of the desert. Some of these 'pyramid towns' temporarily acquired extraordinary importance. One example is the pyramid town beside the valley temple of Teti, first ruler of the 6th Dynasty, in North Saqqara. As far as its situation was concerned it was just a suburb a few kilometres from the Temple of Ptah, but for a certain time during the 1st Intermediate Period it became the politico-administrative centre of Egypt. Similarly, it is

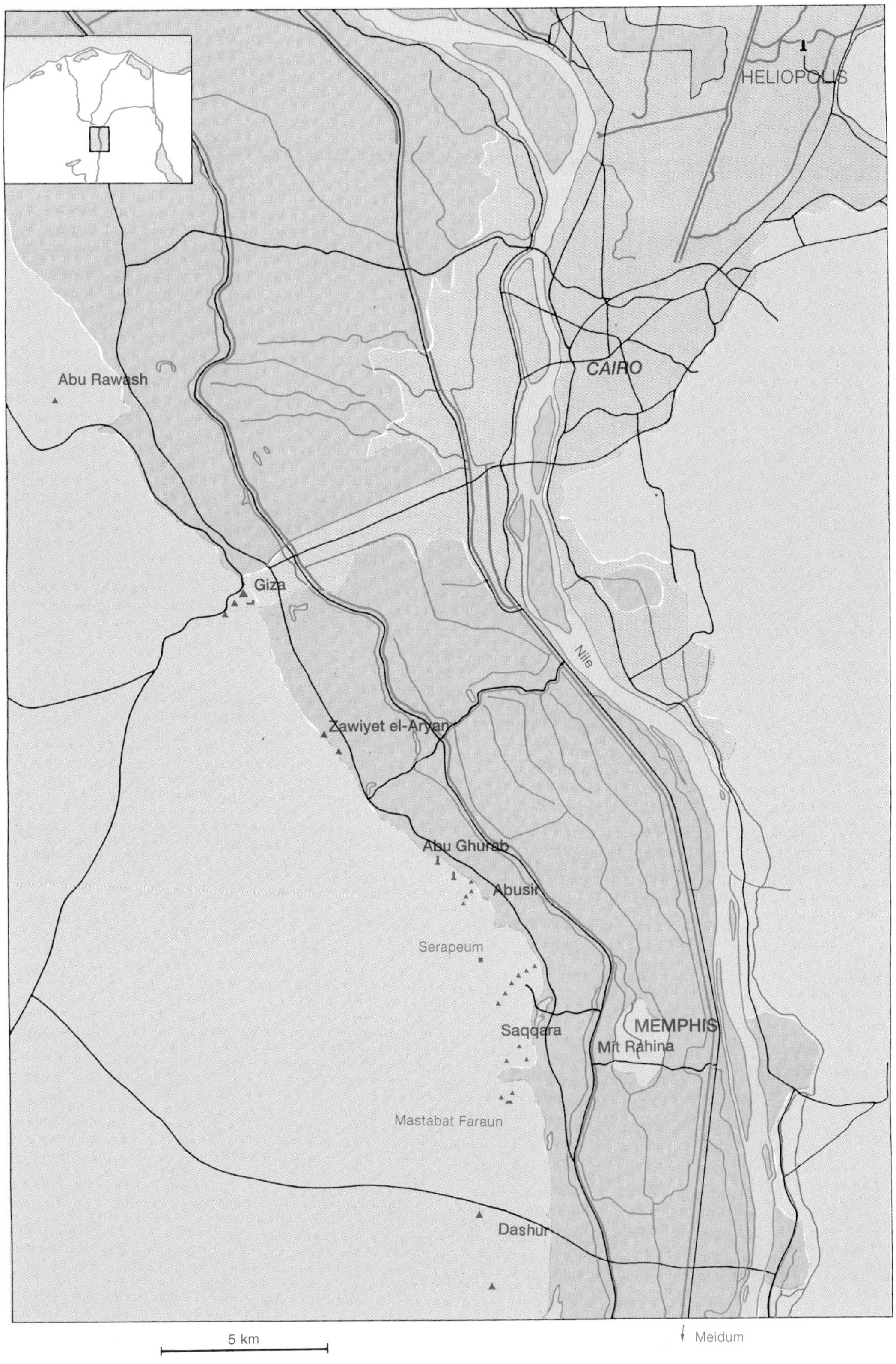

Detail of a map of Egypt showing the pyramid cemeteries of ancient Memphis.

HELIOPOLIS

Abu Rawash

CAIRO

Giza

Nile

Zawiyet el-Aryan

Abu Ghurab

Abusir

Serapeum

Saqqara

MEMPHIS

Mit Rahina

Mastabat Faraun

Dashur

5 km

Meidum

believed that at the end of the 6th Dynasty and especially at the beginning of the Middle Kingdom importance was acquired by that part of the capital which spread out in the environs of the valley temple of Pepi I, in what today is South Saqqara. The pyramid complex of Pepi I was called *Men-nefer-Pepi*, "The beauty of Pepi is enduring". The shortened form of this name, *Men-nefer*, in Greek "Memphis", began to be used to designate the whole capital city from the time of the Middle Kingdom. It is almost symbolic that it was a pyramid which gave the oldest of Egypt's capital cities its name. The destiny of Memphis — its rise, flowering and glory — was inextricably linked to the pyramids and the cemeteries lying at their feet. This relationship was aptly expressed by the Belgian Egyptologists Jean Capart and Marcelle Werbrouck when they entitled their book,

View of the pyramid fields
at Saqqara from the Palace
of Apries.

View of the pyramid fields at Saqqara from the Palace of Apries.

published in 1930, on the oldest capital of Egypt and the period of its greatest flowering, *Memphis à l'Ombre des Pyramides* — "Memphis in the Shadow of the Pyramids."

The royal pyramid cemeteries of former Memphis lie like a string of pearls along the western edge of the Nile valley from the borders of today's Cairo in the north, right down to Meidum at the entrance to the Fayyum oasis in the south. Here, in the places where the sun set and where began the limitless desert from which there was no return, lay the land of the dead — the empire of the god Osiris. The reasons why the ancient Egyptians buried the dead on the edge of the desert on the Western bank of the Nile are evident enough. The same, however, cannot be said of the reasons for their particular choice of sites for pyramid-building. Why, for example, did the founder of the 4th Dynasty, Sneferu, build his first pyramid at Meidum and then abandon the place, building another two of his pyramids approximately 50 kilometres further north at Dahshur? Why did his son Cheops build his tomb, the celebrated Great Pyramid, still further to the north, in Giza? Why did the last ruler of the 4th Dynasty, Shepseskaf, forsake the royal cemetery at Giza and, once again, select for his tomb a faraway site in a deserted spot at South Saqqara? The questions are numerous and,

as a rule, answers to them remain on the level of conjecture.

Some Egyptologists believe that the choice of site for the construction of pyramids was determined by the very practical consideration of proximity to limestone quarries, since this type of stone was the basic building material. The limestone in question was the lower-quality limestone which was to be found on the western bank of the Nile and was used particularly for the so-called 'core' of the pyramid, in contrast to the exterior casing for which it was necessary to transport fine white limestone all the way from the quarries in the hills of Moqattam on the opposite, eastern bank of the Nile. There is certainly some force in this theory. After all, limestone quarries have been discovered near many pyramids. Nevertheless, limestone occurs almost everywhere in the area of the Memphite necropolis and the technical difficulties involved in obtaining it and transporting it to the building site did not vary substantially between the different places chosen.

There is an alternative and quite widespread opinion, first expressed some time ago by the German Egyptologist Adolf Erman. In Erman's view a pyramid would be built in the vicinity of a pharaoh's residence, the location of which could change.

Saqqara in the grip of
a sandstorm.

The Early Dynastic Cemetery in North Saqqara.

Although the offices of the highest organs of state, including the royal palace, were situated in Memphis, the rulers would build their other residences outside the capital city, often with a view to some pressing political, economic or military state interests. One particular variant, or addition, to Erman's theory is represented by the opinion that a ruler would deliberately build his palace near the building site of his pyramid with the aim of being present and personally participating in decisions on the serious organisational matters of the greatest and most important state project of his time — the building of the pyramid. Unfortunately even in the case of Erman's theory we are dealing with pure conjecture, since as yet we have not managed to discover and archaeologically investigate a single one of the royal residences of the Old Kingdom.

The Early Dynastic royal cemetery in North Saqqara is the oldest in the Memphite necropolis. The British Egyptologist Walter Brian Emery, who carried out excavations here for many years, believed that the first rulers of a united Egypt, whose seat Memphis had become, were interred in this cemetery. His theory did not make headway and the prevailing view among Egyptologists is that the first rulers of a united Egypt, the pharaohs of the 1st Dynasty, were still being buried in the old royal cemetery of Upper Egypt at Abydos, at the place which natives of the region call Umm el-Qaab, "Mother of Potsherds". They believe the tombs in the Early Dynastic cemetery in North Saqqara to

be either cenotaphs, false tombs constructed as a symbol of a ruler's presence close to the new capital of the united Egypt, or, more probably, the tombs of the highest state officials and members of the royal family who held their posts in the newly founded capital Memphis. The Early Dynastic tombs in Saqqara take the form of mastabas (from the Arabic — *mastaba,* an elongated rectangular clay bench) of large dimensions. They were built of mudbricks and the outer surfaces of their walls, decorated with niches, were brightly painted to resemble a light construction of wooden poles and matting. The remains of rich burial equipment have been discovered in the underground chambers of several of these tombs.

The tombs of the rulers of the 2nd Dynasty, which for the most part have not yet been discovered, represent one of the greatest problems of Egyptian archaeology. It is believed that the majority of these were located in the Saqqara cemetery near the Step Pyramid. Two enormous underground galleries discovered to the south of the Step Pyramid's enclosure wall are considered to be the underground section of the tombs of the 2nd-Dynasty kings. The period when this dynasty governed was unsettled and the stability of united Egypt extremely fragile. There was probably even a breakdown in the unity of the country with consequent internal conflicts and the despoliation of the royal cemetery in Saqqara. Stabilisation of conditions was only achieved by the last 2nd-dynasty ruler Khasekhemui, whose tomb lies in Abydos but to whom is also attributed one of the two already mentioned underground galleries discovered south of the Step Pyramid at Saqqara.

The beginning of the 3rd Dynasty brought a fundamental innovation in the design of royal tombs. As a result the appearance of the royal cemeteries to the south of Memphis underwent a basic change. The founder of the dynasty Netjerykhet, later called Djoser, built his tomb in the Saqqara cemetery not far from the underground galleries of his predecessors of the 2nd Dynasty. Originally, the tomb took the form of a mastaba of relatively modest dimensions. In subsequent building phases, however, it was extended and remodelled as a six-stepped pyramid more than 60 metres in height and the first monument of its type. The architect of the Step Pyramid and a whole complex of other buildings of symbolic religious and cult

The Step Pyramid. Saqqara.

The monumental gate of
Djoser's pyramid complex.
Saqqara.

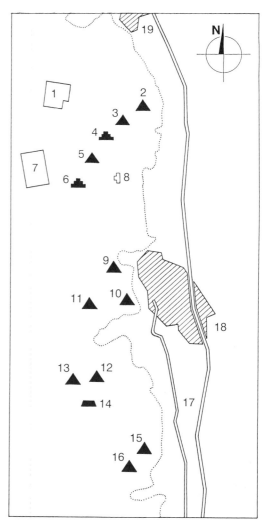

In Djoser's pyramid
complex.

Plan of the pyramid cemetery at Saqqara.
1 Serapeum, 2 Teti, 3 Userkaf, 4 Djoser, 5 Unas, 6 Sekhemkhet, 7 "Great Enclosure", 8 Monastery of Apa
Jeremias, 9 Pepi I., 10 Djedkare, 11 Merenre, 12 Ibi, 13 Pepi II., 14 Shepseskaf (Mastabat Fara'un),
15 Khendjer, 16 Pyramid of Dyn. XIII, 17 Water canals

North-south section of the
Step Pyramid
(by J-Ph. Lauer).

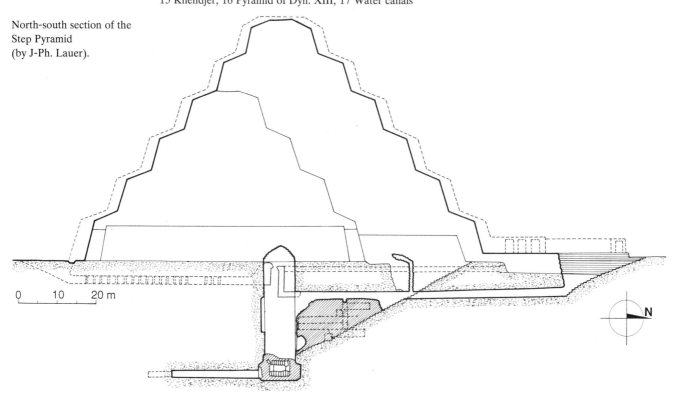

The undergound gallery leading from the south into the heart of the Step Pyramid was a later addition of the Saite Period.

significance was Imhotep, who was probably Djoser's son. Later generations venerated him as a sage and the son of the god Ptah. On an area 545 × 278 m Imhotep created a posthumous symbolic residence for the king, from which rose the Step Pyramid — a gigantic stairway by which Djoser's spirit would make its way heavenward. The whole complex of buildings, including a high enclosure wall, was built of shining white limestone. The pyramid could be seen from a distance and was more than just a tomb; it was the visible expression of the pharaoh's power. The Step Pyramid complex in Saqqara, which is considered the oldest work of monumental stone architecture, became a great source of inspiration for Djoser's

The statue of the pharaoh Djoser located in the *serdab* at the northern foot of the Step Pyramid is a copy; the original is in the Egyptian Museum in Cairo (JE no. 49158).

Model of Djoser's pyramid complex by J-Ph. Lauer.

Unfinished standing white-limestone statue of Djoser in the so-called court of the *sed*. Step Pyramid complex. Saqqara.

View of American and Egyptian excavations in South Giza. In the background is the silhouette of the unfinished 'Layer Pyramid' in Zawiyat el-Aryan.

successors. They too started to build their tombs in the form of pyramids. His immediate heirs, the 3rd-Dynasty rulers, built step pyramids. Djoser's successor Sekhemkhet began building his tomb immediately beside the Step Pyramid although he did not complete the task. Also unfinished was the pyramid of Khaba, who abandoned the cemetery in Saqqara and chose for his pyramid a place only a few kilometres to the north by what is today the village of Zawiyet el-Aryan. The tombs of the remaining few rulers of the 3rd Dynasty have yet to be discovered.

The last pyramid to be designed and built in step form lies approximately 60 kilometres to the east of Saqqara near the modern village of Meidum. The last ruler of the 3rd Dynasty, Huni, has sometimes been credited with initiating the building but archaeological finds have shown that it was the work of the 4th-Dynasty ruler Sneferu. Sneferu probably selected the site for the pyramid with a view to the strategic significance of the area in the Nile valley near to the entrance to the Fayyum Oasis. The pyramid was built first in seven and later in eight steps. For reasons that are not quite clear it was decided to change it into what is called a 'true' pyramid. Sneferu, however, was never buried in this pyramid even though a large cemetery containing the tombs of members of the ruling family was established around it. The German-American physicist Kurt Mendelssohn was

Field with *saqiya* in Saqqara.
The Step Pyramid rises in
the background.

Irrigation canal with water
buffalo. On the route from
Zawiyat el-Aryan to Abusir.

'Meidum geese' (detail).
Fragment of stucco painting.
4th Dynasty. Egyptian
Museum, Cairo.

Meidum geese.

Mastaba no.17. 4th Dynasty.
Meidum.

Cemetery at Meidum.

This statue of the seated prince Rahotep, son of the pharaoh Sneferu, was found at Meidum in 1871 together with a statue of the princess Nofret. Polychrome limestone, height 120 cm. Egyptian Museum in Cairo (CG. no. 3).

Princess Nofret, wife of Prince Rahotep. Polychrome limestone, height 118 cm. 4th Dynasty. Egyptian Museum in Cairo (CG 4).

pyramid's external casing. Although this theory sounds quite seductive archaeologists have rejected it and shown that the pyramid at Meidum, like many others, was gradually destroyed by the people who for centuries exploited it for stone just as if it were a quarry.

The reasons that led Sneferu to abandon the pyramid together with the residence and the town in its neighbourhood have not yet been explained. He chose a new site for pyramid construction approximately 50 km further to the north and near modern Dahshur. The pyramid that he decided to build in Dahshur was from the very beginning designed as a true pyramid. The chosen angle of inclination of the pyramid walls — 60 ° — proved in the course of construction to have been too

Detail of the partially restored facade of a mudbrick mastaba from the 4th Dynasty. Meidum.

Ruins of the mastaba of Rahotep. 4th Dynasty. Meidum.

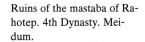

inspired by a visit to Meidum and a view of the peculiar configuration of the ruins of the pyramid to formulate an interesting theory. According to Mendelssohn a catastrophe must have occurred during the final stage of building and in the construction of the external casing, i.e. during the conversion of the step pyramid into a true pyramid. Wrong calculations and faulty binding of the limestone blocks caused what is known as a "flowing effect" and the collapse of the

Ruins of Sneferu's pyramid at Meidum.

steep. At the same time the base on which the pyramid was built was not very stable. The problem was that the foundation was not rock but a compact gravel and sand layer which was unable to bear the pressure of the increasing mass of the pyramid. The walls of the burial chambers began to crack, not in the underground section but in the heart of the pyramid. For this reason it was decided to reduce the angle of inclination in the upper part of the pyramid and so considerably lessen the pressure on the inner chambers. As a result of this experimentation and improvisation the pyramid is today called the Bent or sometimes the Rhomboidal or Two-Slope Pyramid. It is unique among pyramids not only for its shape but also for its two entrances, from the north and the west, and the very unusual layout of its inner rooms.

Lake and pyramids at Dahshur viewed from the south-east.

Pyramids at Dahshur viewed
from South Saqqara.

East-west and north-south
section of the Bent Pyramid
(by A. Fakhry).

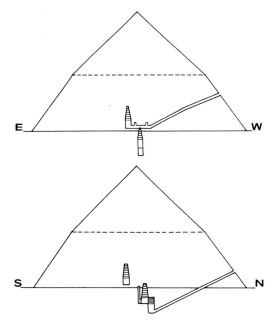

It was undoubtedly as a result of the complications during the construction of the Bent Pyramid and in view of the impaired stability of its inner chambers that work was started, a little way away, on building another pyramid for Sneferu with a relatively small angle of inclination for the outer wall. This is today named the Red Pyramid after the colour of the stone of which it was built. It was probably in this pyramid that Sneferu was buried. In the environs of both of the Dahshur pyramids a new cemetery was established containing the tombs of other members of the royal family and high state officials.

It seems incredible that Sneferu had yet another pyramid built, although this was much smaller than the preceding ones. It stands in Seila, perhaps 10 km west of the Meidum pyramid and on a small hill overlooking the depression of the Fayyum Oasis. This pyramid had no inner or underground chambers and was not planned as a tomb but probably simply as a symbol of royal power. The total volume of masonry for all of Sneferu's pyramids amounts to approximately 3.6 million m³, a building record which none of the Egyptian pharoahs were ever to overtake. The technical, organisational and administrative significance of this figure can be fully grasped only when we remember

The Red Pyramid. Dahshur.

The Bent Pyramid. Dahshur.

Sneferu's Pyramid at Seila.

Irrigation canal near Giza.

that in Sneferu's time the whole of Egypt from the Mediterranean Sea to the first Nile cataract at Aswan had no more that 1 to 1.5 million inhabitants.

Whether because Dahshur was no longer a suitable place to build further great pyramids, or because the local limestone quarries did not meet requirements, or for other reasons, Sneferu's son Cheops decided to found a new cemetery at Giza, perhaps 30 km north from Dahshur. The site selected consisted of a rocky area on the easternmost promontory of the Libyan Desert above the Nile valley just where it begins to spread out into the broad delta. Cheops' pyramid measured about 230.4 m. along each side of

its square base. With a wall gradient of 52 ° it reached a height of 146.5 m. It is the largest of the Egyptian pyramids and is justly called the Great Pyramid and one of the Seven Wonders of the World. Its unique system of internal chambers, especially the so-called Great Gallery and King's Chamber, is from the point of view of construction one of the most ingenious ever created in Ancient Egypt. In volume the Great Pyramid is approximately 2.5 million m^3 and until recently it was believed to have been built with limestone quarried from the rocky massif near the site. The latest geophysical researches carried out by French scientists have shown, however, that the core of the Great Pyramid

Plan of the Giza necropolis (by G.A. Reisner).
1 Cheops
2 Chephren
3 Mycerinus
4 Khentkaus
5 Great Sphinx
6 West Field
7 East Field
8 Central Field

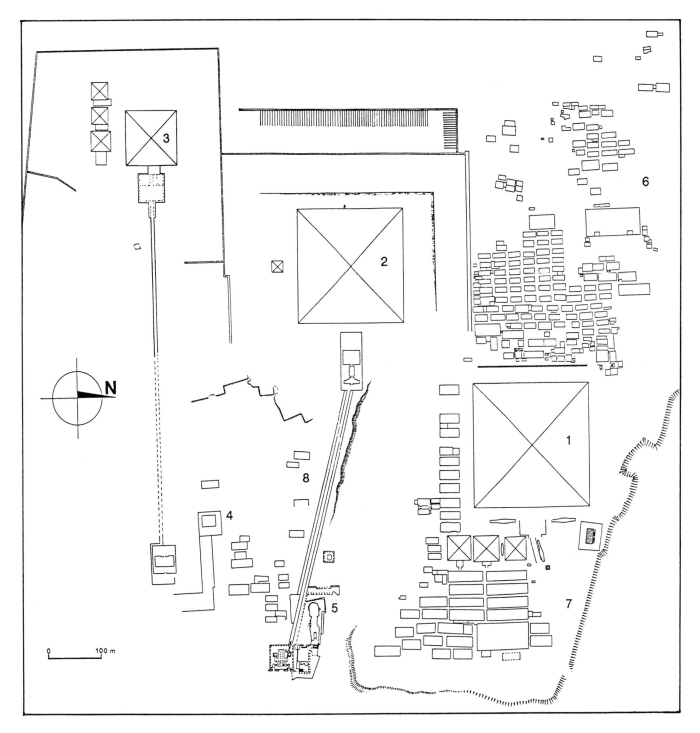

View of the pyramids at Giza from the south-west.

probably consists of a system of chambers constructed from stone blocks and filled with sand. This method was not only very economical and time-saving but also helped to increase the stability of the Great Pyramid during the earthquakes to which Egypt is sometimes prone. A number of other buildings were components of Cheops' tomb and together with the pyramid made up an integrated whole: the valley temple (already discovered but not yet investigated), the causeway, the mortuary temple at the eastern foot of the pyramid (today almost nothing remains of this except remnants of paving), the small cult pyramid, five pits for the symbolic burial of boats (one of the two

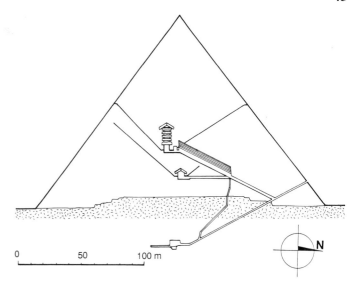

North-south section of the Great Pyramid.

Pyramid of Cheops. Giza.

In the ruins of Radjedef's
pyramid complex.

boats which were preserved was raised in
1954) and the three small pyramids of the
queens.

Cheops' son and heir Radjedef abandoned
the cemetery established by his father and
started to build his pyramid complex approximately 7 km further north, by modern Abu
Rawash. But the complex remained unfinished because the king died prematurely.
Archaeological finds of numerous fragments
of statues of Radjedef, heaped in the pit for
the funerary boat, supported the idea that
the tomb had been deliberately destroyed as
an expression of religio-politically motivated
conflict within the ruling house. This theory
is not, however, universally accepted.

Another of Cheops' sons, Chephren, who
ascended the throne after Radjedef, turned
back to Giza. His tomb almost achieved the
heights of his father's pyramid. The complex
of buildings belonging to it likewise recalled
his father's monument in its basic character-
istics. In Chefren's pyramid complex the
valley temple has been preserved in what is
a relatively very good state and today it is
considered another of the supreme works of
ancient Egyptian architecture. In this temple,
built out of enormous blocks of limestone
and red granite, discoveries have included
a seated diorite statue of Chephren, with the
falcon god, Horus, shielding his head from
behind with outspread wings. Today this

statue is one of the most famous exhibits in the Egyptian Museum in Cairo. Also part of the Chephren complex is the Great Sphinx, the lion deity with the human head symbolically guarding not only the ruler's pyramid complex but the whole Giza cemetery.

The third and smallest pyramid was built in Giza by Chephren's son Mycerinus. Despite the much smaller dimensions of his pyramid Mycerinus failed to complete the whole complex of buildings making up the tomb, and including the three small pyramids for the queens, during his own lifetime. This was accomplished by his successor Shepseskaf. Nevertheless, during excavations at the Mycerinus pyramid complex an American archaeological expedition led by George Andrew Reisner managed to find what is so far the largest group of royal statues of the Old Kingdom to be recovered. These masterpieces of ancient Egyptian sculpture are today on permanent exhibition in museums in Cairo and Boston.

Just as the members of the ruler's family and the highest state officials lived their lives in the proximity of their lord and god, so they wished to rest in the shadow of his pyramid and to enjoy his favour and protection even after death. Similarly, the Pharaoh himself wished to be forever surrounded by his court,

Boat pit.
Radjedef's pyramid complex.
Abu Rawash.

View of the remains of
Radjedef's mortuary temple.
Abu Rawash.

Detail of a statue of the
pharaoh Chephren, his head
shielded from behind by the
outstretched wings of the
falcon god Hor. Diorite, 168
cm in height. Found in 1860
in the pharaoh's valley temple at Giza by the French
archaeologist Auguste
Mariette, the statue is now
one of the most famous
exhibits of the Egyptian
Museum in Cairo (CG 14).

his relatives and his officials. Thus, around
the pyramids at Giza there grew up large
cemeteries of private tombs which had been
partially planned and built in accordance
with the original project. Many of these
tombs, and especially those in the vicinity of
the pyramid of Cheops, have been excavated
by the American Reisner expedition,
another Austrian expedition led by Hermann
Junker, an Egyptian expedition led by Selim
Hassan, and others. In the so-called Western
Field to the west of the pyramid of Cheops lie
the tombs of the ruler's courtiers, among
them the biggest of the Giza mastabas,
G 2000, unfortunately anonymous and only
identified by a number on the archaeological
plan of the cemetery. Later tombs are also
located here, for example that of the famous
Senedjemib Inty, vizier and royal architect in
the reign of Djedkare. In the Eastern Field,
again in rows, are the equally large mastabas
of the highest-ranking members of the royal

Chephren's pyramid. Giza.

The pillared hall of Chephren's valley temple. Giza.

The tomb of the magnate Seshemnofer from the period of the end of the 5th and beginning of the 6th Dynasty. Giza.

A new housing development on the western edge of Cairo already encroaching dangerously on the cemetery at Giza from the north west.

The rock-cut tomb of Kakherptah on the eastern edge of the East Cemetery. 5th Dynasty. Giza.

family, for example prince Ankhhaf, vizier in the reign of Chephren, whose celebrated and splendid bust is today exhibited in the museum in Boston. Also to be found in a dominant position here is the mastaba of Khufukhaf, which belonged to none other than the future pharaoh Rakhef (Gr. Chephren) be-

fore he became king and changed the element "Khufu" (his father's name — Gr. Cheops) in his own name to Re, the name of the sun god. Members of the royal family, courtiers and officials from the reign of Chephren were buried in the Central Field, in the central part of the Giza cemetery south of the

causeway leading from the valley to the pharaoh's pyramid. A rather small cemetery established in the reign of Mycerinus consists of mastabas and rock-cut tombs lying in an area of former quarries south-east of the pharaoh's pyramid. Despite long years of intensive archaeological researches and excavations, however, the royal pyramid cemetery in Giza is still far from being fully explored, a fact which is amply borne out by the surprise discoveries in the area south of the Mycerinus valley temple. Here the Egyptian archaeologist Zahi Hawas found a cemetery containing the tombs of the artisans who built the royal pyramids. Here, subsequently, the American archaeologist Mark Lehner discovered the "provisioning section" of the builders of the Giza pyramids — great storehouses for grain and drink, bakeries etc.

After the death of Mycerinus there were complications in the country's internal political situation. The building of gigantic pyramids had drained off major material resources, and the mortuary cults had tied up much of the labour force and finances; it was a situation that could not but have its effects on economic conditions in the country. The situation was further complicated by succession

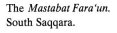

The *Mastabat Fara'un*. South Saqqara.

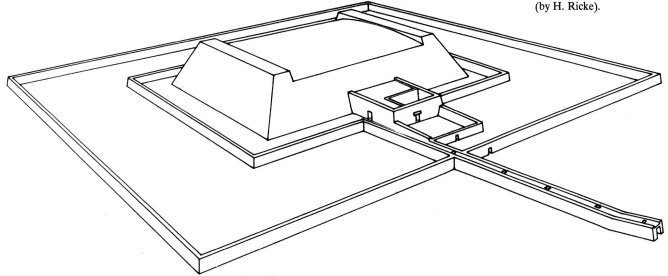

Reconstruction of the original appearance of Shepseskaf's tomb complex (by H. Ricke).

View of South Saqqara and
Dahshur from the north.

Fragment of a limestone
block depicting life in a papyrus thicket. Found by Cecil
Firth during excavations in
Userkaf's mortuary temple
at Saqqara in 1928—29,
the fragment is now exhibited in the Egyptian Museum
in Cairo (JE 56001).

disputes within the royal family and by the
growing importance of the solar cult. This is
the historical background against which we
must interpret the decision of the last 4th-
Dynasty ruler Shepseskaf to build himself
a tomb several kilometres to the south of Giza, in South Saqqara. He did not build it in
the form of a pyramid, as was usual for pharaohs at the time, but as a mastaba and, what
is more, a mastaba resembling a large sarcophagus. The natives call it *Mastabat Fara'un*,
the "Pharaoh's bench". In comparison with
the pyramids of Shepseskaf's predecessors it
was a very small and relatively modest tomb.
Its unusual design has led Egyptologists
to speculate whether it did not represent
a deliberate religiously-motivated renuncia-
tion of the pyramid shape that was so
intimately linked with the solar cult. If this
was the case then Shepseskaf was making
a protest against the growing power of the
priests of the sun god Re, who were ultimately to prevail with the accession of the 5th
Dynasty.

Userkaf, Shepseskaf's successor and the
first 5th-Dynasty ruler, did not abandon Saqqara; nevertheless he had his tomb, again in
pyramid form, built near the north-east
corner of the stone wall surrounding the Step
Pyramid. Userkaf's small pyramid complex
— its valley temple and causeway still as yet

Userkaf's pyramid. Saqqara.

View of the pyramids at Abusir from the western edge
of the Nile valley.

Irrigating a field at Abusir.

Herd of cattle crossing a ford. Low relief with polychrome remains (the water and unsubmerged parts of the bodies of the cattle are in low relief, the submerged parts are only indicated by colour). Ti's mastaba. 5th Dynasty. Saqqara.

unexcavated − attracts attention not only by its eloquent siting near Djoser's pyramid but by reason of two particular features. First, the mortuary temple was not built at the eastern foot of the pyramid, as one would expect from the religiously-motivated east-west orientation of the whole complex, but at its southern foot. The unusual siting of the temple was almost certainly influenced by the existence of a broad and deep ditch, called the Great Moat, enclosing the precincts of Djoser's pyramid complex. The ditch ran precisely across the area where under normal circumstances the mortuary temple should have been sited. In order to be buried close to Djoser's pyramid Userkaf was prepared to change the standard plan for his tomb. The second notable feature is Userkaf's wife's independent pyramid complex built to the south of the ruler's mortuary temple. The queen's mortuary temple was the largest of its kind to have been constructed up to that period.

The majority of the 5th-Dynasty rulers had themselves buried in the cemetery at Abusir, established as an indirect result of Userkaf's construction of his sun temple here (see p. 102). Pyramid complexes were built at Abusir by the rulers Sahure, Neferirkare, Raneferef and Niuserre (for further details see p. 68 ff.). In the vicinity of their pyramids several smaller cemeteries grew up for members of the royal families, courtiers and high state officials. It is noteworthy, however, that many of the leading dignatories of the 5th Dynasty did not have their tombs built at Abusir, near their kings, but at Giza or Saqqara. One example is the magnate Ti, who occupied high offices during the reigns of Neferirkare, Raneferef and Niuserre and was even administrator of these pharaohs' pyramids and sun temples, but who built himself a tomb in North Saqqara. Ti's mastaba is

Fragments of a red granite palm column. Mortuary temple of Djedkare's pyramid complex. South Saqqara.

Djedkare's pyramid. Saqqara.

Fragment of the granite gate of the mortuary temple in front of the pyramid of Unas at Saqqara.

Burial chamber and sarcophagus of Unas. On the side walls of the chamber are Pyramid Texts and the ceiling is decorated to resemble a starry sky.

Ptahhotep sniffing a vessel of perfumed ointment. Mastaba of Ptahhotep. Low relief with polychrome, 5th Dynasty. Saqqara.

considered the most beautiful of the tombs of the Old Kingdom yet discovered. This is because of the well-preserved state of its relief decorations, the artistry of their conception, the diversity of the subjects depicted from everyday life and the mortuary cult and, last but not least, the quality of the workmanship.

The tomb of Niuserre's successor Menkauhor has so far not been discovered. Some archaeologists are searching for it in North Saqqara, others in Dahshur. He was not, however, buried at Abusir, and neither were the last two 5th-Dynasty rulers Djedkare and Unas. Djedkare's pyramid complex, including a comparatively small mortuary tem-

ple and the pyramid of the pharaoh's wife, was built at Saqqara, roughly half way between Djoser's pyramid and the Mastabat Fara'un. The complex, already severely damaged in preceding centuries, met with misfortune of a peculiar kind even in the modern period. At the end of the 1940s and beginning of the 1950s two archaeological expeditions carried out excavations there. The results of the work were not, however, made public and a part of the documentation was even lost. The last 5th-Dynasty ruler Unas, like Userkaf, found a place for his tomb near Djoser's pyramid, but at its opposite end.

The ruins of Unas's valley temple at Saqqara.

Scene depicting a range of funerary offerings with boats and unfinished statues of the tomb's owner. Tomb of Iru-kaptah. Wall painting, 5th Dynasty. Saqqara.

Pyramid Texts. Pyramid of
Teti, Saqqara.

Although Unas' pyramid is one of the smallest monuments of its type from the Old Kingdom, it represents a turning-point in Egyptian history. This is because on the walls of the pyramid's undergound chambers are the first recorded religious inscriptions which Egyptologists call the Pyramid Texts. These are a group of spells, litanies, hymns and other writings, apparently dating from various periods but linked into a single whole, and first transcribed in the pyramid of Unas. Their purpose was to ensure the ruler a path to eternity and life among the gods in the other world. In the vicinity of Unas' mortuary temple and causeway lies a cemetery containing mastabas and rock-cut tombs, many of which belong to members of Unas' family, courtiers, high state officials and the priests who maintained the ruler's mortuary cult. In this cemetery lies the rock-cut tomb of Nefer with the best preserved mummified body from the Old Kingdom, and also, among many others, what is known as the Tomb of the Two Brothers, Nyankhkhnum and Khnumhotep, a tomb which is outstandingly well-preserved and original in its relief decoration.

The pharaohs of the 6th Dynasty built their tombs exclusively in Saqqara. The first of these, Teti, had his tomb constructed in the northern part of Saqqara near the Early Dynastic royal necropolis. His pyramid complex closely resembles that of Unas, and includes the Pyramid Texts. These texts are, in fact, to be found in all the later pyramids of the kings and even in some of the pyramids of the queens right up to the 8th Dynasty. Around Teti's pyramid, and especially north of the monument, a large cemetery was established for magnates and officials and this contains the famous tombs of the Vizier

Feeding a hyena. Tomb of Mereruka. Low relief with remains of polychrome. 6th Dynasty. Saqqara.

Dancers. Tomb of Mehu. Low relief with remains of polychrome. 6th Dynasty. Saqqara.

Ankhmahor. Tomb of
Ankhmahor. Sunken relief.
6th Dynasty. Saqqara.

Remains of the mortuary temple and pyramid of Pepi I in South Saqqara.

Jean-Philippe Lauer with *reis* Abdu al-Qereti and *reis* Mutaal al-Qereti during re-construction work in the substructure of the pyramid of Pepi I in South Saqqara.

Mereruka, the vizier Kagemni, the physician Ankhmahor and many others. The relief decorations preserved in these tombs are astonishing for the variety of the subjects depicted, although the quality of execution does not reach the level of the masterpieces of the 5th Dynasty, for example the tomb of Ti in North Saqqara or of Ptahshepses at Abusir.

The pyramid complex of Pepi I is located in South Saqqara, not far from that of Djedkare. Research there, carried out by a French archaeological expedition led by Jean Leclant, has recently brought the surprising find of four small pyramids and the mortuary temples of the wives of Pepi I; and the possibility that still more may be discovered is not to be ruled out.

The last great pyramid complex of the Old Kingdom was built at the end of the 6th Dynasty by Pepi II. The complex, already excavated before the Second World War, and later by another French expedition, this time led by Gustav Jéquier, lies at the southernmost edge of Saqqara, close by the Mastabat Fara'un. In layout it resembles the tombs of Pepi II's predecessors of the 6th Dynasty. Its components also include three small pyramids and the mortuary temples of the queens Neith, Iput and Udjebten. There is even a small cult pyramid sited near the

Red granite gate with picture of the queen Iput, wife of Pepi II. South Saqqara.

Plan of the pyramid complex of Pepi II (by G. Jéquiér).

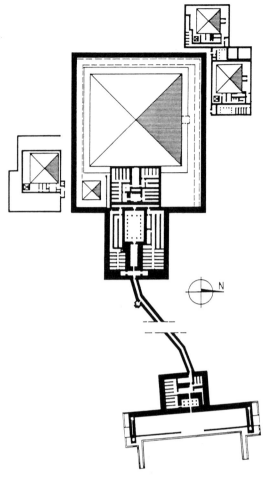

Alabaster offering table of the queen Udjebten near the south-eastern corner of the pyramid of Pepi II in South Saqqara.

south-eastern corner of the pharaoh's pyramid. During investigation of what were hardly the most numerous remains of relief decoration in the mortuary temple it was demonstrated, surprisingly, that its creator

had been inspired by the ʹreliefs from Sahure's mortuary temple at Abusir. This is indirect proof of the high artistic level of the decoration of Sahure's complex, an achievement which became the example for subsequent generations of artists and craftsmen. The same is true, in another form and at another time, of the monument of Pepi II in South Saqqara. This too was later to become a source of inspiration for the builders of the pyramids of the Middle Kingdom pharaohs. These, however, were for the most part not sited in the Memphite necropolis and, at the time when they were built, Memphis had ceased to be the capital city of Egypt.

The sun setting behind the
Step Pyramid and the pyr-
amid of Userkaf.

Abusir - The Destiny
of One Royal Cemetery

2

Until not long ago both specialist and popular publications would inform the reader that Abusir was the cemetery of the 5th Dynasty kings. Today this assertion is not regarded as entirely accurate. Archaeological research and excavations that have been underway particularly in the last two decades have added substantially to our knowledge of this important Egyptian archaeological location and rendered it much more precise. The archaeological picture of Abusir has been enlarged and its contours have become clearer.

"The archaeological past" of Abusir began a very long time ago, many thousands of years before the period in which the great cemeteries were established. Evidence of what is so far the oldest archaeologically documented period in the area is provided by the flint tools and weapons which are to be found in abundance in the desert around

the Abusir pyramids and on the small hills which surround them. They date from the middle Palaeolithic age, a time when the landscape around Abusir looked very different. The Nile was much broader and wilder than it is today, and along its banks, from which green vegetation spread deep into what is now desert, moved herds of wild animals. These provided subsistence for a few groups of prehistoric hunters. Approximately at that time the Nile started to be affected by the rhythm of the annual inundation linked to regularly repeating climatic changes in the East African area and the melting of the snows in the Abyssinian highlands. These life-giving periodic inundations indirectly left their mark on the fortunes of Abusir. At the foot of the raised desert plateau on which the Abusir pyramids stand today there was a slight depression which during the floods filled with water. The water

Theoretical reconstruction of the pyramid cemetery at Abusir by L. Borchardt.

Archaeological spring in a cemetery at Abusir: for a short time a green carpet covers an as yet unexcavated mudbrick tomb south of the pyramid of Neferirkare.

But spring lasts only a few days at Abusir.

then remained there even after the Nile had returned to its normal course. This year-round natural reservoir, in modern times called the Lake of Abusir, ceased to exist only relatively recently, after the building of the Aswan dams and the end of the periodic flooding of the Nile on Egyptian territory. Since the distant past the edges of the Lake of Abusir, recorded in the last century by a German archaeological expedition led by Karl Richard Lepsius, shifted somewhat. This change was linked to the regular deposit of Nile mud in the flood areas, approximately 1 mm annually. In the course of millennia the boundary between the Nile valley and the desert to a certain extent fluctuated.

There is a great deal of evidence that this Abusir lake, at the end of the prehistoric age and the beginning of the historic age, played a significant role in relation to the establishment of the cemetery and the development of burial and religious cults in the area of modern Northern Saqqara and South Abusir. The Lake of Abusir is sometimes even identified with the mythical lake of *Pedju* mentioned in the Pyramid Texts — the oldest group of Ancient Egyptian religious texts. It is also thought that the cult of the Falcon god Sokar, the god of the dead and ruler of the local cemeteries, and the deity to whom Saqqara owes its modern name, arose in close proximity to the Abusir Lake. The area with undergound catacombs south and south-west of the Lake of Abusir is identified by some researchers as the mythical *Rosetau*, the Elysian Fields of the Ancient Egyptians and the realm of Osiris, god of the dead. After all, the name "Abusir" is only the Arabic version of the Greek place name *Busiris*, which conceals the original Egyptian *Per-usire*, "the place of the worship of Usir (Gr. Osiris)".

Leaving aside the speculations of Egyptologists, however, the archaeological fact remains that as early as the end of the prehistoric age, and especially from the beginning of the historic age, large and rich burial grounds grew up on the slopes above the south and south-western edge of the Lake of Abusir. The oldest and most important of these is what is known as the Early Dynastic royal cemetery in North Saqqara. Mention has already been made of the British archaeologist Emery's conviction that it was in this cemetery, in huge mudbrick tombs, that the earliest kings of a united Egypt were buried. These were the pharaohs of the 1st

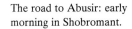

The road to Abusir: early
morning in Shobromant.

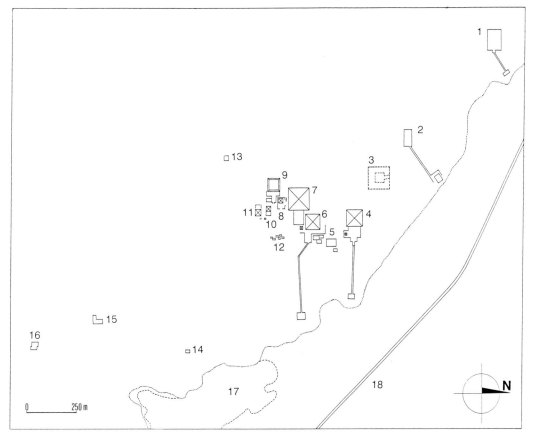

Plan of the Abusir necro-
polis.
1 Sun Temple of Niuserre
2 Sun Temple of Userkaf
3 Unfinished Pyramid (of
  Shepseskare ?)
4 Sahure
5 Ptahshepses
6 Niuserre
7 Neferirkare
8 Khentkaus
9 Raneferef
10 Pyr. no. XXIV
11 Pyr. no. XXV
12 Field of mastabas (Khekeretnebty, Hedjetnub,
   Mernefu, Neserkauhor,
   Idu, etc.)
13 Udjahorresnet
14 Tomb of Dyn. IV, Shedu,
   etc.
15 Fetekta, Hetepi, Isesiseneb, Raotep
16 Kaaper, Ity (?)
17 "Lake of Abusir"
18 Water canal

Dynasty, whose residence was the *White Wall,* precursor of Memphis and lying in the Nile Valley within sight of the later city. On the periphery of this "royal cemetery" the members of lower social strata were buried. At the beginning of the 3rd Dynasty — if we pass over the rather mysterious and archaeologically as yet obscure chapter of the royal tombs of the 2nd Dynasty — the centre of the Saqqara cemetery was shifted to an area south of the Early Dynastic cemetery, towards the Step Pyramid. Until very recently

Small bowl made of fine earthenware with red slip. Early Dynastic Period. Cairo University excavations at Abu Ghurab (published by kind permission of Prof. Ali Radwan).

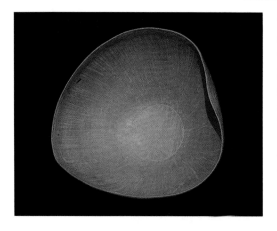

nobody supposed that the Early Dynastic cemetery could also have been extended in a northerly direction. The latest archaeological excavations by the Czech Egyptological expedition, however, undertaken in South Abusir on the small hills to the west and south-west of the former Lake of Abusir, have led to discoveries of previously en-

tirely unknown tombs built of mudbrick and dating from the middle of the 3rd Dynasty, the beginning of the 4th Dynasty and from later periods (see below in the text of this chapter). These finds link up with the discoveries made during excavations carried out by Ernst von Sieglin's German expedition only a few hundred metres to the east, near the modern moslem cemetery of Abusir village. This expedition discovered chamber tombs dating from the Early Dynastic Period and belonging to members of a lower social stratum than those buried in the immediate neighbourhood of the so-called Early Dynastic royal cemetery in North Saqqara. It is a pity that investigation of the cemetery by the modern moslem burial ground has not yet been completed, although in the mid-1980s an Egyptian expedition led by Holeil Ghaly tried to do so. Completion is important for the reconstruction of the

Plan of Ity's (?) mastaba and the mastaba of Kaaper in South Abusir (by M. Bárta).

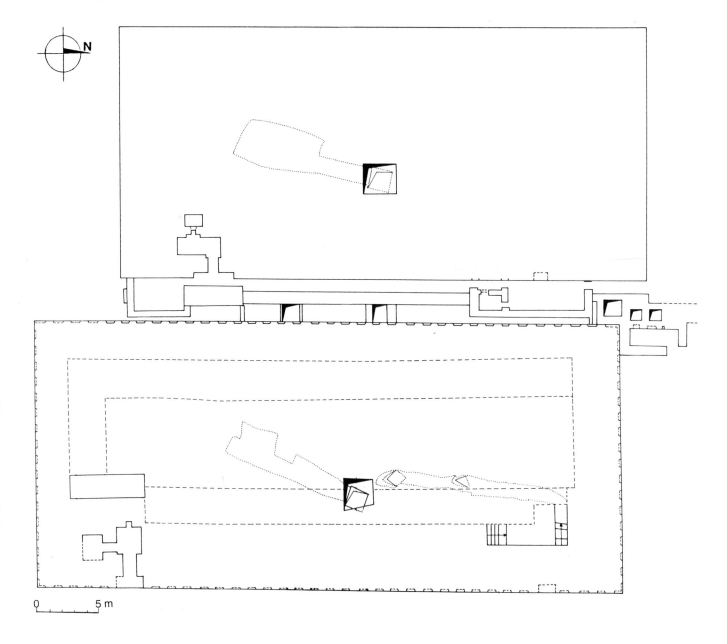

0   5 m

Remains of the facade of the mastaba of Ity (?), Administrator of Both Granaries. 3rd Dynasty. South Abusir.

archaeological map of the cemeteries of the oldest royal seat of a united Egypt in North Saqqara and South Abusir. The most recent discoveries made by the Czech expedition during excavations at South Abusir nevertheless supplement the last finds of the Cairo University archaeological expedition led by Ali Radwan. This Egyptian expedition found a cemetery of the middling ranks of society dating from the 1st Dynasty north of the causeway to Niuserre's sun temple in Abu Ghurab, approximately 1 km to the north of the Abusir pyramids. Among the remarkable archaeological discoveries at this cemetery were the ritual interments of asses near the tombs. In Egyptian conditions ritual interments of asses are unusual and are known principally from the Hyksos Period in the area of the Eastern Delta where there was an indigenous population of non-Egyptian origin.

In the Early Dynastic Period, then, Abusir was definitely not a deserted place. At this time it already had a cemetery, especially for the middle social ranks, and this was extended in the following 3rd and 4th Dynasties. The major turning-point in the history of the Abusir cemetery occurred, however, at the beginning of the 5th Dynasty. The Pharaoh Userkaf selected the place as a site for the construction of the first sun tem-

ple in the Memphite Necropolis. The reasons for this choice of a place approximately 3 km north of his pyramid complex in Saqqara have not yet come to light, and there are only conjectures (see below p. 102). The presence of Userkaf's sun temple, however, was

In the undergound section of the mastaba of Ity (?).

Overall view of the uncovered part of the cemetery discovered on the slope above the western edge of the former „Lake of Abusir".

undoubtedly a decisive factor in the later foundation of the royal cemetery in Abusir.

The first pyramid complex was built in Abusir by Sahure who, it is believed, was very probably Userkaf's son. Part of the evidence for this identification is Sahure's deliberate selection of the site of his pyramid in close southern proximity to Userkaf's sun temple. Even though Sahure's pyramid complex was not outstandingly large, it represents a turning-point in the development of royal tombs under the Old Kingdom. In comparison with the 4th Dynasty the volume

of material used for the pyramid was reduced and there was striking change in the layout of the mortuary temple. The reduction of the amount of stone employed, undoubtedly a result of economic considerations, was compensated for by the better quality and diversity of the types of stone. At the same time the relief decoration — what is called the pictorial scheme of the mortuary and valley temples and the causeway — is so rich in subject matter, artistic conception and quality of workmanship that it represents the highest level of the genre that has yet been

An Abusir workman during excavation work.

Remains of the causeway leading to the pyramid of Sahure.

The ruins of Sahure's valley temple at Abusir are today overgrown with palms and rushes.

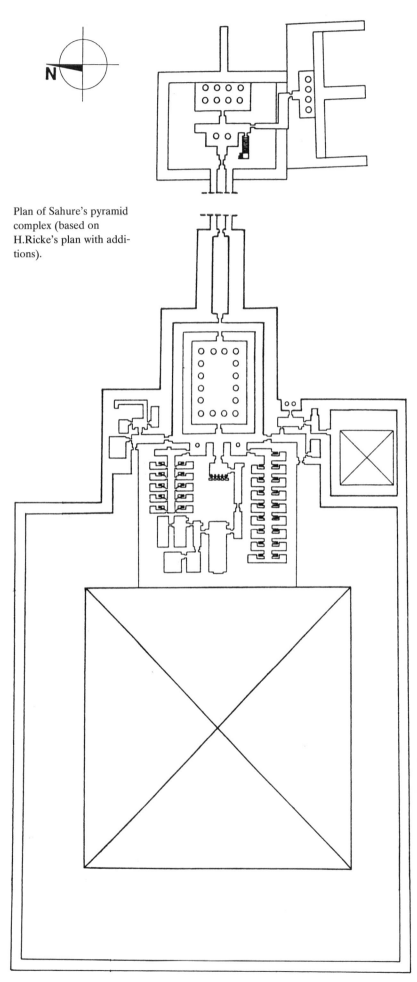

Plan of Sahure's pyramid complex (based on H.Ricke's plan with additions).

discovered from the Old Kingdom. It is therefore no wonder that Sahure's pyramid complex, its architectural plan and scheme of relief decoration, became the conceptual starting-point for the designers of the later royal tombs of the 5th and 6th Dynasties.

The entrance to Sahure's pyramid complex led through the valley temple which was at the same time a monumental gate into the underworld "palace of the spirit" of the deceased ruler. The temple stood at the boundary between the Nile valley and the desert on what was, for the Ancient Egyptians, the symbolic border between the World of the Living and the World of the Dead. Its floor lay perhaps 5 m under the level of the desert surface today — graphic evidence of how far the build-up of deposits of micro-strata of mud through annual flooding since, roughly, the 25th century BC has raised the level of the Nile valley at Abusir. Sahure's valley temple has two landing ramps — one giving access from the east and one giving access from the south. As a rule there would only be one, eastern, landing ramp allowing access from the Nile by way of an artificial channel. It was the opinion of Ludwig Borchardt, who excavated Sahure's pyramid complex at the head of a German archaeological expedition in the early years of this century, that the unusual Southern ramp was perhaps linked to the existence of a so-called 'pyramid town' — the residence of the officials, priests and artisans responsible for the construction of the complex and for

Fragment of a red granite column. Sahure's mortuary temple, Abusir.

the subsequent maintenance of the mortuary cult of the pharaoh — in the area south of the valley temple. Borchardt's theory has proved to be quite well-founded since a pyramid town with the same name as the ruler's whole pyramid complex — "In glory comes forth the soul of Sahure" — lay in all likelihood in the neighbourhood of the valley temple. But at the same time it is possible that while the valley temple's eastern landing ramp was linked directly to the Nile by artificial channel, the southern landing ramp was linked by canal to the Abusir Lake which for the whole year, even after the subsidence of the flood waters, was an important reservoir. The porticos to which each landing ramp led were decorated with granite columns. The walls of the porticos and the rooms inside the temple were covered with coloured pictures in low relief. Reliefs also adorned the inner walls of the causeway, i.e. the corridor which linked the valley temple to the mortuary temple. The predominant themes depicted were images of the ruler in the likeness of a sphinx treading underfoot the defeated foes of Egypt, series of captive and bound enemies of Egypt, and others. They were images of a mythological character, *apotropaia*, which even at the entrance to Sahure's tomb were meant to drive away approaching evil and, at the same time, to elevate the ruler's mythic godlike and sovereign role.

In Sahure's mortuary temple we find for the first time the arrangement of rooms that was later to become the basis for the layout of temples of this type in the Old Kingdom.

The mortuary chapel of Sahure's pyramid complex at Abusir.

Model of Sahure's mortuary temple and pyramid (by Ludwig Borchardt, drawing by Karel Vilgus).

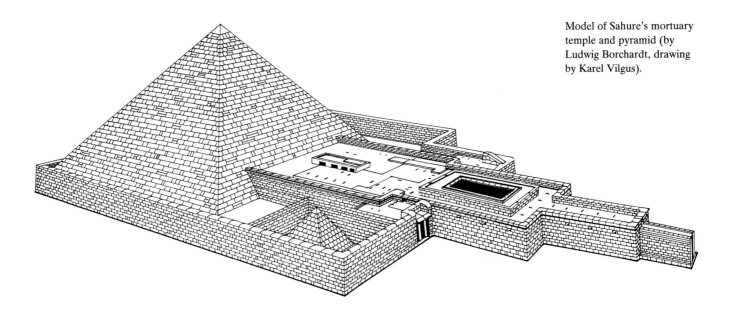

Reconstruction of Sahure's valley temple by Ludwig Borchardt.

Cartouche with the name of the pharaoh Sahure. Red granite, sunken relief. Sahure's mortuary temple. Abusir.

Remains of a staircase in the magazines of Sahure's mortuary temple.

Access to the temple was given by a long entrance hall in which the theme of relief decoration was the welcome to the other world given to the pharaoh by the magnates "of his time". A large open court made up the central part of the temple and a cloister ran along its sides. The ceiling of the cloister was supported by palm columns made of red granite and decorated with the ruler's names and symbols of the protective goddesses of Upper and Lower Egypt, the vulture Nekhbet and the cobra Wadjet. Between the columns there originally stood statues of the pharaoh. The lower part of the lateral walls of the roofed court consisted in what is called a *dado* of red granite while the upper part of the walls was made of white limestone decorated with polychrome scenes in low relief. Predominant among the subjects depicted was the pharaoh's victory over the Asian and Libyan enemies of Egypt and the rich plunder which this had brought to the country. Sacrifices, including burnt offerings, would be offered up on an alabaster altar in the north-western corner of the court.

A transverse corridor running north-south divided off the eastern, so-called 'public' part of the temple from the western, so-called 'intimate' part. This corridor was paved with black basalt and above the dado of red granite there again rose limestone walls covered with relief decoration of which only fragments depicting a sea-battle and the return of trading ships from Asia have been preserved. The 'intimate' part of the mortuary temple included a room with five niches, deep recesses of red granite in which were placed statues depicting the ruler in his various sovereign, i.e. divine forms. The paving of the room was of alabaster as were the low steps leading to the individual recesses. A passage, which only the funerary priests could use, led from the five recesses to the most distant, westernmost, and in cult terms the most important room in the whole temple — the offering hall. On an altar in front of what is called the 'false door', through which the pharaoh's spirit could come from the other world, priests would make offerings and the prescribed rituals of the mortuary cult would be performed. The offering hall, like the rest of the intimate part of the mortuary temple, was sunk in darkness. The basic layout of the mortuary temple was augmented by groups of magazines in which offerings and temple instruments would be stored.

The pyramid which rose above the burial chamber where the mummy of Sahure rested in a basalt sarcophagus reached, when complete, a height of perhaps 47 m. It was therefore incomparably smaller than the pyramids of the 4th-Dynasty pharaohs. It was also constructed in a much simpler way. Research on the analogically constructed but unfinished pyramid of Raneferef on the south-western edge of the Abusir cemetery (see p. 139 f.) has given us a detailed picture of this building method. If we also take into consideration the fact that the material employed in its construction, with the exception of the external casing, was low-quality and only very roughly worked limestone from nearby quarries west of Abusir, then we can understand why Sahure's pyramid, in contrast to the pyramids in Dahshur or Giza, is in such a woeful state and from a distance resembles no more than a heap of stones. The same is true of the other remaining Abusir pyramids.

The complex of buildings making up Sahure's tomb included yet another, miniature pyramid. It stood near the south-eastern corner of the pharaoh's pyramid and had only a cult significance. What precisely that significance was is a question which to this day generates disputes among experts. Cult pyramids, also sometimes called satellite

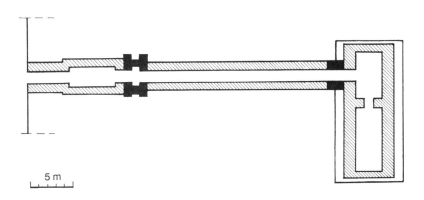

5 m

In Borchardt's model a cross-section of Sahure's pyramid along its north-south axis illustrates the German archaeologist's conception of how the masonry and chambers inside the pyramid were constructed and arranged.

Plan of the substructure of Sahure's pyramid (by V. Maragioglio and C. Rinaldi).

Approach road to the Abusir cemetery.

The South portico of Sa-
hure's mortuary temple.
Abusir.

Remains of a scene of Kaaper's funerary feast. Eastern
wall of the chapel of Kaaper's mastaba. Low relief. 5th
Dynasty. South Abusir.

pyramids, are considered by some to be so-
called 'southern tombs' — royal tombs that
are symbolic in character and represent
a grave which ought to be located in the
oldest cemetery of the Egyptian kings at
Umm el-Qaab in Abydos in Southern Egypt.
Others believe that statues of pharaohs were
laid in these pyramids, and so forth.

The Borchardt expedition did not investigate the surroundings of Sahure's pyram-

id. The tombs of the immediate members of
Sahure's family ought to be located here,
especially that of his wife Neferkhanebty and
his sons Netjeryrenre, Haremsaf, Khakare
and Nebankhre. These tombs, and particularly the inscriptions on their walls, could
provide valuable historical data and answers
to many questions relating to the reign of Sahure. It would, for example, be very interesting to know more about the fate of Sahure's
first-born son Netjeryrenre and why it was
not he who inherited the throne, but Neferirkare, whose origin is as yet the subject of no
more than conjecture.

The reign of Sahure saw the completion of
the great tomb of Kaaper, Scribe to the
Royal Army and holder of many other titles.
It is at the opposite, southern end of the Abusir cemetery, almost on the edge of North
Saqqara. The tomb is a mastaba in type, built
of limestone blocks to a height of perhaps 5
m on a ground plan of roughly 40 × 20 m. It
stands on a small hill which is literally
crammed with tombs dating from the period
from the 3rd to the 6th Dynasty (see above,
p. 66). It is interesting, even if it sounds paradoxical, that Kaaper's mastaba was known to

View of South Abusir and North Saqqara from the North.

Kaaper in the embrace of his wife. Based on H.G. Fischer's drawing of a relief.

View of Neferirkare's mortuary temple and pyramid from the summit of Niuserre's pyramid.

North-south cross-section of Neferirkare's pyramid with a reconstruction of what are believed to have been its building phases.

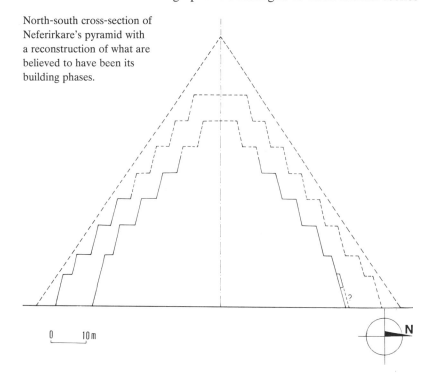

Egyptologists before it was actually found. Around the mid-1950s officials of the Antiquities Inspectorate in Saqqara arranged for several photographic shots of the walls of the offering room of a tomb which thieves had broken into a short time before. When the photographs were obtained, however, the officials forgot to record the precise location of the discovery on a map. The photographs had managed to catch several scenes in low relief with hieroglyphic inscriptions and pictures of the owner of the tomb and members of his family. Among them was a unique representation of Kaaper in the embrace of his wife — a picture which at the time had no parallel among the reliefs known from other tombs. On the basis of the photographs the American Egyptologist Henry George Fisher later published a remarkably precise study of Kaaper and the reliefs from his tomb. The tomb itself, however, was long regarded as lost. It was found only recently by the Czech expedition during archaeological survey of the southern part of the Abusir cemetery. Kaaper's mastaba — the fact that the name is identical with that of the owner of the famous wooden sculpture in the Egyptian Museum in Cairo called *Sheikh el-Balad* ("village headman", in Arabic) is a pure coincidence — lies immediately next to the mudbrick mastaba of Ity, the administrator of the granaries from the mid-3rd Dynasty. Ity's mastaba has already been mentioned and is the oldest building yet discovered in the Abusir cemetery.

If we estimate the length of Sahure's reign at perhaps fourteen years, then the reign of Neferirkare was undoubtedly shorter. The latest year of rule which can so far be attributed to Neferirkare is probably recorded in a cursive inscription found on a block of stone in the masonry of the pyramid of the ruler's wife Khentkaus in Abusir (see below p. 121). On the basis of this inscription Neferirkare's reign could be considered to have lasted ten years. In the opinion of some Egyptologists he was Sahure's brother. This belief rests on the small but interesting additional change made to one scene in a low relief. The Borchardt expedition found fragments of this relief during excavations in Sahure's mortuary temple. It depicts Sahure surrounded by courtiers, but has been amended: the figure of one of the courtiers standing immediately beside the pharaoh has had the royal insignia carved on his head and breast, and the name of Neferirkare added beside him in a cartouche (see p. 124). The celebrated German Egyptologist Kurt Sethe, who worked on and published the fragments of relief decoration discovered by Borchardt at Sahure's mortuary temple, was the first to present the theory that Neferirkare was Sahure's brother and that the relief had been amended after he had ascended the throne. The addition does not, however, bear unambiguous interpretation. At the very least, one other interpretation is possible. Sahure and Neferkirkare need not have been related as brothers at all; they could have been unrelated and the addition to the scene could have expressed a subtle but sufficiently plain allusion to the fact that in the time of Sahure's reign there existed a person who was the legitimate ruler but who for circumstantial reasons could not exercise that office. In Egyptian history we know of cases of usurpation of the throne and protest against the usurper could then find expression in the deliberate defacement of his monument, and especially his name. There are, in fact, other relevant pieces of historical and archaeological evidence. For example, in the Canon of Turin, a List of Kings written on a papyrus and dating from the 19th Dynasty, Neferirkare is considered the founder of the new dynasty. At the same time the latest archaeological discoveries in Abusir indicate that apart from Sahure's pyramid all the other pyramids in this cemetery make up a whole that is architecturally and functionally very closely connected with Neferirkare's pyramid. We are apparently dealing with a cemetery of Neferirkare's family — his wife, sons and daughters-in-law. The character of Neferirkare's pyramid itself, its unusual original design and the alterations subsequently made to it, also fit in with this scheme.

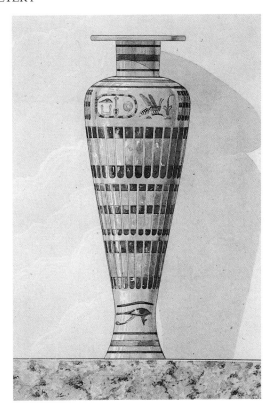

Reconstruction of a symbolic wooden cult vessel decorated with coloured faience and gold. The vessel was found during Borchardt's excavations in Neferirkare's mortuary temple at Abusir.

The archaeological survey recently carried out by the Czech expedition has shown that Neferirkare's pyramid was originally conceived and nearly completed as a step pyramid. This is a very significant discovery, since the era of step pyramids had come to an end in the 3rd Dynasty, long before Neferirkare's reign. Neferirkare's pyramid originally had six steps and reached a height equal to 100 Egyptian cubits, i.e. approximately 52 m. Its casing was not, however, completed. When it had been cased up to roughly ten metres above the ground the decision was taken to change the stepped into a true pyramid. The whole construction was slightly extended and since the angle of inclination selected for the walls was 54° the modified pyramid should have reached a height of perhaps 72 m. But this project also remained unfinished due to the pharaoh's premature death; only the lowest levels of the red granite blocks in which the pyramid was to have been cased were put into place. Even so, Neferirkare's pyramid, entitled "Neferirkare is a soul", was the largest building in Abusir. Since it stood on a small hill perhaps 30 m above the Nile valley, i.e. perhaps 10 m higher than Sahure's pyramid, it dominated not only the Abusir cemetery but a wide area around it. The mortuary temple at the foot of the eastern side of the pyramid was only completed by Neferirkare's heirs Raneferef

A view of Neferirkare's pyramid from the south west eloquently illustrates the building phases that went into the monument's construction.

Aerial view of the family cemetery that grew up around Neferirkare's pyramid and which includes the tomb complexes of Neferirkare's wife Khentkaus and his sons Raneferef and Niuserre (the photograph is a gift of the expedition of Waseda University, Tokyo).

and Niuserre. For reasons of economy and time-saving mudbricks and wood were used for its construction. Even the columns put up inside the temple were made of wood. While the temple plan included the basic elements which, in precisely defined and mutually balanced form, had already been incorporated into the royal mortuary temple in Sahure's time, its overall appearance was branded by the quick and "cheap" execution both of the construction and of progressive reconstruction. It is also significant that it has no causeway leading up to it. Neferirkare's sons considered it their duty speedily to complete their father's tomb and the place of his mortuary cult, i.e. the pyramid and mortuary temple, but not the causeway and valley temple. This was despite the fact that both uncompleted elements of Neferirkare's pyramid complex must, at the moment of the ruler's death, have been partially built, as is clear from the plan of the neighbouring pyramid complex of Niuserre which included a part of the foundation ramp of Neferirkare's causeway and a site originally destined for Neferirkare's valley temple.

The fact that Neferirkare's pyramid complex is only composed of a pyramid and a mortuary temple has had one important practical result. The funerary priests, who under normal circumstances would have lived in a pyramid town in the environs of the

valley temple, took up residence directly by the mortuary temple. Their simple dwellings, also constructed of mudbricks and rushes, soon merged into one whole with the mortuary temple. It is to this unusual development that we owe the fact that the papyri of the Neferirkare temple archive have survived up to this day. Had there existed a causeway and valley temple, then all written materials would have been archived in the administrative buildings of a so-called 'pyramid town' on the edge of the Nile valley. Today they would long have been buried under a layer of mud several metres deep and far below the sub-surface water level, and no trace of them would remain. There were similar reasons for the preservation of remnants of the papyrus archives of the mortuary temples of Raneferef and the royal mother Khentkaus, which are both situated in the neighbourhood of Neferirkare's pyramid (see below p. 169). Apart from the pyramid complexes of Neferirkare's wife Khentkaus and his eldest son and heir Raneferef, the cemetery of the pharaoh's family contains another three pyramid complexes — one large, belonging to Niuserre, and two small, which apparently belonged to the royal wives.

Niuserre's pyramid complex is most unusual in many respects. Its very siting is curious. Had the basic axis of the Abusir cemetery been respected — an axis running

Neferirkare and Niuserre's pyramid at Abusir. Visible in the foreground is a series of mastabas (Djadjamankh's, Userkafankh's and the „Nameless" mastaba) dating from the beginning of the 5th Dynasty and probably already standing on the site before Niuserre's pyramid was built.

through the north-western corners of the pyramid complexes of Sahure, Neferirkare and Raneferef — Niuserre's pyramid would have had to be built to the south-west of Raneferef's. This, however, would have meant a site deep in the desert and more than a kilometre away from the edge of the Nile valley. The costs of construction would evidently have risen above a tolerable level. We should not forget that on his ascent to the throne Niuserre took on the obligation of completing the three half-built pyramid complexes of his predecessors and the nearest members of his family, i.e. his father, mother and elder brother. The pharaoh therefore decided to use the modest free space close to his father's tomb and build his pyramid and mortuary temple near the north-eastern corner of Neferirkare's pyramid. He took over the site for his valley temple and parts of the causeway from the building project for the tomb of his father. This decision, which also reflected filial piety, significantly influenced the building project. Moreover, the plan had also to respect the small group of mastabas that had already been built to the east of the site of the future pyramid of Niuserre in the time of Sahure.

All these topographical and archaeological factors were reflected in the layout of the mortuary temple. For this reason the overall plan of Niuserre's pyramid complex, which bears the poetic name, "Enduring are the Places of Niuserre", is so atypical.

Niuserre's pyramid was approximately as large as that of Sahure. Even its substructure did not differ very much from the substructures of the pyramids of the ruler's predecessors Neferirkare and Sahure. The underground sections were accessible by a passage sloping downwards approximately along the north-south axis of the pyramid and from the northern foot of pyramid roughly as far as a point directly under its summit. The passage opens into an anteroom connected with the burial chamber. The ceiling of both underground chambers was built of three layers, each composed of gigantic limestone blocks placed one on top of another, and braced against each other in the form of an upturned "V". This bold and technically demanding construction could successfully resist the enormous pressure exerted on it by the stone material of the pyramid. It did not, however, manage to resist the stone thieves who centuries ago opened up the pyramid and, as in neighbouring pyramids, caused large-scale devastation to the underground chambers. They concentrated particularly on the very high-quality fine white limestone from which the ceiling and facing of the underground chambers had been constructed. The activity of thieves in the underground parts of all the Abusir pyramids has thus created a dangerous situation; today they are either impossible to enter or, where access is still possible, a question of special permission and only at one's own risk. At the end of the 1960s the Italian researchers Vito Maraglioglio and Celeste Rinaldi carried out the last measurements to be made in the underground parts of the Abusir pyramids. During the work they did not dare to speak for fear that the resonance of the sound would loosen the portions of broken ceiling blocks hanging over their heads. When necessary they exchanged directions and opinions written on pieces of paper.

Niuserre's valley temple did not differ fundamentally from the neighbouring temple of Sahure in its layout, except in the fact that

Vito Maragioglio.

it had only one landing ramp, located on the south side. The causeway, which for more than half its length follows the direction of the ascent ramp originally destined for

Remains of a basalt dado, the lower section of the facing of side walls, in the entrance hall of Niuserre's mortuary temple at Abusir.

Basin for waste water, reddish quartzite. Niuserre's mortuary temple at Abusir.

Princess Khekeretnebty looking on as funerary offerings are brought. Mastaba of Khekeretnebty. Wall painting. End of the 5th Dynasty. Abusir.

Neferirkare, turns aside, bends away toward the north-west and finally leads into Niuserre's mortuary temple. If the basic outline of the standard mortuary temple of the 5th or 6th Dynasty resembles the letter "T", then Niuserre's mortuary temple can be said to bear more resemblance to the letter "L". But despite this modification of basic layout, which was influenced by the topographic and archaeological factors already mentioned, the temple contains all the fundamental elements already established as the pattern for this kind of building in the reign of Sahure: entrance hall, open columned court — in Niuserre's temple the columns, in contrast to those of Sahure's temple, were of red granite and in the likeness of bunches of papyrus stalks with buds — , a transversal corridor, a room with five niches, offering hall and several groups of magazines. However, two interesting new features have appeared. One of these was a small room on the boundary between the so-called 'public' and 'intimate' parts of the temple. In this room was placed a large red granite statue of a lion, the symbolic guardian of the pharaoh's privacy in the underworld. The second was a small rectangular room between the five niches and the offering hall, which from this time on became a permanent element of the layout of mortuary temples and for which Egyptologists have come to use the term, *antichambre carrée*. The walls of the temple rooms were originally richly decorated in low relief not differing greatly in subject matter or quality from that of Sahure's mortuary temple. Many fragments of these reliefs, together with those from Sahure's temple, are today exhibited in German museums. In Niuserre's mortuary temple we meet with yet another architectural innovation which was later to have a marked influence on the appearance

Plan of the cemetery with the mastabas of the princesses and high officials from the end of the 5th Dynasty on the slope south-east of Niuserre's mortuary temple at Abusir.
1 Khekeretnebty
2 Hedjetnebu
3 "L"
4 Mernefu
5 Neserkauhor
6 Idu and Khenit

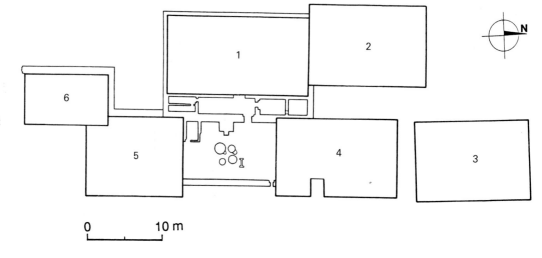

Statue of the princess Hedjetnebu, shortly after it was discovered. Wood with remains of stucco and polychrome. End of the 5th Dynasty. Abusir.

Detail from the false door of Tisethor, daughter (?) of the princess Khekeretnebty.

of Ancient Egyptian architecture. High tower-shaped buildings with slightly sloping outer walls were erected at the north-east and south-east corners of the temple. At the top these terminated in flat terraces accessible by staircase. In these gigantic corner buildings we can see the prototype of pylons, the monumental gates of later Ancient Egyptian temples and palaces.

A number of other significant buildings were also constructed in the Abusir cemetery at approximately the same time as the Niuserre pyramid complex. These include two small pyramids on the southern margin of the pyramid field. While research on these is only just beginning it is believed that they were the tombs of Niuserre's wives. Since their owners have so far not been identified the designations used for the pyramids are L no. XXIV and L no. XXV, shortened forms of the serial numbers allocated to them in the 1840s by the Lepsius expedition. Both pyramids have been damaged severely and no sensational finds can be expected in them. Nevertheless their investigation could provide answers to several questions relating to the history of the 5th Dynasty in the reigns of Niuserre, Menkauhor and Djedkare. Another

monument of the same period lies north-west of Niuserre's pyramid. It is the tomb constructed for the ruler's children and identified by Borchardt, who uncovered it, as the Mastaba of the Princesses. Also a monument from Niuserre's time is the huge

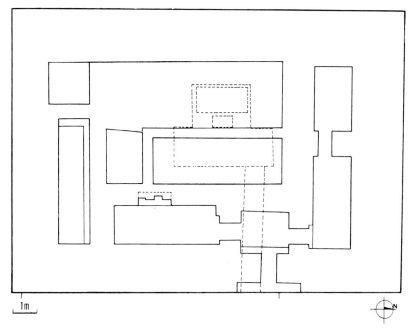

Plan of the mastaba of the princess Nebtyemneferes (by M. Balík).

Bandages from a mummy found in the mastaba of the princess Khekeretnebty at Abusir. On the bandages is a cursive, semi-hieratic inscription containing the name and titles of the overseer of the workshop in which the lines was produced.

mastaba of the pharaoh's son-in-law Ptah-shepses, chief director of all the royal building works including the ruler's Abusir pyramid complex (see below, pp. 173—192).

The origins of the unfinished pyramid discovered by the Czech archaeological expedition at the beginning of the 1980s in the area between Sahure's pyramid and Userkaf's sun temple are very obscure. It is not really a question of an unfinished pyramid in the true sense of the term but of scarcely begun and rapidly abandoned pyramid foundation work. Work was discontinued at the stage when the desert terrain had been levelled and a large trench dug out in the form of the letter "T" — the trench in which the underground chambers would have been constructed had work proceeded. The abandoned site represents the results of no more than a few weeks labour. In what circumstances was work on this building project commenced and so rapidly abandoned? Whose was the pyramid to have been? Only one ephemeral pharaoh of the time is a serious candidate here: Shepseskare. His name is documented in only one Ancient Egyptian list of kings, the Saqqara List. To judge by the negligible amount of evidence he reigned for a very short time. During excavations in Raneferef's mortuary temple

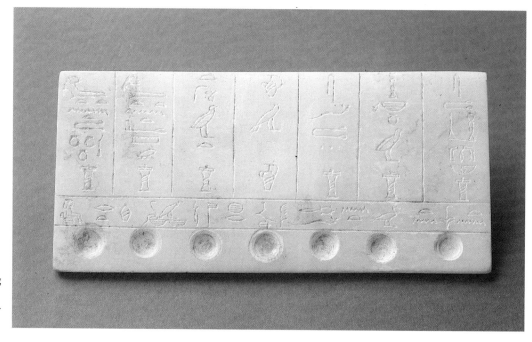

Tablet of „the seven offering oils" found in the mastaba of the princess Khekeretneb-ty at Abusir.

two fragments of clay sealings bearing one of Shepseskare's names — his Horus name — were found in the area of its earliest building phase. Can we infer, on the basis of this isolated find, that it was this pharaoh who was responsible for the improvised completion of Raneferef's tomb and at least for the provisional site of the ruler's mortuary cult? If so, then not Niuserre but the mysterious Shepseskare was the direct successor of Raneferef. Was he then responsible for the pyramid building, abandoned so shortly after its initiation, on the northern margin of the Abusir cemetery? This building is notable for a site almost exactly half way between Sahure's pyramid and Userkaf's sun temple. Userkaf and Sahure are believed to have been father and son. Did the builder of the early abandoned building wish to express, in its very location, his close — family ? — relationship with these two rulers? If this is the case and the building belonged to Shepseskare, would this mean that it was through him that Userkaf's, i.e. Sahure's, branch of the royal family regained power at the expense of the Neferirkare branch? The questions multiply, since they arise from what is not entirely contemporary evidence apparently testifying to the disturbed conditions and complex dynastic relationships which accompanied the whole period of the 5th Dynasty and, after Neferirkare's death, probably reached one of their critical moments. In any case, in conditions that are still far from

Miniature symbolic alabaster vases found in the sarcophagus chamber of Khekeretnebty's mastaba at Abusir.

This miniature crystal vase and basalt conical vessel were used in the ceremony of the Opening of the Mouth. The vessels were found in the sarcophagus chamber of Khekeretnebty's mastaba at Abusir.

Miniature copper bowls found in the sarcophagus chamber of Khekeretnebty's mastaba at Abusir.

This group of mudbrick offering tables was a subsequent addition to the court in front of the entrance to Khekeretnebty's mastaba at Abusir.

This model of a sexual organ was originally tied to Mere-fu's mummy.

This mace was originally part of a statue of Mernefu, director of the royal palace. Mastaba of Mernefu. Wood. 5th Dynasty. Abusir.

clear it was finally Neferirkare's younger son Niuserre who gained the upper hand. During his more than thirty-year rule the Abusir cemetery attained its highest grandeur, the nearby sun temples built by several rulers of the 5th Dynasty only giving it further lustre (see pp. 99—102).

After the death of Niuserre everything changed. His successors Menkauhor and Djedkare abandoned Abusir and built their monuments elsewhere. Abusir ceased to be the royal cemetery. This loss of status was interrupted by perhaps one, so far mysterious exception. On the slope to the southeast of Niuserre's mortuary temple Djedkare founded a cemetery for the members of his family and high officials. This was a rather puzzling decision since the closest members of the royal family as a rule desired to be buried „in the shadow" of the ruler's pyramid. The Czech expedition discovered this cemetery in the mid 1970s and has so far managed to excavate and investigate the tombs of the princess Khekeretnebty and her daughter Tisethor, the princess Hedjetnebu, the prince Neserkauhor, the director of the royal palace Mernefu, the scribe of the royal children Idu and his wife Khenit, and one unnamed tomb. From the point of view of design most of these tombs are in many respects very similar. They are mastabas constructed cheaply from poor quality limestone and dried bricks. In the above-ground sections there is usually an ante-chamber, a cult chamber, storage chamber and the so-called *serdab* (Arabic for "cellar"), a closed room for statues of the deceased. In the underground sections, accessible by a vertical shaft and not far beneath ground level, was a single burial chamber with sarcophagus. All the tombs had already been pillaged in ancient times. However, one of them — that of Khekeretnebty — had only been despoiled in part. This was because one of the limestone ceiling

Group of half-disintegrated wooden statues found in the *serdab* of the mastaba of the princce Neserkauhor from the 5th Dynasty at Abusir.

The inscription, recorded on the limestone sarcophagus of Idu, Scribe to the Royal Children, was deliberately hacked off during the ancient Egyptian period. Mastaba of Idu and Khenit. End of the 5th Dynasty. Abusir.

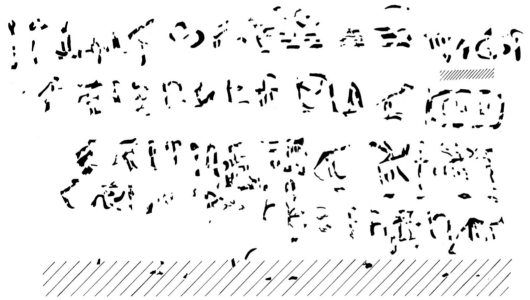

"6th (?) day, 3rd month of winter, 14th census (i.e. 28th regnal year). w'b-priest of the pyramid 'Kakai — is — the Soul', the scribe of the royal children Idu. The inspector of the priests of the Mother of the King of Upper and Lower Egypt (acting as) the King of Upper and Lower Egypt Khentkaus, Idu. The judge, the scribe of the temple, the King's acquaintance . . . Idu."

slabs in her burial chamber had cracked shortly after the interment of the deceased in the sarcophagus, and rubble and sand had poured down from the filling material of the tomb's superstructure. Part of the princess's burial equipment was under the debris. The thieves who subsequently broke into the tomb did not dare to remove the heap of rubble since they justifiably feared that this would lead to a a greater cave-in. Several beautiful small objects from Khekeretnebty's tomb — symbolic alabaster and copper vessels, symbolic miniature copper instruments and others — are today on exhibition in the Egyptian Museum in Cairo.

The cemetery established by Djedkare was gradually extended towards the east and almost up to the edge of the Nile valley, a limit which it reached during the 6th Dynasty. By this time Abusir had become no more than a local cemetery in which members of the lower middle ranks from neighbouring areas built their simple tombs, often in the vicinity of the older and larger mastabas of the 4th and 5th Dynasty. These were, among others, people employed to maintain the royal mortuary cults at the pyramids. Their simple family tombs, usually built of dried bricks and characterised by a number of burial shafts and a single common cult location, gradually filled up the eastern slopes of the desert hills between Abusir and Saqqara. Among them are the tomb of Shedu, chief confectioner at Niuserre's

Remains of wooden statues
of Shedu, Chief confectioner
in Niuserre's pyramid complex, and of his wife and
son.

mortuary temple, Fetekta, administrator of the stores, Hetepi, administrator of the stores, Rahotep, priest of Unas's mortuary temple, and many others discovered during Czech excavations over recent years.

After the break-up of the Egyptian state at the end of the Old Kingdom there followed what is called the 1st Intermediate Period of Egyptian history, during which the country was shaken by social unrest, armed conflicts and sometimes even anarchy. Not even the royal cemeteries escaped the consequences of these upheavals — and looting and tomb robbing occurred. It was at this period that not only did the mortuary cult of the pharoahs buried at Abusir die out but their pyramids were desecrated and pillaged. The robbers at this point contented themselves simply with looting the rich burial equipment in the underground chambers of the pyramids and the precious cult instruments in the magazines of the mortuary temples, and sometimes with damaging royal mummies while searching for personal jewellery. There was no effort to demolish the pyramid complexes themselves; paradoxically this was something which began only in later periods of domestic tranquillity and the development of the country under the New Kingdom. After the victory of the local rulers from Thebes in Upper Egypt, the re-unification of Egypt and the consolidation of state power at the end of the 11th Dynasty, the beginning of

Offering table of Shedu, Head confectioner in Niuserre's pyramid complex. Limestone. End of the 5th Dynasty. Abusir.

Remains of one of the burials found in the family tomb of the farmer Gegi. 6th Dynasty. South Abusir.

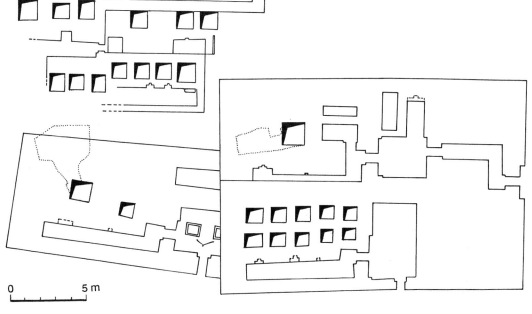

0   5 m

Plan of the cemetery of members of the lower-middle social strata in the vicinity of Fetekta's tomb in South Abusir (by J. Krejčí and K. Smoláriková).

The pillared vestibule of Fetekta's tomb in South
Abusir is buried under sand again after the season
of 1992. The walls of the vestibule and the pillars
were still decorated with superb wall paintings in
the 1840s.

the Middle Kingdom also saw the renewal of
the mortuary cults of the pharaohs buried at
Abusir. The priests who were active here had
their own tombs built directly on sites inside
parts of the already half-disintegrating and
sand-clogged pyramid complexes and, above
all, in the mortuary temples and their surroundings. At the beginning of this century
the Borchardt expedition managed to discover, during excavations in the vicinity of
Niuserre's mortuary temple, a number of intact tombs belonging to these priests. Many
such tombs were constructed in artificially
made cavities in the foundation ramp of Niuserre's causeway. The finds from these tombs
made their way, yet again, to German

Facsimile of inscriptions and pictures on the false
door of Rahotep, priest of the goddess Wadjet.

Conservation specialist
Yusef rescuing the remains
of wall paintings in Fetekta's
tomb.

Wall painting with a scene depicting vineyard workers. Documented in Fetekta's tomb by the Lepsius expedition in the 1840s, the painting is no longer in existence.

This famous scene from Fetekta's tomb — "At an Ancient Egyptian Market" — has also not survived.

Museums since conditions in the Egyptian Antiquities Organisation still allowed such export at the beginning of the century. An example was the richly ornamented wooden coffin with the mummy of the priest Herish-efhotep, one of the most precious exhibition pieces at the Egyptian Museum in Leipzig.

The renewed mortuary cults at the Abusir pyramids survived, however, for only a short period and then died out forever. Abusir fell into complete oblivion for almost half a millennium. People returned there only at the beginning of the New Kingdom when the cult of the goddess Sakhmet developed in the ruins of Sahure's mortuary temple. It is possible that the stimulus to this cult was given by the relief of the lion goddess which once adorned the wall of the cor-

Facsimile of an inscription on the false door of Isesiseneb, priest of the pyramid complex of Unas.

ridor around the temple's open court, and the precise significance of which was not quite grasped by simple people. The cult of the so-called 'Sahure Sakhmet' rapidly acquired an importance which transcended the level of popular culture. It endured until the end of the New Kingdom. Interestingly, it was on exactly the same spot that a small Coptic shrine appeared much later.

The New Kingdom period, however, saw yet another chapter in the history of the royal cemetery's decline. No major scruples inhibited moves to dismantle the huge stone constructions of the 5th-Dynasty Kings. The quickly and cheaply acquired materials were taken to other places in the Memphite necropolis and used for building new tombs. In the context of this period a dissonant note was sounded only by the isolated and generously conceived efforts of Prince Khamwese, the son of Ramesses the Great and the High Priest of the Temple of Ptah in Memphis. These were devoted to the reconstruction of damaged royal monuments throughout the whole Memphite necropolis. Fragments of Khamwese's "restoration inscriptions" have been found near several pyramids. The fascination of the Memphite necropolis finally led the wise prince to his decision to build his own monument on a hill on the south-west margins of the Abusir cemetery. This was by far the highest placed site and from here it was possible to look out over the whole

Block with the remains of a wall painting found in Fetekta's tomb during excavations in 1991.

Reis Muhammad Talal and reis Ahmad al-Qereti, foremen of workmen at the excavations, above the site of the discovery of the limestone false door of Rahotep, priest of goddess Wadjet, dating from the end of the 5th and beginning of the 6th Dynasty. South Abusir.

ravishing panorama of all the pyramids stretching from Abu Rawash, Giza, Zawiyet el-Aryan, Abusir, Saqqara and up to Dahshur. The ruins of Khamwese's monument are today being investigated by a Japanese archaeological expedition from Waseda University.

The social consciousness of the Egyptians, at least as it appears to us from our modern standpoint, was full of contradictions. How else can we explain, for example, the fact that under the New Kingdom, at the very time when the vast burial monuments of the rulers of the Old Kingdom were being unscrupulously dismantled without reverence for forefathers and with full official approval, it was precisely these disintegrating and sand-choked pyramids, temples and graves

Fragment of a limestone block with an Aramaic inscription found in Neferirkare's mortuary temple by the Borchardt expedition.

that were becoming, for a wide spectrum of social ranks, sought-after sites for final resting-places. People had come to believe that all these grand monuments of the past were the work of gods and mythical rulers. Hand in hand with this idea came the desire to be buried near these fabulous beings, to rest in their ,,shadow" and enjoy their favour and protection. In Abusir too it is this period that saw the beginnings of the cemetery for the common people, which gradually spread, in the upper sand levels, over the whole area of the field containing the pyramids, temples, mastabas and family tombs of the Old Kingdom. The deceased, inhabitants of the nearby villages of the Nile valley, were interred in simple wooden coffins which were sometimes roughly anthropoid in shape, very primitively decorated and occasionally "inscribed" with a copied formula manifestly transcribed by an illiterate ignorant of hieroglyphic writing. Sometimes the dead were buried in oval coffins of baked clay or were simply swathed in a mat. The poverty of the deceased was often attested by very modest burial equipment, made up of a ceramic

vessel, a couple of faience amulets and beads, shells etc. Often, however, there was none at all. The development of the commoners' cemetery received a new stimulus in the Late Period when in nearby North Saqqara, only two or three kilometres from the Abusir pyramids, an important religious centre grew up — not only for the Memphite necropolis but for the whole of Egypt. Here there were underground catacombs and the tombs of sacred animals, above all bulls, cows, ibises, jackals, falcons and others. The most important site was the Serapeum — the cemetery of the sacred bulls of Apis, who were regarded as the earthly incarnations of Ptah, the chief god of Memphis.

The existence of the Serapeum and the other religious buildings in its vicinity probably provided the impulse for the writing of the last magnificent chapter in the history of the Abusir Cemetery. At the end of the 26th Dynasty, known as the Saite Dynasty, a new cemetery was established midway between the Abusir pyramids and the Serapeum, and already a relatively long way from the Nile valley. The founder was none other than

In the fields by Abusir.

Abusir laundresses.

Udjahorresnet, the very shadowy and historically controversial leading figure in Egypt towards the end of the country's age of independence and at the beginning of the period known as the First Persian Domination (see below, pp. 195—208).

The history of the cemetery in Abusir closes in the 4th century BC with an archaeologically somewhat obscure episode. This is represented by the small Greek cemetery with interments in wooden coffins that was discovered during Borchardt's excavations in the area to the east of Niuserre's mortuary temple. In addition to the coffins of Greek type, other objects were found making up part of the grave equipment, such as pottery, coins slipped into the mouth of the deceased before the final journey, and other items. Despite the range of discoveries and typological analysis of the coffins, the dating of the Greek cemetery is still a matter of dispute. The dominant view is that it dates from the 4th century BC — the period after the Alexander the Great's conquest of Egypt in 332 BC. It has also been argued, however, that it may be older and connected with the Greek military colony which already existed in the vicinity of Memphis from the 26th Dynasty.

It is not without interest that Udjahorres-net, the owner of the previously mentioned huge shaft tomb on the south-west margins of the cemetery was, among other things, the commander of the Greek soldiers enlisted in Egyptian services. It is also not without significance here that it was in the Abusir cemetery that a German expedition managed to discover, at the beginning of 1920, one of the earliest Greek literary records in Egypt — a papyrus with the manuscript "Timotheos, The Persians".

Scattered Greek coins; the remains of the Coptic sanctuary in the ruins of Sahure's mortuary temple; a few isolated vestiges left by the Coptic pilgrims who once congregated in the ruins of Khentkaus's mortuary temple; at Neferirkare's pyramid a stray bronze arrow loosed by a Mamlouk soldier, or an Arabic inscription carved into a corner block of Raneferef's unfinished pyramid, perhaps from the time when General Amr Ibn el-Aas gathered the Arab forces beside the Abusir pyramids for their final assault on the Byzantine stronghold of Babylon and a future of complete control of Egypt; all this represents the epilogue in the history of the Abusir cemetery. It was an epilogue which already concerned the cemetery itself no more than indirectly.

Under the Sign of the Sun

3

From ancient times man has looked up at the sun with a mixture of wonder, fear, respect and hope; from ancient times man's spirit has been drawn towards that huge and mysterious radiant heavenly body which brings both benefit and destruction, life and death. Yet rarely has fascination with the sun reached the level that it did in Ancient Egypt. Undoubtedly a factor contributing to this was the particular natural environment of Egypt, a fertile strip of land stretching along the banks of the Nile from south to north and closed in to east and west by unending and eternally scorched desert. The fertile valley and the desert, water and sun — so sharp yet so imperceptible a border between prosperity and wretchedness, good and evil,

life and death. Here terror and measureless respect flowed together in man into a feeling of absolute dependence on the sun, ruler of the world.

We can only guess at the beginnings of sun worship in the Nile valley. Undoubtedly they reach back far into prehistory. The earliest direct evidence, however, is to be found with the first development of Egyptian writing at the watershed between the prehistoric and historic eras. The oldest hieroglyphic writing already shows the sun denoted by the simple yet very realistic sign of a disc. This pictorial semantic sign, an ideogram, could also be transcribed by means of phonograms and then sounded as *re* (the vowel *e* is not transcribed with complete precision since it refers

The Egyptian sun.

to a sound value resembling the Arabic *ayin* (Hebrew *yodh*), a guttural sound resembling our *e, a* and *o* all at once). Philologists suggest that its meaning is possibly connected with the Egyptian word *ier* which meant „to rise", or „come forth". The etymology of the word *re* has not, however, been satisfactorily identified. Also obscure are the beginnings of the deification of the sun and the development of its cult. It appears that in the earliest times the cult of the sun was popular mainly among people of the lowest social strata and that in the second half of the 4th millennium BC the sun god Re was overshadowed by other more significant deities. If we leave on one side the rather debatable evidence for the theo-form character of the names of two 2nd-Dynasty rulers, in which the word *re* is an element, then it seems that the real, one might almost say unstoppable, advance of the sun god and his cult began from the 3rd Dynasty with the reign of Djoser, who was the founder of the strictly centralised state known in the periodisation of Egyptian history as the Old Kingdom (approximately from the 28th-22nd century BC).

Re was pictured as a man with the sun disc on his head. Later he acquired other attributes and could be depicted in other forms such as a sitting cat or man with the head of a cat. Gradually Re became not merely the object of a cult but the subject of complex theological speculations, the highest state deity and the corner stone of Ancient Egyptian statehood. The basic ideology of the Ancient Egyptian state consisted in the idea that Egypt was the work of the gods, an island of order and justice surrounded by an endless sea of chaos. The Egyptian ruler, the Pharaoh, who was the only god to live among men on earth, was the guarantee that hostile forces of internal and external evil would not prevail over the forces of order and good. Order, truth and justice were embodied by Re's daughter Maat pictured as a seated woman with an ostrich feather in her hair. The ostrich feather, having the same sound value *maat*, became the symbol of the goddess and, together with her, of order, truth and justice. In theological constructions Re emerges as a universal cosmic deity, the creator, ruler of the gods, god of the dead and ruler of the other world. He played an important role in myths and magery. According to an ancient myth the sun god was born each morning from the sky goddess Nut on the eastern horizon, in the form of the god Khepre. Here he began his daily journey across the heavenly ocean in a barge called *mendjet,* so that in the evening on the western horizon he could descend as the god Atum. At night his journey continued in the night sky through the underworld, in a barge called *mesketet.* And so on and on continuously from the creation of the world until its end.

In various of his aspects, or in combination with other gods, Re was worshipped in many places in Egypt. The oldest, and in the Old Kingdom at the time of the pyramid builders also the most important centre of the cult of Re was *Iunu*, later called Heliopolis, "the solar city" in Greek. This lay on the eastern margins of modern Cairo. Here the best known and largest temples of Re were built, and especially what was known as the "High Sand" giving material form to the mythical hill which at the creation of the world first emerged from the primeval waters and on which the radiance of the sun first shone. In the sacred places of the temple called the "House of Benben" worship was offered to *benben,* an ancient stone fetish in the shape of a pyramid which symbolized the summit on which the sun was born daily. The shape of this particular fetish is usually linked to the original form of the royal tombs of the Old Kingdom — the pyramid. The priests of Re from Heliopolis gained ever greater importance and influence, especially Re's High Priest who in the earliest period was called "One who sees the Great One (i.e. the God)", and later the "Greatest of those who see (God)". Another significant centre of the cult of Re was the Ancient Egyptian *Sakhebu,* a place not as yet precisely located but probably lying on the south bank of the Nile opposite Heliopolis and near modern Zat el-Kom. Both of these places played an important part in the obscure period of the fall of the 4th Dynasty and rise of the 5th Dynasty and in connexion with the establishment and development of the royal cemetery at Abusir. Abusir was, after all, chosen as their final resting-place by the 5th-Dynasty pharaohs who were sometimes termed "Solar Kings". Several of these kings also built what are known as 'sun temples' here.

The English traveller and collector of antiquities Henry Westcar, during his stay in Egypt in the mid-nineteenth century, acquired a papyrus which to this day bears his name and represents a highly significant

Ancient Egyptian literary source. On the papyrus, which dates from the Hyksos Period, four stories have been preserved which are in fact only a fragment and copy of an original apparently older and longer text. The first of these tales is set in the time of the 4th Dynasty and takes place at the court of the famous Pharaoh Cheops. It describes how the sons of the Pharaoh came into his presence and related the remarkable things that had occurred in the reigns of his predecessors Nebka and Sneferu. The account also mentions the magician Djedi. The hundred and ten year-old Djedi is at last summoned and asked to demonstrate his arts to the Pharaoh. During one of the wonders which he performs Djedi predicts the miraculous birth of three kings — founders of a new dynasty. He was thus indirectly informing the Pharaoh of the extinction of his line. The alarm that seizes the Pharaoh is such that Djedi can then do no more than comfort him with the words: "Your son, his son, (and only then) one of them". Another two generations of the line of Cheops were to follow each other

on the throne of the pharaohs. According to the prophecy of Djedi, the new rulers — Userkaf, Sahure and Neferirkare — would be born through the supernatural union of the sun god Re himself and an ordinary woman named Rededet, the wife of a priest of Ra from Sakhebu.

Egyptological literature has taken up the designation of "Solar Kings" for the new rulers who founded the 5th Dynasty. It seems that beneath the apparently innocent story or fairytale from the Westcar Papyrus there lies a hidden political and propaganda purpose. This was perhaps to give additional explanation for and justify the changes in the leadership of the state and the rise of a new dynasty. To speak of a "new dynasty" is not perhaps quite accurate; it might be more appropriate to speak of a partial violation of the strict rules governing succession to the throne which served the interests of a collateral branch of the royal family. The prophecy of Djedi was in any case not entirely accurate since after the death of Cheops three successors who were demonstrably his

The ruins of Userkaf's sun temple. In the background the Abusir Pyramids are visible.

heirs followed on the throne — his two sons Radjedef and Chefren and his grandson Mycerinus in that order. Only after the death of Mycerinus did the reign of the 4th Dynasty meet its so far still obscure end. For other reasons as well the story from the Westcar Papyrus cannot be regarded as a direct historical source but only as a literary reflection on historical events which probably originated at the end of the 4th Dynasty and beginning of the 5th Dynasty.

Obscurity also surrounds the reasons that led the first pharaohs of the 5th Dynasty to found the new royal necropolis in Abusir, at the time a by no means outstandingly significant place between Saqqara and Giza. Some Egyptologists believe that Abusir was chosen because it was the southernmost spot from which it was still possible to glimpse the sun shining on the top of the obelisk of Re's temple in Heliopolis. The first to start building in Abusir was Userkaf, the founder of the 5th Dynasty and a man of uncertain origin, possibly a son (collateral?) of the royal fami-

ly, possibly High Priest of Re from Heliopolis, or even both. Userkaf provided the impetus for the establishment of the royal necropolis in Abusir, even if he had his own tomb built in Saqqara near the north-eastern corner of Djoser's complex. This is because he built the first sun temple in Abusir. In this way he opened the brief and still in many ways mysterious and obscure chapter of Egyptian history represented by the sun temples built in the Memphite necropolis — only during the 5th Dynasty and only by some of its rulers.

"Re's Stronghold"; this was the name given to Userkaf's sun temple. Its ruins are to be found today on a hill north of Sahure's pyramid at Abusir. The name of the temple is taken from Nekhen, a stronghold in Upper Egypt and the seat of the earliest, still prehistoric, kings whose achievements led to the victorious conclusion of the efforts to unite Egypt. Did Userkaf, in using this name, want to give symbolic expression to the final victory in the struggle to assert the cult of Re

Horizontal plan and lengthwise cross-section of the building complex of Userkaf's sun temple (by H. Ricke).

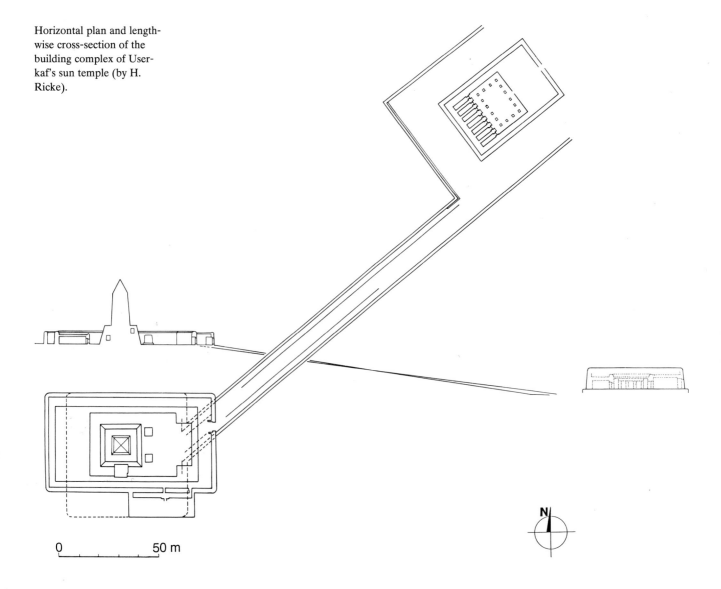

0 _____ 50 m

and the invincibility of the stronghold of the new faith? The building in some respects resembles a pyramid complex. It consists in a valley temple on the edge of the desert, a causeway and a temple erected on a hill above the Nile valley. Here, of course, the likeness ends. The design of the complex of buildings making up the sun temple differs completely in both overall conception and detailed execution from the contemporary royal tomb in the form of a pyramid. Above all there is the strikingly different orientation of the sun temple complex. Only the temple with the obelisk, erected on a hill roughly 20 m high, is precisely oriented in an east-west direction. The other elements in the complex — the valley temple and the causeway leading to the temple with the obelisk — were not oriented by the cardinal points. This fact is particularly surprising in the case of the valley temple. This building on the edge of the Nile valley was not, after all, simply a monumental „gate" to the whole complex but a genuine temple, albeit one atypical in its layout. It was rectangular in shape and was made up of an ante-chamber, middle section with an open court with pillars and finally of seven niches in the rear section. In Ancient Egypt precise orientation to the cardinal points was, however, an integral part of the rituals accompanying the establishment of a temple, whether the axis of the temple was east-west or north-south. The peculiarities of this valley temple led Herbert Ricke and his colleagues on the joint Swiss-German archaeological expedition which excavated the Userkaf sun temple complex in the mid 1950s to the theory that it was a temple older than the rest of the complex into which it had then been incorporated. They even considered the possibility that it had originally been a sanctuary of the goddess Neith, an idea based on the discovery of the head of a statue made of black slate and with a partially preserved Lower Egyptian crown. By chance this statue fragment was found only a few hours before the completion of excavations in the precincts of Userkaf's sun temple. Ultimately, however, the theory was rejected because more detailed analysis showed that there was a moustache under the nose and therefore it was not a portrait of the goddess Neith but most probably of the pharaoh Userkaf himself with a Lower Egyptian crown on his head (the statue is now exhibited in the Egyptian Museum in Cairo). This explanation does not, of course, answer

Head of colossal red granite statue of Userkaf. The Egyptian Museum, Cairo.

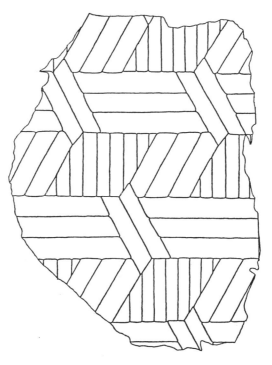

Ornamental sculpture pattern resembling matting made from plant materials. Fragment of a diorite naos (shrine) for a statue from Userkaf's sun temple (by H. Ricke).

the basic question of the unusual layout and orientation of the valley temple of Userkaf's complex at Abusir.

Also unusual in position and orientation is the causeway, a sort of open ramp which linked the valley temple to the temple with the obelisk located on higher ground. The causeway does not lie along the main axis of either of the two temples. It is a pity that we are unable to compare the causeway of Userkaf's sun temple complex with that of his pyramid complex in Saqqara. This is because neither the valley temple nor the causeway of the latter complex has yet been excavated. The position of Userkaf's causeway in Abusir does, however, indicate that its architects to a certain extent drew inspiration from the tomb complexes of Userkaf's predecessors Mycerinus in Giza and Shepseskaf in South Saqqara.

The most significant part of Userkaf's complex in Abusir was the temple with the obelisk. The temple gradually underwent extensive reconstruction and this markedly changed its appearance. Originally it had a square ground plan, but it was then extended and the ground plan was modified to a rectangular design, oriented east-west. The greater part of the temple, roughly its eastern half, was filled by a large open court. In the western half there was a large stone-built obelisk, the symbol of the sun cult. Archaeological research into its construction, however, has resulted in the very surprising discovery that the obelisk was not a part of the original temple but was erected as a later addition. Originally a low building resembling a mastaba in shape had stood there, possibly supporting a wooden column with an image of the sun disc. Here there was evidently once an altar accessible by a low staircase. After the reconstruction the altar, on which offerings were made, was positioned in front of the eastern side of the base of the

huge obelisk. From written sources we know that the obelisk was of red granite and that it was the ruler Neferirkare who caused it to be erected in Userkaf's temple. On two sides of the altar, to the north and south, shrines of diorite were built in which probably stood statues of Re and Hathor, the deities venerated in the sun temple. The temple also included magazines. It was surrounded by a huge enclosure wall with rounded outer corners. It is not yet established whether this rounded effect had a merely constructional-functional significance, i.e. to provide greater resistance to damage, or perhaps also a religious meaning, i.e. to resemble the Primeval Hill on which the sun had shone at the creation of the world.

Only a few hundred metres to the north of the Userkaf sun temple, at a place called Abu Ghurab which in Arabic means "Father of Ravens", lie the ruins of the second sun temple to have been found and investigated archaeologically — that of Niuserre. Excavations were carried out here as early as the end of the last century by the German archaeological expedition led by Friedrich Wilhelm von Bissing. The member of the expedition entrusted with the task of documenting and processing the architectonic

Niuserre's sun temple in Abu Ghurab. The pyramids at Giza can be seen in the background.

Guard at Abu Ghurab.

discoveries was Ludwig Borchardt, the architect and archaeologist who was later to contribute significantly to archaeological investigation of the neighbouring pyramid cemetery at Abusir.

Niuserre's sun temple bore the very exalted name "Delight of Re". Again, it was composed of three parts: a valley temple, a causeway and a temple with an obelisk. This temple too was not precisely aligned to the cardinal points. Here, however, as had not been the case with Userkaf's complex, the von Bissing expedition was able to uncover the surroundings of the valley temple. As excavations proceeded it was shown that the huge stone enclosure wall of a city, which had apparently extended far towards the east in the Nile valley, abutted on the valley temple. Of course, even the existence of this city — whether contemporary with or older than Niuserre's complex, does not explain the disharmony in the orientation of the valley

Fragment of a relief with a rare picture of an elephant from the so-called 'Chamber of Seasons' from Niuserre's sun temple at Abu Ghurab (by E.Edel and S. Wenig).

Alabaster bowl from the so-called 'Great Slaughterhouse' of Niuserre's sun temple at Abu Ghurab. View from above and cross-section (by L. Borchardt).

temple to the cardinal points. Niuserre's valley temple was simpler than neighbouring Userkaf's in layout. It might be more appropriate to speak of it as a matter of a monumental gate to Niuserre's complex than as a valley temple. A huge structure made of limestone blocks, it had pillared porticoes on three sides: a main entrance approached from the north-west and decorated with two pairs of palm columns of red granite, and side entrances on the north-west and south-east each decorated with only one pair of these columns. The gate allowed access to the open causeway built in technically demanding conditions: a 16 m. vertical difference had to be overcome over a relatively short distance and also over very uneven ground. Limestone blocks were also the material used for construction of the causeway.

The hill on which Niuserre's temple with the obelisk stood was comparatively small. Before construction of the temple it was necessary to extend the summit with a system of artificial terraces. The temple has a rectangular layout with an east-west orientation defined by a huge periphery wall built

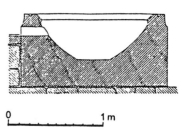

of limestone blocks. Roughly the south-eastern quarter of the temple was taken up by a large open court. The north-eastern quarter consisted in a series of storage chambers and an open space which Borchardt called the Great Slaughterhouse. This was because here he discovered several large

Ground plan of Niuserre's sun temple at Abu Ghurab (by L. Borchardt and H. Schäfer).

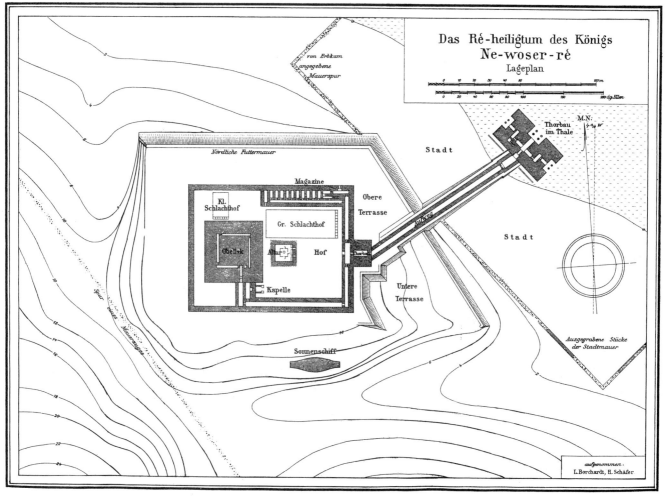

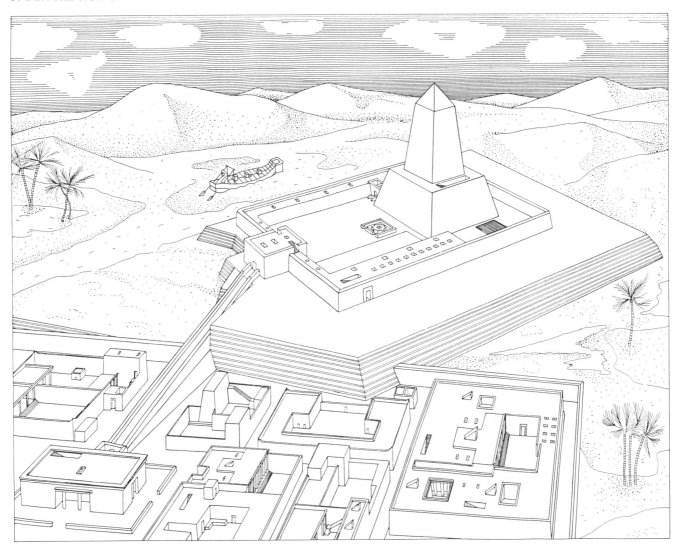

Reconstruction of Niuserre's sun temple at Abu Ghurab (by L. Borchardt).

View of the remains of the court and the base of the obelisk in Niuserre's sun temple at Abu Ghurab. In the foreground is a series of alabaster purification basins.

Remains of a gate of reddish
quartzite. Niuserre's sun
temple at Abu Ghurab.

alabaster basins — circular bowls carved out of a roughly cubical block — which were positioned in cascading order one after the other so that the blood of the sacrificial beasts could flow freely down them. The limestone paving of the slaughterhouse was provided with grooves which would, at the same time, facilitate the run-off of liquid. In his reconstruction of the original layout Borchardt postulated the existence of a second similar but smaller slaughterhouse in the northwestern corner of the temple. However, Borchardt's interpretation of both the spaces mentioned as slaughterhouses has one serious weakness. Neither in the Great or Small "Slaughterhouse", nor anywhere else in the whole temple, has there been found any unmistakeable archaeological evidence of the killing of sacrificial animals. In particular, there has been no sign of the characteristic conical stone blocks with a hole, and anchored in the ground, to which the prone and bound beasts were tied before slaughter. Such blocks, with their eloquent archaeologi-

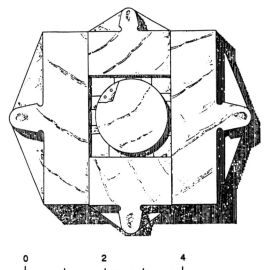

View from above of the alabaster offering table from Niuserre's sun temple at Abu Ghurab
(by L. Borchardt).

cal testimony, have been found in the "Sanctuary of the Knife" in the precincts of the Raneferef pyramid complex in Abusir. Niuserre's temple has also yielded no other kinds of evidence characteristic for slaughterhouses, such as animal bones, flint knives,

Alabaster offering table at the eastern foot of the base of the obelisk of Niuserre's sun temple at Abu Ghurab.

etc. It appears that rather than being used for the slaughter of animals these spaces were employed for the ritual purification of the offerings, including meat, to be laid on the altar of the sun god. The altar stood in the open court almost at the centre of the temple. It was made of five enormous alabaster blocks, the central block having an upper surface circular in form and the four lateral blocks, facing the cardinal points, having surfaces carved in the form of the hieroglyphic symbol *hetep*, which means "offering" or "offering table". The altar, which has remained to this day in a relatively good state of preservation, represents the most beautiful example of its type not only from the Old Kingdom, but from Ancient Egypt in its entire history.

The altar stood at the eastern foot of an immense stone pedestal, 20 m high, from which a 36 m obelisk soared toward the sky. The pedestal was in the form of a truncated pyramid. It was built of limestone blocks and its outer walls were faced with red granite blocks. A corridor led through it, slanting upward to allow access to the top of the pedestal at the foot of the obelisk. The corridor walls were decorated with exquisite scenes in low relief, of which, alas, only a part has survived. Among these were found the unique pictures known as the seasons; these depict the changing natural background during the Ancient Egyptian seasons of inundation and harvest. The scenes from the third part of the year, the season of emergence (of the fields from the flood), have not survived. The von Bissing expedition removed the reliefs and took them to Germany where today they are one of the most valuable of the exhibits in the Egyptian Museum in Berlin (the Weltkammer). In the ruins of the pedestal the German expedition also found fragments of scenes of the festival of *sed*, an important religious ceremony in which the ruler would celebrate the jubilee of his ascent to the throne and at the same time would be reconfirmed in his office. Only fragments of the obelisk, which once towered to a height of 36 m, have survived. It was not made from one piece of stone but from limestone blocks. This facilitated its later destruction when the temple became an easily accessible quarry.

Outside the temple and near its southern side the German expedition discovered a large building resembling a boat. It was built of mudbricks, plastered, whitewashed and coloured and augmented with several other elements made of other materials, for example wood. It had a purely symbolic character and is believed to have been a representation of the so-called, 'solar boat' in which, according to the Ancient Egyptian conception, the sun god was supposed to float across the heavenly ocean. There is no reason to doubt that the "boat" was symbolic in character and that it was part of the building complex making up Niuserre's sun temple. Nevertheless the interpretation of this unique archaeological find so far presented somewhat oversimplifies the case. We know from written sources that the sun god had two boats on his eternal journey — one for the day and one for the night. In the first he travelled with his retinue across the diurnal heaven, "the ocean of day" and in the second across the night's "underworld ocean". In Niuserre's sun temple in Abu Ghurab, however, only one boat has been found and at the nearby sun temple of Userkaf, despite very thorough survey of the whole area, not a single boat has been discovered.

The sun temples of Userkaf and Niuserre are the only two monuments of their kind yet to have been discovered and archaeologically investigated. Contemporary written sources, however, and especially inscriptions in the tombs of magnates and high officials from the 5th Dynasty, as well as papyri from the archives of the Abusir pyramid complexes, mention six sun temples. The temples were build only by rulers of the 5th Dynasty and not even by all of these. The earliest was the sun temple of Userkaf which has already been described. The second sun temple, "Field of Re", built by Sahure, has not yet been found. A few limestone blocks bearing the name of the temple have, however, been discovered in the masonry of Niuserre's mortuary temple in Abusir. Perhaps these were blocks which were left over after the completion of Sahure's temple, or perhaps Sahure's sun temple was never completed and material prepared for it was used for other purposes. Whatever the answer, Sahure's sun temple apparently did not stand far from Abusir. Archaeologists are also still looking for the "Place of Re's Pleasure", the sun temple of Neferirkare. This was probably the largest of the sun temples built under the 5th Dynasty, and, in any case, the one most frequently mentioned in contemporary inscriptions. Raneferef's sun temple called "Re's Offering Table" has also so far proved impossible to find. This is not perhaps so surprising, since this ruler reigned for too short a time for his sun temple to have been completed. Either this temple, mentioned only once in inscriptions from the famous tomb of the magnate Ti in Saqqara, was abandoned shortly after building had commenced, or the site was used by one Raneferef's successors. In this connexion research on the remains of the huge brick buildings which the von Bissing expedition found under the ruins of Niuserre's sun temple at Abu Ghurab is interesting and certainly worth more thorough archaeological investigation. If we leave aside Niuserre's sun temple, which we have already discussed, then we come to the last monument of this kind, built by the little-known Pharaoh Menkauhor. His sun temple named "Horizon of Re" or "The Place where Re Issues Forth" has likewise still not been found. The last rulers of the 5th Dynasty, Djedkare and Unas had given up the construction of sun temples.

The reasons which lay behind the building of sun temples at the beginning of the 5th Dynasty and the reasons why such building ceased towards the end of the dynasty have not yet been satisfactorily explained. Undoubtedly the task has been made difficult by the fact that of the six sun temples it has so far proved possible to locate and archaeologically investigate only two. Information is incomplete and there exist only a series of more or less plausible suppositions. It is clear from the names and design of the two temples as yet discovered that these temples were closely connected with the solar cult; the central cult symbol in both was an obelisk, the solar symbol *par excellence*. The fact that the temples — both those already located and very probably the others as well — were built on the west bank of the Nile in places where the sun set and in the middle of the Memphite necropolis nevertheless shows that they were also linked to conceptions of the after-life and above all to the royal mortuary cult. This is, in any case, amply confirmed by the new information provided by papyri from the Abusir temple archives. From these we know that it was from the sun temples that many of the sacrifices — especially meat, vegetables etc. — would come to the royal mortuary temples. The offerings would first be placed on the altar of Re in a sun temple and only then distributed to serve the needs of royal mortuary cults. It is interesting that a sun temple would not

only supply the mortuary temple of the ruler who had built it, but would supply those of other pharaohs as well. The sun temple was, then, not only the place of the setting sun, i.e. the mortuary temple of the "dying sun", but in both religious and economic terms an integral part of the building complex of a ruler's tomb and his mortuary cult. It also appears that the short history of sun temples was closely linked with the destiny of the royal cemetery in Abusir. This was because the sun temples were built above all by the rulers buried in Abusir. Moreover, two out of the six sun temples have already been found in the immediate neighbourhood of Abusir.

Just as the foundation of the royal cemetery in Abusir was evidently influenced by Userkaf's decision to build the first of the sun temples in that place, so the abandonment of the Abusir cemetery by Djedkare was probably one reason why sun temples

Jean-Philippe Lauer by the red granite pyramidion of an obelisk discovered in April 1974 near the south-western corner of the mastaba of Ptahshepses.

ceased to be built. There must, nonetheless, have been still more weighty reasons. Was one of these Djedkare's fundamental reorganisation of the royal mortuary cults at the Abusir cemetery (for a detailed account see p. 164)? Was one factor the administrative-political interests that lay behind the pharaoh's transfer of not only the royal cemetery but also the royal residence to another place — to what today is South Saqqara? Or were the decisive reasons religious and linked to the popularization of the burial cult and the rise of the cult of Osiris which occurred just at the time of Djedkare ? There are many unanswered questions but the greatest question, and the real challenge to present and future generations of Egyptologists, is posed by the four still undiscovered sun temples lying under the sand and almost certainly within sight of the summits of the Abusir pyramids.

The Step Pyramid on the
boundary of day and night.

The Royal Mother

The visitor to the royal cemetery at Giza, who stands awestruck in front of that wonder of the world, the Great Pyramid, is usually convinced that its owner Cheops was the greatest of the Egyptian pyramid-builders. He was not. That pre-eminence belongs to his father Sneferu, who built no less than four pyramids with a total volume that exceeds the work of Cheops by roughly a third. It was on the orders of Sneferu that the pyramid in Meidum, the Bent Pyramid and the Red Pyramid in Dahshur and the small pyramid in Seila were raised toward the heavens.

Altogether an incredible 3.6 million cubic metres of stone! Sneferu, later represented by the Ancient Egyptians as a wise and beneficent king, founded the dynasty whose rule and whose feats were to make the deepest impression on the memory of generations succeeding each other on the banks of the Nile. It was an impression to which the sheer "weight" of the Giza pyramids undoubtedly contributed. The names of Sneferu, Cheops, Radjedef, Chephren and Mycerinus marked out the 4th Dynasty's glorious path like milestones and it seemed that there could be

View of the pyramid cemetery at Giza from the southeast. The "bridge" in the foreground was in fact the great gate of a stone ceremonial wall which protected the royal cemetery from the south.

no limits to its power. Neverthelesss the dynasty met with sudden decline and fall, and ended in circumstances still more obscure than those in which it attained power. The mysterious tomb of the last ruler of the dynasty Shepseskaf, which in Arabic is called the Mastabat Fara'un, represents an almost symbolic question-mark at the end of one famous era. But besides Shepseskaf there was yet another figure who came to the fore during the obscure and confused period which set in at the end of the 4th Dynasty. This figure was the Queen Khenthaus. In almost every respect she is surrounded by mystery, beginning with her origins and ending with her unusual tomb. Nevertheless, with the progress of archaeological excavations new information has come to light which makes it ever more apparent that this woman played a key role not only at the end of the 4th Dynasty but also in the inauguration of the new 5th Dynasty.

When in 1932 the Egyptian archaeologist Selim Hassan began archaeological research on the so-called 'Fourth Pyramid' at Giza, surprises followed in rapid succession. "The Fourth Pyramid", a mysterious two-stepped building on the eastern margins of the Giza cemetery near the Great Sphinx, had attracted the attention of archaeologists as early as the last century. For a time it was even

considered to be the tomb of the little-known pharaoh Shepseskaf mentioned above. In the 1930s and shortly before Hassan's excavations this was still the belief of such famous experts on the royal cemetery in Giza as Uvo Hölscher, the German archaeologist and architect who led the investigations of the pyramid complex of the pharaoh Chephren, and the American Egyptologist and archaeologist George Andrew Reisner whose name is inseparable from research on the pyramid complex of Mycerinus. The first surprise brought by Hassan's excavations was the discovery that the 'Fourth Pyramid' was not a pyramid at all but originally a rock-cut tomb of mastaba type extended by a superstructure which transformed it into a stepped construction. We should immediately add that this construction is highly individual, and has no parallels among contemporary or indeed any other Ancient Egyptian tombs. The second surprise was that it belonged to Queen Khentkaus. It seemed that light would finally be shed on the mysteries surrounding Queen Khentkaus and the fall of the famous dynasty.

Even in its original form, Khentkaus's tomb at Giza was a remarkable and unique building. It was entirely carved out of a rock outcrop and its groundplan, surprising and unusual in tombs of mastaba type, was

The stepped tomb of the royal mother Khentkaus at Giza.

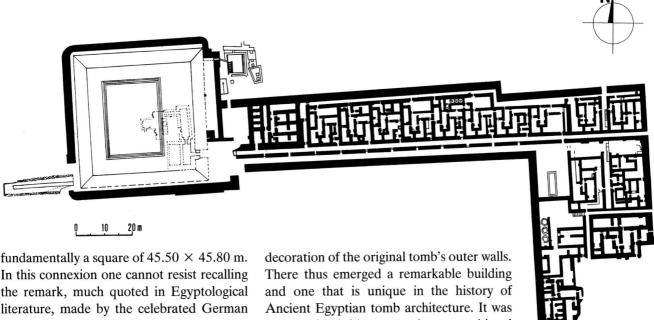

Plan of the tomb complex of Khentkaus at Giza (by Salim Hassan).

fundamentally a square of 45.50 × 45.80 m. In this connexion one cannot resist recalling the remark, much quoted in Egyptological literature, made by the celebrated German archaeologist and architect Ludwig Borchardt in a discussion with the young, and later equally famous French architect and archaeologist Jean-Philippe Lauer: "Jeune homme, vous ne m'apprendrez pas l'archéologie, un mastaba n'est jamais carrée!" This was Borchardt's ironic response, during a visit to Saqqara at the end of the 1920s, to Lauer's enthusiastic description of the discovery that a mastaba with a square ground-plan was the earliest building phase of the Step Pyramid. The exterior face of the side walls of the superstructure of Khentkaus's tomb were sloping at an angle of 74° and adorned with a pattern of niches, a motif taken up from the Early Dynastic architecture which had mainly employed dried bricks, wood and light plant materials. The niches resembled stylised, symbolic door apertures representing entrances to the tomb. They were set all around the tomb and this was related to the concept of ever-multiplying gifts offered to the spirit of the deceased remaining in the tomb.

At a later stage another step, built from limestone blocks, was added to Khentkaus's rock tomb. This extension was not square but rectangular in ground plan and oriented along a lengthy axis toward the north-east. It was not placed over the centre of the original building but shifted markedly toward its western part, and its surmounting surface was not horizontal but slightly rounded to facilitate the run-off of rainwater. The whole two-stepped structure, reaching a height of 17.5 m., was finally finished with a smooth casing of smaller blocks of fine white limestone which covered up even the original decoration of the original tomb's outer walls. There thus emerged a remarkable building and one that is unique in the history of Ancient Egyptian tomb architecture. It was a kind of hybrid representing a transitional form between the private tomb of mastaba type and the royal tomb of pyramid type. This unusual form of tomb did not come about by accident but, as we shall see, developed as a result of the extraordinary circumstances accompanying the life of the queen.

The generally unconventional impression made by the outer appearance of the tomb is reinforced by its internal design. The mortuary cult chambers were concentrated in the south-eastern part of the lower, older layer of the tomb. There were three of these and they were only accessible from the east, via a great gate of red granite originally equipped with heavy wooden doors. On the front face of the gate Selim Hassan found remnants of hieroglyphic inscriptions with the partially preserved titulary, name and picture of the queen. From the original relief decoration of the walls of the three cult chambers, which are linked in series from south to north, only a few fragments have survived; among them is a remnant of the so-called 'false door', the symbolic passage between this world and the other world, which was set into the western wall of the northernmost chamber. The underground part of the tomb was laid out in a way that in some respects resembles the substructure of Mycerinus's pyramid. This similarity perhaps reflects something more significant than the simple proximity of these monuments in time. The underground part — an extensive ante-chamber, several narrow magazines and above all the burial chamber — was devastated and pillaged by thieves in ancient times, evidently repeatedly. Of the alabaster sarcophagus in which the queen's mummy was once interred only tiny fragments have been found.

The tomb complex was, however, much larger than the foregoing description suggests and it included other additional and archaeologically very interesting features. Among them was a long narrow trench at the south-west corner of the tomb which had originally contained the so-called 'funerary boat', by which the spirit of the deceased was to depart for the other world and float across the heavenly ocean. At the south-east corner of the tomb there was also a pool which was used for purification ceremonies and perhaps even during the mummification of the dead queen. The most noteworthy element was, of course, the residential area lying in front of the anterior, eastern wall of the tomb. This contained the dwellings of the priests who maintained the mortuary cult of the queen in the period of the 5th and 6th Dynasties. Khentkaus's whole complex, in the broadest sense, also included a number of neighbouring tombs which were the burial places of people connected with the queen either by family ties or mortuary cult duties. Khentkaus's two-step tomb became the centre of a small but independent cemetery which grew up gradually on the eastern margins of the Giza necropolis. From the archaeological viewpoint this is a very remarkable phenomenon; elsewhere in the Giza necropolis it is a demonstrable pattern only in the case of rulers, whose pyramid complexes always represent the centres of satellite cemeteries of relatives, courtiers, officials and priests — everyone, in short, who desired and was entitled to be close to his sovereign even after death. The siting of Khentkaus's tomb very close to Mycerinus's valley temple is a further indication of a possible close relationship between the two individuals. This is a possibility which can only be strengthened by the discovery in Mycerinus's valley temple of a fragment of a stone stela with a damaged hieroglyphic inscription which suggests that Khentkaus was the pharaoh's daughter.

Among the many extraordinary archaeological discoveries from Khentkaus's tomb complex one in particular produced amazement and even a sensation. This was the inscription on a fragment of the granite gate which has already been mentioned and which contained the never before documented title of queen. Its discovery immediately raised a fundamental controversy among Egyptologists since from a purely grammatical point of view two interpretations were possible, Some translated the title as "Mother of the Two Kings of Upper and Lower Egypt" while others rendered it as "King of Upper and Lower Egypt and Mother of the king of Upper and Lower Egypt". The first interpretation was put forward by Vladimir Vikentiev, the Russian Egyptologist and emigrant who at that time lived in Cairo, and the second by the Austrian Egyptologist Hermann Junker, who at just that period had started the ambitious Austrian excavations in the cemeteries lying "in the shadow" of Cheops' pyramid. It is paradoxical that Vikentiev's opinion prevailed for such a long time when the discoverer of Khentkaus's tomb, Selim Hassan, inclined immediately to Junker's interpretation. This was perhaps a result of the influence of the Westcar Papyrus, according to which the first three 5th-Dynasty rulers were brothers. On the basis of all the data gathered during excavations Selim Hassan drew remarkable historical conclusions. He considered the shape of the tomb, and especially the second step which resembled a huge sarcophagus, to be similar to Shepseskaf's Mastabat Faraun. From this formal resemblance he deduced that Khentkaus and Shepseskaf, two figures from the last years of the 4th Dynasty, had been married. Moreover, he saw in the shape of both tombs, so ostentatiously differing from the pyramid form which prevailed for royal tombs of the period and represented almost a religio-political obligation, an expression of opposition by the ruling royal line to the ever-growing influence of the solar religion and the might of the priesthood of Re. He inferred that after the death of her husband, Khentkaus finally bowed to the priests of Re and was even forced to marry their High Priest, Userkaf, with whom she then founded the 5th Dynasty. She refused, however, to be buried next to her second husband and so built her own tomb at Giza in the eternal resting-places of her famous royal ancestors.

It is hardly necessary to emphasize that Selim Hassan's researches and his theory attracted not only attention but mixed reactions. One of the first to make a stand was Ludwig Borchardt. Having spent long years of archaeological research in the neighbouring necropolis at Abusir, Borchardt

immediately realised that the name of queen Khentkaus was familiar to him. The name Khentkaus, adorned with the title "Royal Mother", appeared on several fragments of papyri which had earlier been discovered in Abusir and which, it was later ascertained, had made up part of the archive of the pyramid complex of the 5th-Dynasty pharaoh Neferirkare (see p. 163 ff.). Not only these fragments of papyri but also a number of other archaeological finds, such as an alabaster offering table with the remains of an inscription bearing the titles and name of the queen, provided indirect evidence of the cult of Khentkaus at Abusir. A fragment of an inscription on a piece of relief from Mersetjefptah's tomb at Abusir even makes express mention of Khentkaus's mortuary temple, which was evidently located somewhere in the Abusir cemetery. The historical conclusions drawn by Borchardt in many respects augmented Selim Hassan's theory, but they also modified it. According to Borchardt, Shepseskaf was not of royal origin, and gained power only thanks to his marriage to Khentkaus. Their two sons, Sahure and Neferirkare, became legitimate rulers and founded the 5th Dynasty. The first 5th-Dynasty king, Userkaf, gained the throne only through the premature death of Shepseskaf at a point when the two legitimate heirs to the throne were too young to assume power. Borchardt's conviction that Sahure and Neferirkare were brothers was undoubtedly influenced by the adjustments to the relief decoration which he discovered during his research in Sahure's pyramid complex at Abusir (see above, pp. 77 and 124)

Not long after Borchardt, Bernhard Grdseloff, the Polish archaeologist living in Egypt, expressed his opinion on the whole question and gave it a new historical dimension. Grdseloff looked at Khentkaus's career in the wider context of the development of the royal line in the course of the 4th Dynasty. He based his opinion on the premise that the premature death of Cheops' son, Crown Prince Kawab, unexpectedly brought to the throne his younger brother Radjedef. Grdseloff believed that Hetepheres (II), Radjedef's wife, had been the daughter of a princess of Libyan origin. In this way the so-called 'Libyan branch' of the royal family temporarily rose to power. Ultimately, however, the main branch of the line, represented by Chephren, Mycerinus and Shepseskaf with his wife Khentkaus, enforced its claim.

The prematurely widowed Khentkaus herself ruled for a certain period in place of her as yet immature sons Sahure and Neferirkare. Grdseloff argued, however, that she finally married a prince from the Libyan branch of the family — Userkaf, the founder of the 5th Dynasty — and brought the unharmonious branches of the royal family into concord.

Yet despite the efforts of Selim Hassan, Ludwig Borchardt and Bernhard Grdseloff, and partly as a result of their theories and speculations, the fall of the 4th Dynasty in fact became ever more obscure. For many years the theme seemed to have been exhausted. Only after more than a quarter of a century, at the beginning of the 1970s, did the problem receive fresh attention, this time from the German Egyptologist Hartwig Altenmüller and from a surprising new philological, literary-historical viewpoint. It occurred to Altenmüller that there could be a concrete connexion between Queen

Detail from a relief depicting the goddess Nekhbet, protectress of the crown of Upper Egypt, with the vulture diadem on her head (by L. Borchardt).

Khentkaus and the celebrated Ancient Egyptian literary work preserved in the Westcar Papyrus (see pp. 100 f.). He expressed the opinion that the name Rededet, the earthly woman with whom Re had intercourse and who became the mother of the kings Userkaf, Sahure and Neferirkare, was a pseudonym for none other than Queen Khentkaus. He then considered the coming to power of her sons as the rehabilitation of the adherents of the solar cult and as the resumption of the rule of the main branch of this ruling family.

Neither Altenmüller's theory nor various other attempts to explain the tangled circumstances of the fall of the 4th Dynasty and rise of the 5th Dynasty were free of inconsistencies; nor did they meet with general acceptance. On the one hand there was an ever-growing tendency to regard the Royal Mother as a personal link between the two dynasties, but on the other she remained the symbol of a complex historical problem: the mysterious fall of a mighty royal line and the no less puzzling rise of a new ruling family and opening of a new epoch in Egyptian history. The confusing array of different historical sources, and of theories attempting to interpret them, finally earned the question its own lapidary title in Egyptological literature: the Khentkaus problem. Most Egyptologists came to believe that the Khentkaus problem could not be solved unless new information came to light. It was anticipated that any breakthrough would come either from as yet unpublished written sources lying in the depositaries of world museums, for example, or from new finds made during archaeological excavations. This second possibility is the one that has proved fruitful since finds from the Czech archaeological excavations in Abusir in 1978 and the years following have apparently brought the desired turning-point in relation to the "Khentkaus problem".

It is puzzling that the Deutsche Orient-Gesellschaft expedition led by Ludwig Borchardt did not pay more attention, during its work at Abusir, to the ruins of a large

Fragment of a relief from the tomb of Mersetjefptah at Abusir, with the remains of an inscription mentioning the mortuary temple of the royal mother (by H. Schäfer).

View of the pyramid complex of the royal mother Khentkaus at Abusir (bottom right and in the background are the two small pyramid complexes L no. XXIV and L no. XXV, likewise just before excavations were started.)

Neferirkare, and the record made late in his reign and probably shortly before his death. Or, alternatively, the ruler in question could have been his younger son and second heir, Niuserre; in this case it would constitute a record of the renewal and completion of the building works after a long interruption of approximately twelve years. Yet another serious modification occurred, however, as is again shown by one of the building inscriptions, on which the word "Mother" has been added above the word "Wife" in the title of the tomb's owner. The tomb was therefore completed for a woman who was no longer "the King's Wife" but had already become "the King's Mother".

On completion the pyramid was perhaps 17 m high, with sides 25 m long and walls with an angle of inclination of 52°. The remains of the pyramid that have survived to this day reach a height of perhaps 4 m. In the devastated burial chamber underneath the pyramid no demonstrable fragments of the queen's physical remains have been discovered, if we do not count a few shreds of linen bandaging which perhaps once swathed a mummified body. A similarly indirect piece of evidence is the small fragment of a sarcophagus made of red granite found in the ruins at the foot of the pyramid.

The mortuary temple, built in front of the eastern face of the pyramid for cult reasons, was constructed in two major building phases. The first-phase temple was modest in dimensions although built out of limestone blocks. This earlier "stone phase" of the

temple was so extensively destroyed by ancient stone thieves that today it is very difficult to reconstruct even a rough approximation of the main elements of its original design. The entrance to the temple was originally from the east, near the south-eastern corner, and decorated with twin pillars — limestone monoliths coloured red and bearing on the exterior side a vertical hieroglyphic inscription in sunken relief with the queen's titulary, name and picture. The front, eastern half of the temple was taken up by an open court decorated with similar pillars. The centre of the queen's mortuary cult was in the western part of the temple in an

Limestone pillars, one standing, one fallen, with remains of hieroglyphic inscriptions containing the name and titles of the queen Khentkaus. Khentkau's pyramid complex at Abusir.

A half-standing, half-fallen limestone pillar with remains of hieroglyphic inscriptions containing the name and titles of the queen Khentkaus. Khentkaus's pyramid complex at Abusir.

This inscription on a clay sealing from the reign of Djedkare mentions the unique title "Mother of the King of Upper and Lower Egypt (exercising office as) King of Upper and Lower Egypt".

View of the entrance section of the extended mortuary temple of the queen Khentkaus at Abusir. In the background rises Neferirkare's pyramid.

This small limestone column capital in the form of a lotus flower in full blossom was found in the mortuary temple of the queen Khentkaus at Abusir.

Detail of a relief from Sahure's mortuary temple with the subsequently altered picture of the pharaoh Neferirkare (by L. Borchardt).

offering hall with an altar and false door made of red granite. The false door was embedded in the western wall of the chamber and directly adjoined the pyramid. In front of it offerings would be placed by the mortuary priests. Beside the offering hall and in the westernmost part of the temple were three deep recesses in which there originally stood statues of the queen. A staircase in the southwest corner of the temple gave access to the temple's roof terrace on which the priests would conduct astronomical observations and certain ceremonies day and night.

The rooms in the western part of the temple were decorated with scenes and inscriptions in coloured low relief. The temple's so-called 'decorative scheme' covered an astoundingly wide spectrum of subjects, above all scenes of sacrifice, agricultural work, processions of personified funerary estates bearing offerings to the queen, and others. Among them there are also absolutely exceptional themes, such as a scene, unfortunately preserved only in several small

Detail from an inscription
on a standing pillar in the
mortuary temple of the
queen Khentkaus at Abusir:
the queen Khentkaus is sitting on the throne, holding
the sceptre *wadj* in her right
hand and with the uraeus on
her forehead.

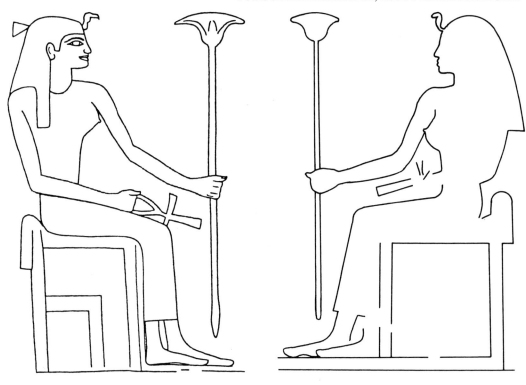

Detail of a picture of the queen Khentkaus with the uraeus on her forehead. Mortuary temple of the queen, Abusir.

Detail of a picture of Khentkaus on a pillar at the original entrance to the queen's mortuary temple at Abusir.

fragments, probably depicting the ruler Niuserre and members of his family standing in front of the queen. On the fragment with the scene, just as on a number of others, the queen's name is preceded by a title which is identical to the historically unique title of the Khentkaus buried in the step tomb at Giza: "Mother of the Two Kings of Upper and Lower Egypt" or "King of Upper and Lower Egypt and Mother of the King of Upper and Lower Egypt"! The remains of inscriptions on the one pillar still standing in the temple court brought another unexpected surprise. The vertical hieroglyphic inscription with remnants of titles and the name Khentkaus terminates in a picture of the queen sitting on the throne and holding a sceptre, the *wadj* in her hand. The queen's brow is adorned with a cobra rearing to attack, the uraeus. At the

time when the queen lived, the right to wear the uraeus on the forehead was the exclusive privilege of the ruling sovereign or of the gods. The ruler was in any case a god according to the ideas of Ancient Egyptians — the only god living on earth among men. This image of the queen was not, however, to be the last of the surprising discoveries made during the archaeological uncovering of Khentkaus's pyramid complex.

According to the original plan the pyramid and the stone mortuary temple should have been enclosed by a high wall built of limestone blocks. However, construction of the surrounding wall was never completed and such parts as had been erected were partially dismantled during the reconstruction and extension of the pyramid complex. The materials obtained from the original wall

This limestone cylindrical seal belonging to the administrator of the granaries was discovered in the magazines of the mortuary temple of Khentkaus at Abusir.

were used in the building of a diminutive so-called 'cult pyramid' near the south-east corner of the older stone part of the temple. Reconstruction also included the basic extension of the temple towards the east. A new monumental entrance, again adorned with twin limestone pillars, was erected, this time precisely on the east-west axis of the pyramid complex. A small stone basin immediately by the entrance reminded the visitor of the duty of ritual purification before entering the temple. The spacious entrance hall was an important crossroads because it allowed access to a group of five magazines in the south-east corner of the extended part of the temple and to a group of dwelling rooms in the north-eastern corner; finally, towards the west, it gave access to the so-called 'intimate' part of the temple containing the cult rooms. Limestone blocks were not used for the extension of the temple but, this time, the much more economical material of mud-

rank of a ruler. The discovery of fragments of papyri originally from the archives of the queen's mortuary temple has provided additional indirect evidence that this was the status of Khentkaus's pyramid complex. On some fragments the queen is depicted with the ruler's sceptre, the *was*, in her hand.

The mortuary cult of Queen Khentkaus lasted, if in gradually diminishing form, for perhaps three centuries up the end of the 6th Dynasty. During the ensuing 1st Intermediate Period and disruption of state power Khentkaus's pyramid was pillaged. Centuries went by and the abandoned, half-ruined, sanded-up pyramid complex became a convenient quarry from which, as early as the 19th Dynasty, stone was already being taken for building other tombs not far away. Individual stone-cutters built simple dwellings from fragments of stone in the ruins of the temple.

The surprising discovery of Khentkaus's pyramid complex at Abusir invested the whole series of historical problems known as

Clay sealing with hieroglyphic inscription and cartouche of the pharaoh Djedkare.

Facsimile of inscription on the clay sealing.

bricks. The mudbrick walls were, of course, plastered and whitewashed, and sometimes adorned with paintings which at first sight and for a limited time softened the contrast between the results of the two different building phases.

The meaning of the entire reconstruction project lay in a fundamental change of the conception behind the queen's pyramid complex. Originally an appendage of the great pyramid complex of Neferirkare it became the architecturally and functionally "independent" tomb of a person with the

Amulet in the shape of a so-called 'sacred eye' found during excavations in Khentkaus's pyramid complex. Faience with coloured glaze. Late Period.

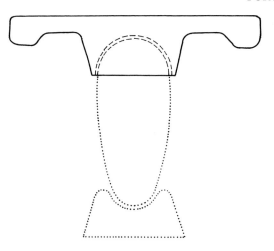

Reconstruction of a potter's wheel, from a surviving turning plate found during excavations in Khentkaus's mortuary temple at Abusir.

the „Khentkaus problem" with a new urgency. In particular, two basic questions came to the fore:

1. Are the Khentkaus from Giza and the Khentkaus from Abusir one and the same person or two different people?

2. Did the Khentkaus from Abusir and/or Giza hold monarchic office and exercise the powers of ruler?

Thorough investigation of this problem seemed to demand, if this was at all possible, a re-examination of the archaeological monuments discovered by Selim Hassan during his research on the step tomb of Queen Khentkaus at Giza.

The individual finds that Hassan had not publicised were lying, long forgotten, in some archaeological storehouse in Giza or in the depositary of the Egyptian Museum in Cairo and it was not feasible to get hold of them again. What then remained was only the tomb itself and especially the section in which the remains of inscriptions were still to be found, primarily on the fragment of the granite gate. Careful examination of this inscription, when undertaken with an eye to

the information gained in Abusir, nonetheless led to a surprising discovery. Selim Hassan had overlooked a few very small but enormously important details and he had published an imprecise transcription of the inscription! Just as at Abusir, at the end of the inscriptions on Khentkaus's granite gate at Giza there is a picture of the queen under her name. On the north and south parts of the gate the queen is depicted sitting on a throne. The picture of her on the northern section is damaged but on the south section the picture is complete. Examination of the complete picture showed that to the queen's head, with its long wig, had been added the so-called vulture diadem, the ornament of Egyptian queens and goddesses, and also a short ritual beard evenly trimmed at the bottom. The ritual beard, fastened to the pharaoh's face, was of course the exclusive privilege of ruling sovereigns. To the queen's hand, placed on her breast, a royal sceptre had been added! It is likely that all these additions to the queen's portrait were made during the reconstruction of her Giza tomb into a two-step building.

The unexpected discovery at Giza and the no less unexpected discoveries at Abusir led to the conclusion that Queen Khentkaus had in her time been considered a true ruler. This, however, seems contradicted by the fact that there is not a single example of her name written in an oval cartouche, as was the rule in writing down kings' names. Her name

Detail from inscription on the granite gate of Khentkaus's tomb at Giza. The picture of the royal mother has been augmented with the vulture diadem, beard and mace.

Fragments of a large storage vessel decorated with geometrical *motifs* and a small bird. These come from the Coptic stratum in Khentkaus's mortuary temple at Abusir. Red baked clay, remains of polychrome.

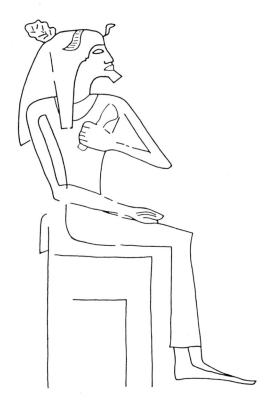

also appears in none of the surviving Ancient Egyptian king lists. There exists, however, an entirely logical explanation for this apparent contradiction, which is that Khentkaus exercised kingly power *de facto* but not *de iure*. At this period, in line with the basic conception of the Ancient Egyptian state, only a man, the pharaoh, could occupy the highest office in the land. He only was the single living god among men. Probably, under the exceptional circumstances of the evidently premature death of the pharaoh when his legitimate heir was too young to exercise power, the authority of the Royal Mother —

the Regent, came to the fore. Her rule was apparently long and energetic enough to allow some of her sovereign attributes, at least to a certain extent, to be commemorated after her death. If this interpretation of the new information that has come to light is correct, then we can answer the second of the questions posed above and translate Khenkaus's unusual title as "Mother of the King of Upper and Lower Egypt (holding office as) King of Upper and Lower Egypt". It seems, therefore, that in the original debate it was Hermann Junker's translation of the title which was nearest to the truth.

Detail of inscription on a fragment of the granite gate in front of the southeast corner of the tomb of the royal mother Khentkaus at Giza: additional features were added to the picture of the queen sitting on the throne (see the drawing on p. 128).

Anthropoid wooden coffin from a burial of the Late Period found during excavations in Khentkaus's pyramid complex at Abusir.

An answer to the second question does not, of course, throw light on the first question: are we dealing with one person or two different people? Neither the physical remains of the queen nor any archaeologically persuasive relics of these remains have been discovered at either Giza or Abusir. In both places, however, there is solid evidence of the long-term existence of the mortuary cult of Khentkaus, "Mother of the King of Upper and Lower Egypt (holding office as) King of Upper and Lower Egypt". If we are dealing here with one and the same person, then one of the tombs should be considered as what is known as a cenotaph, or symbolic tomb. If there were two different people, then this would mean that during a very short period of perhaps one or two generations the same exceptional historical situation in the royal family occurred twice, and the land found itself twice, in rapid succession, under the *de facto* rule of a royal mother — regent.

There exists, however, a third possibility which appears, on the basis of all the information currently available, to be the most probable. This is that there were two different women bearing the same name, separated from each other by perhaps one or two generations, and that a cult for the elder, Khentkaus I from Giza, was established in the mortuary temple of the younger, Khentkaus II at Abusir. There must have been very weighty reasons for such an unusual step, and these were probably dynastic-political in character. It was apparently necessary to draw support from the authority of the famous Queen Khentkaus I, the primal mother of the dynasty and its undoubted direct blood link — the "full blood royal", as George Reisner put it — with the pharaoh Mycerinus and so with the old royal line founded by Sneferu. The cult was established by Niuserre and there can be no dispute about this dating because it is archaeologically demonstrable that the reconstruction of Khentkaus's pyramid complex took place in his reign. This became both the tomb of Niuserre's mother Khentkaus II and at the same time the location of the cult of his primal mother Khentkaus I. Niuserre's measures can be understood in the context of the dynastic disputes which after the premature death of Raneferef evidently broke out again between the two rival branches of the royal family — the Sahurean and the Neferirkarean. The protagonists of the two branches struggling for the throne would later probably have been Shepseskare and Niuserre. Niuserre finally prevailed, perhaps with the help of appeal to the authority which had been enjoyed by Khentkaus I, the mother of the dynasty, whose direct descendant he evidently considered himself to be. We also cannot exclude the possibility that the two queens, Khentkaus I and II were mother and daughter, or grandmother and granddaughter. The inheritance of the throne through the distaff side in the main branch of the family was apparently more legitimate than its inheritance through males in the collateral branch. However, the evidence for this answer to part of the "Khentkaus problem" is not unambiguous. Archaeological excavations currently in progress at various sites in the Abusir necropolis, especially in the pyramid complexes from the 5th Dynasty, may bring discoveries no less unexpected than those which this locality has already yielded up.

The Secret
of the Unfinished Pyramid

Partly submerged in sand and almost co-alescing with the surrounding desert terrain is the lowest step of a pyramid core which lies only a few dozen metres south-west of Nef-erirkare's pyramid. For a long time it re-presented what was, for Egyptologists, one of the mysteries of the Abusir cemetery. Some attributed the building to the little-known 5th-Dynasty pharaoh Raneferef while others considered it the work of the still lesser-known ruler of the period, Shepses-kare. There were also those who hesitated to make any identification of its owner. They all, however, agreed that it was an unfinished pyramid, that this construction, abandoned shortly after work had commenced on it, never served the purpose for which it had been planned and that nobody was buried in it. It acquired the name of the Unfinished Pyramid at Abusir and apart from a few occasional visitors to this forgotten corner of Memphite necropolis nobody expressed any interest in it.

The Unfinished Pyramid became a pri-ority interest of the Egyptological expedition of Charles University in Prague when in 1974 the Czech team obtained the conces-sion which allowed it to carry out archaeo-logical research in an extensive area south of Neferirkare's and Niuserre's pyramid com-plex. There were several reasons for the in-terest. Above all it was just at this time that papyri from the archive of Neferirkare's mortuary temple were published by Paule Posener-Kriéger in the series of the French Institute of Oriental Archaeology in Cairo. In one of the small remnants published was a fragmentary allusion to Raneferef's mortu-ary temple and to the provision of a contrib-ution to Neferirkare's mortuary cult. This al-lusion indirectly confirmed the existence of Raneferef's tomb and a mortuary temple

View of the Unfinished Pyr-amid from the summit of Neferirkare's pyramid just before excavations were started.

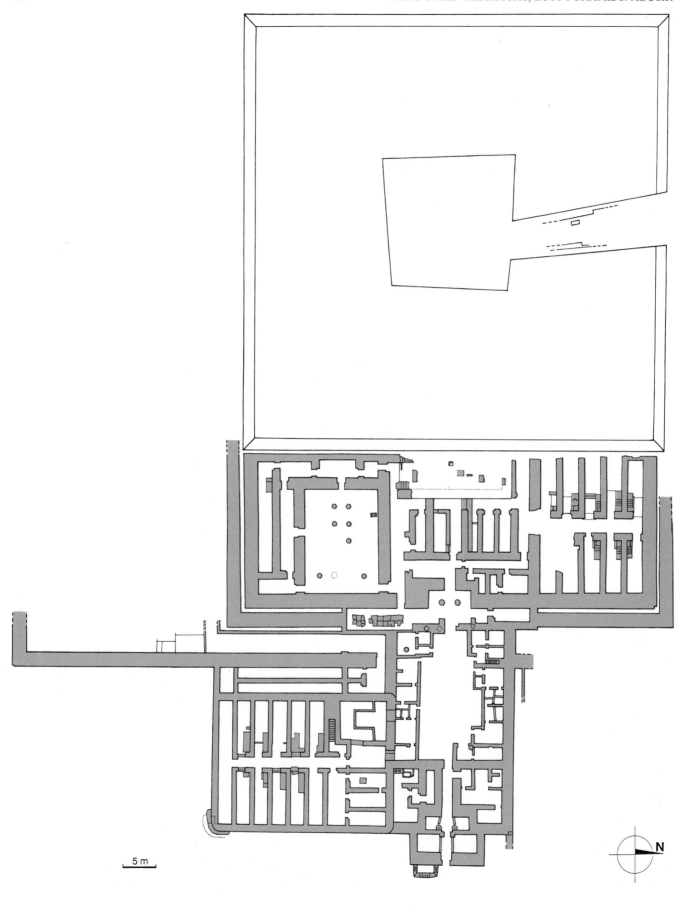

5 m

N

Plan of Raneferef's pyramid
complex (by M. Švec and
O. Vosika).

View of the largely uncovered pyramid complex of Raneferef from the top of Neferirkare's pyramid.

somewhere near Neferirkare's pyramid complex, which had, moreover, to be at Abusir (see below p. 166).

Evidence of another kind, but likewise relating to Raneferef, was a limestone block with the remains of relief decoration discovered not in Neferirkare's pyramid temple, from which it had originally come, but in Abusir village, where it had been used in the construction of a house. On the block was a partially preserved scene depicting Neferirkare's family and indicating that the ruler's eldest son was called Ranefer, "Re is beautiful". It is more than probable that this Ranefer and the later pharaoh Raneferef, Neferirkare's successor, were one and the same person. After ascending the throne the prince simply slightly altered his name to Raneferef, "Re is his beauty", which expressed the status of a pharaoh more appropriately.

Another significant factor was the siting of the Unfinished Pyramid in the cemetery — it was clearly located as the third in a series, after Sahure's and Neferirkare's. The pyramids at Abusir, just as at Giza, were not positioned in the cemeteries randomly but in accordance with a particular scheme which is not yet understood in all its aspects. The fundamental axis of the cemetery at Giza was a line linking the south-east corners of the pyramids there, while at Abusir it was a line linking the pyramids' north-west corners. Both lines, the axes of the pyramid cemeteries at Giza and at Abusir, converge to-

wards one point which lies at Matariya, an eastern suburb of modern Cairo. In ancient times this was the site of the famous centre of the sun cult, *Iunu,* in Greek Heliopolis. It is possible that here was the "fixed point" of the world of the pyramid-builders, in the places where the fetish *benben* was kept and worshipped. This was the symbolic primeval hill which at the creation of the world had emerged from the primeval waters and on which the sun had first cast its rays. The positioning of the Unfinished Pyramid was such that even before excavation work commenced it could be anticipated that it belonged to Neferirkare's direct heir, which in normal circumstances would be his eldest son Ranefer, the later Raneferef.

The written evidence for the existence of Raneferef's mortuary temple — and a mortuary cult presupposed the existence of a tomb — and likewise the well-grounded belief that it was Raneferef who built the Unfinished Pyramid, led to a single conclusion: despite its appearance and the negative results of the trial digging carried out there by Borchardt at the beginning of the century, the Unfinished Pyramid must once have been a real pharaoh's tomb. With this working hypothesis, research commenced at the end of the 1970s with the aim of finally revealing the secret of the Unfinished Pyramid.

The first step on the road to understanding the Unfinished Pyramid was geophysical surveying. In view of the particular condition of

View of Raneferef's pyramid complex from the south-east, from the ruins of pyramid L XXIV.

the terrain and the data required, the method chosen from the varied list of geophysical techniques was that of magnetometry. It was most intensively applied to the extensive sand plain, in no way distinguishable from the surrounding desert, in front of the eastern wall of the Unfinished Pyramid. The results of geo-magnetic measuring were fast, unambiguous and surprising. It was ascertained that under the sand in the space investigated lay a huge, highly articulated building of mudbricks, with a basic external outline resembling the letter "T" seen from above. This shape is characteristic for the basic layout of mortuary temples in the 5th and 6th dynasties. Archaeological excavations, precisely and rapidly targeted on the basis of the results of geophysical measurement, soon definitively confirmed the existence of a mortuary temple. It was demonstrated that the building complex dominated by the Unfinished Pyramid was indeed the tomb of the pharaoh Raneferef.

Ludwig Borchardt had, in fact, been within inches of this discovery at the beginning of this century. He did not wish entirely to ignore the Unfinished Pyramid on the western margin of the Abusir cemetery, and so he had at least carried out trial digging. As an experienced archaeologist and expert on pyramids he decided to dig a trench in the deep open ditch which ran from the north into the centre of the monument and at the bottom of which, in the case of a completed tomb, it would be natural to assume the existence of a passage leading to the sarcophagus chamber. He dug a trench several metres deep in the rubble which filled the ditch right up to its upper edge, but he did not reach the passage or its remains. This negative result confirmed him in the belief that he was dealing with a rough, unfinished building consisting in no more than the lowest step of a pyramid core, and that inside it work had never even started on the construction of what is called the pyramid substructure, i.e. the passage giving access from the north, the passage blockade (a stone portcullis), the ante-chamber, and the burial or sarcophagus chamber situated approximately under the projected apex of the pyramid. The orientation of the passage was closely connected with the idea that after death the pharaoh's spirit would depart to the northern

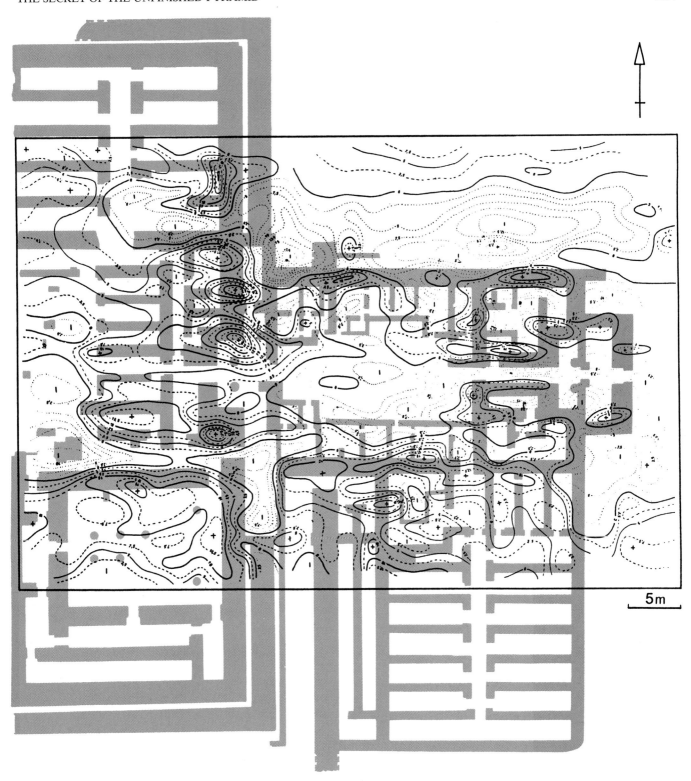

5m

heaven to become one of the never-setting stars around the Polestar. The contrasting east-west orientation of the burial chamber — the sarcophagus at its western wall was, however, once again aligned north-east and the pharaoh's mummy laid in it with his head to the north and face turned to the east, to the rising sun — was dictated by the solar religion. This involved the belief that after death the pharaoh would become a member of the entourage of his father Re and together with

him would float forever on the heavenly ocean.

Was it by mistake or merely by chance that Borchardt did not continue with his probe for at least another hour? Perhaps 1 metre lower than the point where he gave up his probe he would have made two archaeological finds under the rubble and these would certainly have led him to a decision to investigate the Unfinished Pyramid and its surroundings thoroughly. He would, that is,

Projection of Raneferef's mortuary temple on a map drawn up on the basis of geophysical measurements in front of the eastern wall of the Unfinished Pyramid. The projection confirms the accuracy of the geophysical measurements which enabled the expedition to locate the thick mudbrick enclosure walls of the temple (by V. Hašek).

have reached the bottom of the ditch and there discovered, partly still *in situ,* the huge blocks of red granite out of which the port-cullis blockade in the passage giving access to the burial chamber had been constructed. It would immediately have been obvious to an archaeologist as experienced as Borchardt that a substructure had once been completed in its entirety, even though the pyramid superstructure had never been finished. The second discovery was also not one that he could have missed. It was a cursive in-scription recorded in black on a block from the core of the Unfinished Pyramid and con-taining Raneferef's name in a cartouche. The builder and owner of the Unfinished Pyr-amid would then have been known. Bor-chardt's premature negative conclusion had apparently consigned the Unfinished Pyram-id to perpetual archaeological oblivion. This has made the possibility of correcting his conclusion after more than 70 years all the more pleasurable. It is a source of great de-light that the Czech expedition was able to undertake archaeological research on a great royal tomb complex from the Old Kingdom at a time when it looked as if all the pyramids had been more or less investigated and that no further great surprises were to be expected from them.

The excavations in Raneferef's pyramid complex proceeded, with intervals between individual archaeological seasons, through-out the 1980s. During that time the Czech archaeological expedition received invalu-able help especially from the sons of *reis* Abdu el-Kereti, Mohammed Talaal and Ahmad, who from 1978, after their father's death, took over the function of foremen of workers at the excavations. Although some peripheral parts of Raneferef's complex still lie under sand and rubble the main parts have already been uncovered. The basic out-lines of the architectural and functional pic-ture of the monument have emerged. Some unexpected and in many respects unique archaeological discoveries have given us an entirely new view of the pyramid complex, the technical aspects of construction, the stat-us of a royal tomb of that period, the organi-sation of the royal mortuary cult etc. This has been made possible by the coincidence of two chance circumstances. On the one hand, an unfinished building offers an opportunity to look, as it were, backstage and throw light on many previously unexplained questions related to the building of a pyramid. On the other hand, the appearance of this aban-

doned and sand-buried relic of a pyramid apparently held off whole generations of experienced medieval and modern tomb-robbers, and so the mortuary temple in parti-cular could be archaeologically investigated in the state in which it had been left in the era of the pharaohs, untouched by anything save the ravages of time.

On the site destined for the building of Ra-neferef's pyramid (see p. 135), which was already quite some way from the Nile Valley, the ground was levelled and bearings taken for the base of the future pyramid. In the middle of the base a rectangular trench was sunk, east-west in orientation, in which the underground parts of the future royal tomb were to be constructed. Then a deep ditch was dug down into the trench from the north; this was to be the basis of the passage leading down to the underground chambers. It is clear from the unfinished building that work on the underground section of Rane-feref's pyramid began at the same time as work on the first, lowest step of the core of the section above ground. It was a logical ap-proach given the mode of construction of the saddle roof of the undergound chambers. This roof would have consisted of three lay-ers, each layer made up of huge limestone blocks placed one on top of the other, and then the three braced against each other in the shape of a reversed letter "V". The procedure required the presence on the sides of compact masonry to which the roof blocks could be anchored. Roof construction was therefore already to be found at the founda-tion level of a pyramid. Raneferef probably died at the time when the building of the underground parts of a pyramid and the first step of the pyramid core was more or less complete. He was about twenty years old, to judge by a few surviving portraits. Given the prescribed minimum period of seventy days for the preparation of a royal burial, includ-ing essential mummifying rituals, there was not the faintest possibility of finishing con-struction of pyramid which had originally been projected as a matter of many years of work. The first step of the core of the pyram-id, which resembled a truncated pyramid, was therefore hastily faced with blocks of fine white limestone. The outer surface of the building, sloping at an angle of perhaps 78°, was carefully smoothed down. Finally what had been planned as a pyramid became a mastaba, if with an atypical square ground plan.

In appearance the tomb resembled a hill,

a stylised tumulus above a burial. This resemblance was not, of course, purely accidental. In one of the papyrus fragments found in Raneferef's mortuary temple there is evidence that this mastaba was known as the "Mound" to those who built it and to those who served the pharaoh's's mortuary cult in its "shadow". The upward-facing surface of the "Mound" was constructed in a very original way: the whole horizontal terraced roof of the mastaba was covered by a layer of clay several centimetres thick, into which was pressed coarse gravel collected from the surface of the surrounding desert. The roof terrace thus visually merged with the desert, and the weather over four and a half millennia left as little trace on it as on its desert surroundings. Damage to the tomb of Raneferef called the "Mound" only occurred as a result of the activities of stone thieves who started to use it as a convenient quarry at the time of the New Kingdom.

The unfinished state of the Pyramid has provided yet further significant archaeological testimony. It was long believed that the way in which pyramids were built was by the arrangement of the stone masonry of the stepped core into a system of slanted layers, inclined at an angle of 75° and leaning on a central stone spindle around the vertical axis of the pyramid. The effect, therefore, was of masonry arranged into a system of inner casings resembling the layers of an onion. The author of this theory was Richard Lepsius. It is interesting that it was on the basis of study of the Abusir pyramids, especially that of Neferirkare, that he developed his theory of the construction of pyramid cores. Ludwig Borchardt, who had investigated the three biggest Abusir pyramids, embraced the theory as well. Borchardt's, i.e. Lepsius's, opinion also received persuasive support from the published plans of the Abusir pyramids and the model of Sahure's pyramid complex exhibited in the Egyptian museum in Cairo. The Unfinished Pyramid offered a unique opportunity to verify this widespread theory. If the theory was valid, then after the removal of the thin clay and gravel layer protecting the building's roof terrace, it should have been possible to find — as in a cross-section — stone masonry arranged on all four sides in parallel layers. It would be as if an onion not circular, but square, had been sliced across horizontally.

The trench dug in a north-eastern direction in the crown of the Unfinished Pyr-

The gravel roof terrace of the Unfinished Pyramid.

amid showed, however, something different. The outer face of the first step of the pyramid core was formed by a frame made of huge blocks of dark grey limestone up to 5 m long and well bound together. Similarly, there was an inner frame built of smaller blocks, and making up the walls of the rectangular trench destined for the underground chambers of the tomb. Between the two frames pieces of poor-quality limestone had been packed, sometimes "dry" and sometimes stuck together with clay mortar and sand. The core of Raneferef's pyramid, and undoubtedly other large Abusir pyramids as well, had therefore been constructed in a simpler way, less demanding in terms of time and material

Fragment of a faience tablet with cartouche of Raneferef from the pharaoh's mortuary temple at Abusir.

but at the same time sloppier and less safe from the point of view of stability. The core was indeed modelled into steps, but these were built in horizontal layers and only the stone blocks making up the outer surface were of high quality and well joined together. The inner part of the core was filled up with only partially joined rough stones of varying quality and size. For this reason it is no wonder that today the Abusir pyramids, long ago stripped of their casing of high quality white limestone and with their cores denuded and exposed to further human destruction and natural erosion, resemble rather formless heaps of stone.

Horizontal cross-section at the foundation level and north-west cross-section of the Meidum pyramid showing how the stepped core of the monument was constructed with masonry arranged in slanted layers.

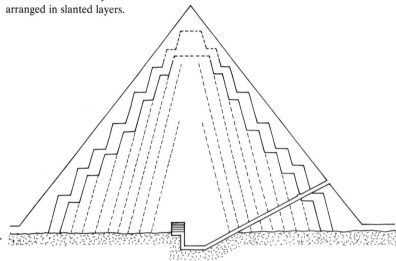

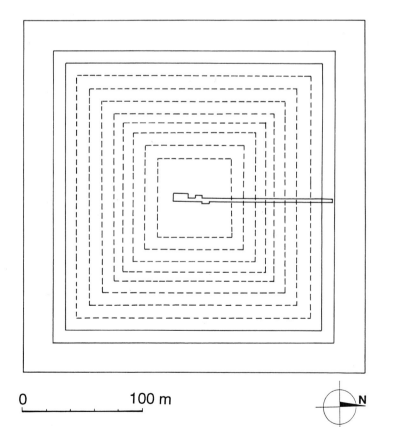

0   100 m

N

On Raneferef's death his heir was faced with a by no means easy task. It was his duty to complete the tomb and, as the new divine pharaoh, to prepare the burial of his equally divine predecessor. The site of the mortuary cult of a pharaoh was at that time usually a large temple erected in front of the east face of his pyramid, the face looking towards the rising sun. In the short time remaining before Raneferef's interment, however, it was evidently impossible even to think of building a standard temple consisting of an architecturally articulated complex planned on the basis of defined religious principles. For this reason a very small temple built of limestone blocks was hurriedly erected in front of the east face of the Unfinished Pyramid and on its east-west axis. The temple stood on the pyramid's base platform, which had been created by two layers of huge limestone blocks. This was because a five-metre strip of free space on the platform remained around the pyramid, the space having been allowed in the original plan for completion of the pyramid's smooth limestone casing.

In its initial phase the mortuary temple's design was simple and rectangular, with a north-south orientation. There was only one entrance to the temple; this was from the south and via a low staired ramp. It led immediately into an open vestibule where the priests carried out the essential purification rituals required on entry to the temple. The rest of the temple was taken up by three rooms. Of these the largest and most important was the offering hall. It was originally submerged in darkness and in its western wall was embedded the false door, probably made of red granite, which represented the central place of the cult. In front of the false door stood an altar on which offerings were placed, and of which at least an imprint has remained on the paving of the chamber. It is possible that each of the two narrow rooms at the sides of the offering chamber originally contained what is known as a funerary boat . The precise meaning of these boats which have been found symbolically interred in royal tomb complexes, such as the celebrated boat of Cheops discovered in 1954 at the Great Pyramid in Giza, is not yet known and is the subject of debate among Egyptologists. A small shaft under the temple's paving yielded the discovery *in situ* of a so-called 'foundation deposit' consisting in symbolic vessels, a piece of fine dark grey clay used for sealing, and the heads of a small bull and a bird sacrificed during the ceremonies connected with the founding of the temple.

As yet we do not know with certainty who built the initial small mortuary temple for Raneferef and who, therefore, was his direct successor. According to a few contemporary written records the almost unknown pharaoh Shepseskare ruled for a short time either immediately before or immediately after Raneferef. Sekhemkhau, his so-called Horus name, appears on two clay sealings which were found near the oldest Raneferef mortuary temple already described above. Was Shepseskare, then, Raneferef's heir? We do not know, but if he was, then it was only for a very brief period (see above, p. 84 f.). When Raneferef's brother Niuserre, who was to rule for more than thirty years, ascended the throne of the Egyptian pharaohs he confronted a series of difficult tasks. One of these was to complete, at least provisionally, the half-finished tomb complexes of the closest members of his family — Neferirkare, Khentkaus and Raneferef. He proceeded step by step, at the same time building his own pyramid complex in the immediate neighbourhood of the unfinished tombs of his forebears. Although we cannot safely identify the builder of the first construction phase of Raneferef's mortuary temple, we can certainly and without qualification ascribe to Niuserre the later phases in which the temple was fundamentally extended and basically modified in design. The building projects show signs of both improvisation

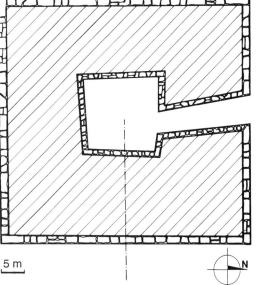

5 m   N

Plan showing a horizontal cross-section across the crown of the Unfinished Pyramid. The broken line indicates the direction in which a trench was dug in the masonry of the monument. The trench confirmed that the core of the Unfinished Pyramid (and probably those of the other Abusir pyramids as well) was not constructed in inner slanted layers. Instead it was built out of irregular pieces of lower-quality limestone. Only on the outside were large precisely fitted blocks of limestone used.

and originality. The result was the emergence of a huge and architecturally unique tomb complex which in its design conception has no parallel among pyramid temples. It received the name "Divine are the souls (i.e. divine is the power) of Raneferef".

With the second building phase there emerged a large temple with a rectangular ground-plan which stretched along the whole eastern side of the Unfinished Pyramid. With the exception of a few architectonic elements it was entirely built of mudbricks, a material much less durable than stone but representing a saving of time and money. The main axis of the second-stage temple was north-south in orientation; no other pyramid temple is aligned in this way, if we set on one

In several places the mudbrick masonry of Raneferef's mortuary temple has survived to a surprising height.

side the older and in many respects dissimilar group of step pyramid complexes of the 3rd Dynasty, and Userkaf's mortuary temple from the early 5th Dynasty, which was atypically oriented as a result of particular topographical conditions. This unusual characteristic was undoubtedly a consequence of the fact that the architect was faced with the singular task of building a royal mortuary temple not in front of a pyramid — the standard type of royal tomb of the period — but in front of a mastaba, albeit one of markedly unusual design. The only possibility was to improvise, making a break with all the previous customs and more or less settled norms of royal funerary architecture.

The entrance to the second-phase temple lay in the middle of the eastern facade. It was adorned with two four-stemmed lotus columns made of white limestone; these held up an architrave placed crossways on which rested the wooden boards of a roof terrace. In the central part of the temple, between the columned entrance and the offering hall with the false door installed in the small stone first-phase temple, there was neither an entrance chamber, an open court nor even a sanctuary with five niches and the pharaoh's cult statues — all features found in other pyramid tombs. Instead, the central part contained, besides the access passages, five large magazines in which the more valuable temple equipment used for cult ceremonies in the offering hall was originally stored. After damage due to an accidental minor fire in the western part of the temple, two wooden cult boats were ritually buried and sprinkled with sand in one of these chambers. They were buried with piety, as is

The hypostyle hall in the south-western part of Raneferef's mortuary temple represents the earliest example of its type in ancient Egypt yet discovered.

shown by the two thousand cornelian beads, perhaps originally strung on a thread, discovered around the boats. This isolated find has led us to reflect on how little we really know of the everyday religious and cult practices in Egypt at that time.

The northern part of the second-phase temple was filled by ten large chambers — storerooms, originally on two storeys. They were arranged in five pairs located opposite each other and accessible from a common passage. The number of rooms was not accidental. This is because the mortuary cult in the temple maintained a priesthood divided into five groups or *phyles* (from the Greek word for "watch", see p. 164). In addition to papyri, somewhat mysterious fragments of fritt tablets and faience ornaments have been discovered in these storerooms. The fritt tablets with depictions of gods and the pharaoh accompanied by hieroglyphic inscriptions are encrusted with a white paste and covered with thin gold leaf. They perhaps originally adorned some cult objects and wooden boxes holding the precious pieces of temple equipment. In contrast, the faience ornaments probably decorated the large wooden symbolic vessels used during temple ceremonies. The storerooms likewise yielded discoveries of vessels made of diorite, alabaster, gabro, limestone and basalt, practical and cult pottery, flint knives and blades and other remains. The apparently modest clay sealings bearing the imprints of inscriptions from cylindrical seals have enormous scientific value. They come from the jar stoppers on vessels and fastenings on boxes containing cult objects, and from doors and even papyrus scrolls. The priests serving in Raneferef's temple, just like Ancient Egyptian officials in general, were obsessed by the bureaucratic longing continually to check and register everything and at every moment to have precise information on what was in the storerooms, who was responsible for it, and what had to be obtained or released. Cheap, easily procurable clay, which could be moulded without difficulty and stuck on the end of a string wound round a chest or the neck of a vessel and which could be imprinted with the text on the cylindrical seal entrusted to the hand of a responsible official, was the almost perfect means to fulfill this bureaucratic obsession. It is thanks to this mania that today we are able, from the sealings bearing the names of kings and officials, gods, temples, palaces and others, to

reconstruct with great precision chronology, the organisation of the administration, economic relations, the mode of keeping accounts and many other phenomena of great historical significance. The discoveries from Raneferef's temple have more than doubled the number of sealings dating from Old Kingdom and so far known.

The greatest architectural and archaeological surprise, however, was brought by excavations in the southern part of the temple. Under what was an almost four-metre layer of sand, disintegrated rubble and fragments of mudbrick, were buried the remains of a large columned hall — a hypostyle. It was an absolutely unexpected discovery since nothing similar had previously been found in any of the known mortuary temples in the pyramid complexes, or indeed in other monuments of the age of the pyramid-builders. The find was the first known archaeological evidence of a columned hall from Ancient Egypt. The hypostyle hall was rectangular in design and oriented east-west. The space in the hall had been divided up by four lines of five columns, aligned in the same east-west direction. Not one of the columns has survived but from the imprint on one of the limestone bases we can tell that they were designed to resemble sheaves of six lotus buds. They were of wood, covered with a thin layer of stucco and multi-coloured, and they had supported the flat wooden ceiling of the chamber at a height of perhaps four metres above the floor. Nothing has survived of the roof either, although from remains of polychrome stucco discovered on the clay floor of the hall we can be almost sure that it was painted blue and decorated with gilded stars. The hall was undoubtedly originally sunk in shadow, as is suggested, for example, by the ceiling decoration. There can also be no doubt that important rites of the mortuary cult were performed there, as several archaeological finds suggest.

In the columned hall itself and in its immediate vicinity were discovered numerous fragments of statues of Raneferef made of diorite, basalt, limestone, reddish quartzite and wood. Among them were six complete portraits of the pharaoh! The smallest and most beautiful of the statues, understandably in fragments and incomplete, was of rose-coloured limestone and was originally cca. 35 cm high. It represented the young pharaoh Raneferef sitting on a throne and holding at his breast the mace or *hedj,* the

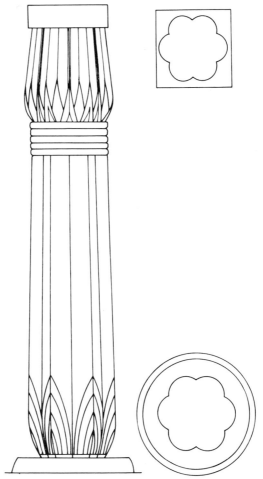

Limestone six-stemmed papyrus column from Niuserre's mortuary temple at Abusir (according to L. Borchardt). Similar columns, although made of wood and smaller im size, originally adorned the column hall of Raneferef's mortuary temple.

emblem of kingly power. The ruler's head, its brow originally adorned with a uraeus, was protected from behind by the outstretched wings of the falcon god Horus. The Egyptian pharaohs considered themselves the earthly incarnations of the highest god of the heavens, Horus, and the statue was therefore expressing, in an original fashion, the linking of earthly and heavenly might in the person of the pharaoh. Previously, the famous diorite statue of the enthroned Chephren from his

The extraordinary artistic and historical value of Raneferef's statue, its head shielded by the falcon god Horus, has been recognised by its reproduction on a postage stamp.

Raneferef sitting on the
throne. In his right hand,
placed on his breast, he
holds the ruler's mace. The
pharaoh is dressed in
a short skirt. A uraeus,
probably made of gold,
originally adorned his forehead. The statue, originally
approximately 35 cm in
height, has a low base. Rose
limestone. Today Ranefer-
ef's statue is stored in the
Egyptian Museum in Cairo.

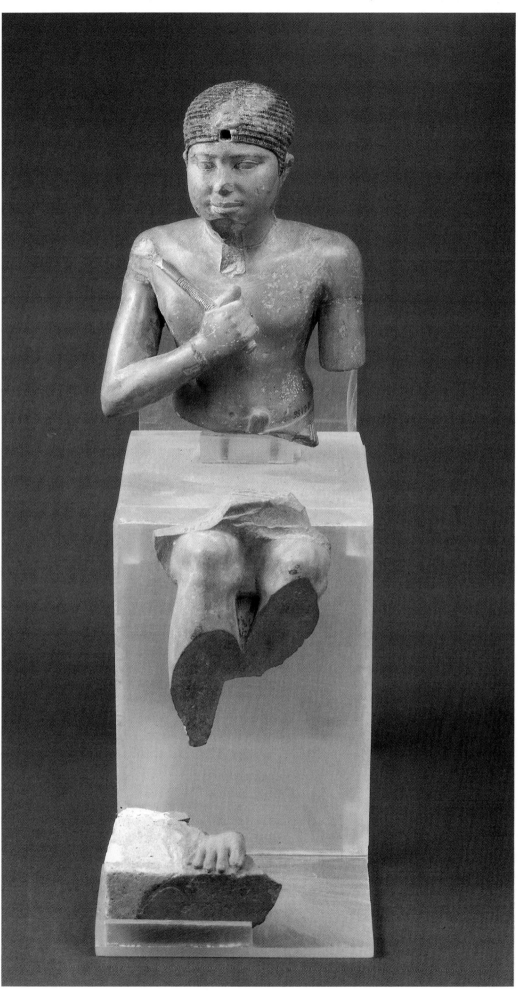

The head of Raneferef's statue is shielded from the back by the outspread wings of the falcon god Horus, whose earthly incarnations the pharaoh was considered to be. The statue thus very eloquently expresses the pharaoh's exceptional position and universal power.

valley temple at Giza, now one of the most celebrated exhibits at the Egyptian Museum in Cairo, had been considered the only evidence of this conception in this type of statue. Other statues discovered in Raneferef's mortuary temple represented the ruler striding with the so-called white Upper Egyptian crown on his head and the sovereign's mace in his hand, or sitting on the throne and wearing on his head the pleated covering called the *nemes*. The largest of the stone statues of Raneferef had been approximately 80 cm in height. All these statues were char-

acterised by perfect craftsmanship in relation to materials, and a masterly artistic shaping of the ruler's likeness and expression of his celestial kingly power. The largest of all the statues found was originally life-size and made of wood. Unfortunately no more than fragments of it survive: a part of the sole with the base, a ritual beard and a part of the hand with the thumb. It was this statue in particular which apparently played an especially important part in the cult ceremonies in the columned hall, as is suggested by several fragments of papyri from the temple archive. The

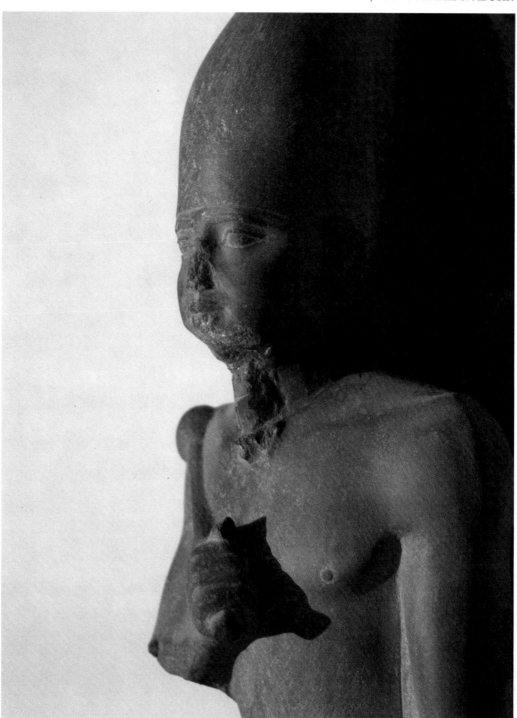

Detail of the head and chest
of the statue of Raneferef
striding. The ruler wears the
crown of Upper Egypt on
his head. In his right hand,
which is placed on his
breast, he holds the ruler's
mace. Basalt. Originally the
whole statue, which now
lacks several pieces, was
approximately 80 cm. high.
The statue is today in the
Egyptian Museum in Cairo
(JE no. 98181).

discovery of Raneferef's statues, which are
today on permanent exhibition at the Egyptian Museum in Cairo, represents in terms of
extent what is so far the third largest find of
royal sculpture from the Old Kingdom. This
find is all the more valuable because it fills
what has up to now been a perceptible gap in
the recorded development of royal sculpture
in Ancient Egypt in the third millennium BC.

Yet further sculptures, however, were
found in the hypostyle in Raneferef's
mortuary temple; these were not of the ruler,
but closely associated with him. They were

small wooden statuettes of the so-called
enemies of Egypt. They represented Asians,
Nubians and Libyans kneeling and with
hands tied behind their backs. The statuettes
originally adorned the royal throne or naos in
which stood the statue of the pharaoh. The
motif of the captured enemies kneeling before the pharaoh is a thoroughly "royal motif" linked with the Ancient Egyptian conception of the arrangement of the world and
the status of the pharaoh within it. As the
only god living among men on earth the pharaoh had continually to ensure that the forces

of evil and chaos were not victorious on earth. If the pharaoh could not vanquish them in reality, then he had at least to triumph over them symbolically. This was the reason why the *motif* of the captive enemies so often adorns objects around the pharaoh. Not only the statuettes of the captive enemies of Egypt but also many other archaeological discoveries — symbolic models of boats, fragments of stone vessels or faience decorations, clay sealings etc. — are allowing us gradually to reconstruct the significance and function of the columned hall in Raneferef's mortuary temple.

The architectonic plan embodied the religious conception and made of the columned hall the place of the other world *par excellence*. Under the heavenly night canopy of the hall flowered the sheaves of lotuses, symbol of resurrection, clasping the columns. The pharaoh, finding his image in a cult statue — and his various sovereign likenesses in his various statues — had made for him here an intimate world of eternal bliss, from which

Reis Ahmad al-Qereti with the find of the first two fragments of the basalt statue of the pharaoh Raneferef striding.

Head of a statue of the pharaoh Raneferef. He is wearing the head-covering *nemes* and a long ritual beard is tied to his chin. Diorite. The head with the beard is 13.2 cm high. The statue is now in the Egyptian Museum in Cairo (JE 98180).

conception behind the cult which was practised in the hall with the precision of a time-table of priestly services. It is also possible that the columned hall resembled the throne hall in a royal palace. To confirm this resemblance it would, of course, be necessary to find and archaeologically investigate at least one royal palace from the age of the

Head of a young man with hair cut short and a moustache. Alabaster. The head is 9.8 cm high. It was found together with fragments of a sculpture of the pharaoh Raneferef but shows none of the symbols of royal office. The identity of the man represented is therefore debatable. Egyptian Museum in Cairo (JE 98179).

he could continue to govern the destinies of "the people of his time", exist as a living god on earth and act as a mediator between the worlds of gods and men. This was the basic

Detail of the upper half of a statuette of a captive Asian chieftain discovered in Raneferef's mortuary temple. The chieftain was represented kneeling and with hands bound behind his back. His shoulder-length hair is tied with a headband and he has a pointed beard. The statuette was originally inserted in a larger object, perhaps a throne or a naos. Wood, 15.5 cm high. Egyptian Museum in Cairo. (JE 98182).

Statuette of kneeling Libyan (?) captive found in Ranef-eref's mortuary temple. The man as his hands bound behind his back and long hair reaching to his shoulders. He is dressed in a short skirt. Wood, 14.1 cm high. Egyptian Museum in Cairo (JE 98182).

Statuette of a kneeling Nubian captive found in Raneferef's mortuary temple. He is dressed in a short skirt and wears a wig. Wood., 14.1 cm high. Egyptian Museum in Cairo.

pyramid-builders. Unfortunately, such a discovery still remains one of the unfulfilled goals of Egyptian archaeology.

While it is true that archaeological ex-

Relief decoration of the captive enemies of Egypt from Sahure's mortuary temple at Abusir (by L. Borchardt).

Bust of the pharaoh Raneferef, his head adorned by the *nemes*. The but is a fragment of a statue which originally represented the ruler sitting on his throne. Basalt. The bust is 23.8 cm high and is now in the Egyptian Museum in Cairo (JE 98177).

amples of royal palaces from the time of the pyramid-builders have not been found and are known only from contemporary Egyptian written records, Raneferef's tomb complex has nevertheless yielded remarkable testimony of a different kind. When the excavations in front of the Unfinished Pyramid were shifted further towards the south-east another large building of mudbrick began gradually to emerge from the sand and rubble. Like Raneferef's mortuary temple it was built in two phases of construction, was rectangular in plan and north-south in orientation. Its dimensions, orientation and rounded outer corners indicated that it was not residential or economic but religious in character. Thorough archaeological research eventually brought its purpose to light: to

Fragment of a fritt tablet with pictures of deities. The raised figures of the deities were modelled with paste and then covered by thin gold leaf. The fragment (8 × 5.5 cm), found in Raneferef's mortuary temple at Abusir, is now in the Egyptian Museum in Cairo.

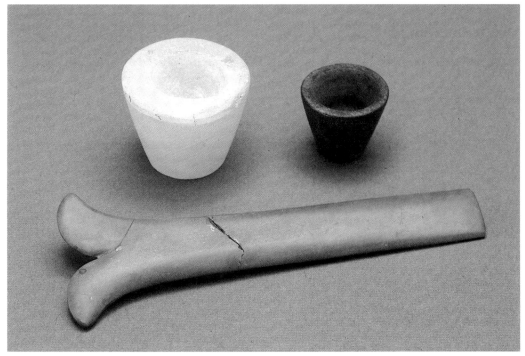

Peseshkef knife in the shape of a swallow-tail, conical limestone bowl and conical basalt bowl. These were cult objects used in the ceremony of the Opening of the Mouth. The knife, made of grey-black slate, is 16.7 cm long, the limestone bowl if 4 cm high and the basalt bowl is 3 cm high. They were all found in Raneferef's mortuary tomb and are now in the Egyptian Museum in Cairo (JE 9730).

serve the needs of the cult of Raneferef a cult slaughterhouse for sacrificial animals had been built in the immediate vicinity of the pharaoh's mortuary temple! From the written records discovered, for example the inscriptions on the vessels for fat, or fragments of papyri in the temple archive, it was ascertained that this cult abbatoir was called "the Sanctuary of the Knife". While this name had been known from other contemporary written sources, its interpretation had been the subject of dispute because archaeological evidence had been lacking.

Raneferef's "Sanctuary of the Knife" had a single, relatively wide entrance from the north through which the sacrificial animals, mainly cattle but also wild goats, gazelles and others, had been led inside. These would then have been ritually slaughtered with the aid of sharp flint knives in the open courtyard in the north-west part of the slaughterhouse. In the chambers in the north-eastern corner of the slaughterhouse the meat would then have been cut up on a wooden chopping board and prepared by heating. The rest of the abattoir — at least two third of the building — was filled with storage rooms. A staircase leading to a roof terrace suggests that this space too fulfilled a particular function in the context of the slaughterhouse; perhaps the meat would have been dried in the sun here. The great capacity of the storage areas of "the Sanctuary of the Knife"

was initially rather puzzling, but only until there had been time for at least a general examination of the newly-discovered papyri of Raneferef's temple archive. On one of the fragments it was possible to read that on the occasion of ten-day religious festivals thirteen bulls would be killed daily to supply the needs of Raneferef's mortuary cult. This means that during individual annual festivals and to meet the requirements of a single royal mortuary cult an unbelievable 130 animals would have been slaughtered! This figure testifies not only to the intensity of the cult and the number of people whose economic life would be linked simply with one mortu-

ary temple, and who would themselves consume the offerings made to the pharaoh's spirit after completion of the ceremonies, but also suggests how great were the material resources tied up, essentially unproductively, in the building of the the the huge tomb complexes and their long-term maintenance. Undoubtedly this was one of the causes of the economic, political and social decline of the Ancient Egyptian state at the end of the Old Kingdom.

"The Sanctuary of the Knife" served its purpose for a relatively short time. Already, during the reign of the Niuserre, the ruler who built it, Raneferef's mortuary cult was reorganised, the supplies of meat for the pharaoh's offering table were secured from elsewhere, and "the Sanctuary of the Knife" became a storehouse. This change occurred at the point when the decision was taken to extend Raneferef's mortuary temple towards the east and alter its design to approximate more to the standard pyramid temple model of the period.

This 3rd major building phase in the temple's development principally involved the construction of a new monumental entrance and a large open columned courtyard. The temple acquired the characteristic form of a "T" in its rough ground plan, and the once

The hieratic sign *nemet* (butcher's block with knife sticking into it), used in writing the name 'Sanctuary of the Knife', appears several times on the potsherds of grease vessels discovered during excavation of Raneferef's mortuary temple.

Flint knife and blades found in Raneferef's mortuary temple.

independent "Sanctuary of the Knife" became an integral part of it. The monumental entrance was placed, as in the preceding building phase, on the east-west axis of the tomb complex. Its roof was supported by a pair of six-stemmed but this time papyrus columns of fine white limestone. Just like the lotus, the papyrus was a plant of great symbolic significance in the religious conceptions of the Ancient Egyptians. In the time of the pyramid-builders dense papyrus undergrowth covered the great flats of the mud banks of the Nile. Papyrus rapidly renewed itself, was always green and fresh, and therefore became a symbol of resurrection, eternal life and permanent prosperity. Religious beliefs also influenced the design conception of the open courtyard, another place of important ceremonies for the royal mortuary cult. The courtyard was rectangular and oriented east-west in layout. Around its sides 24 columns supporting a flat wooden roof were arranged at regular intervals. Not a single column has survived and they have left only a few limestone bases, on one of which is the characteristic circular imprint of the shaft. The circular imprint suggests that the columns were of wood and fashioned to resemble date-palms — the symbol of fertility, abundance and peace. This symbolic meaning was one of the reasons why the legendary palm grove in the venerable Lower Egyptian royal seat Buto became the mythical national cemetery of the Ancient Egyptians.

No vestige remains of the wall paintings which decorated the walls of the courtyard, and the stone, perhaps alabaster, altar which originally probably stood in the north-west part of the courtyard, and on which burnt offerings would be presented has also vanished without trace. At the latest at the be-

Diorite bowls at the moment when they were discovered in Raneferef's mortuary temple.

On the inner surface of two of the three diorite bowls from Raneferef's mortuary temple are visible traces of red ochre.

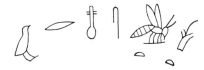

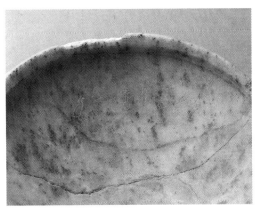

On the edge of the inner surface of one of the diorite bowls the inscription, „Sneferu, King of Upper and Lower Egypt" is lightly incised.

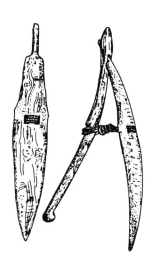

Wooden implements used in the era of the pyramid builders: a hoe, mallet and dragsleds (H. Schäfer and L. Borchardt).

Fragment of the anthropoid coffin of the funerary priest Khuiankh. The priest was buried at the beginning of the Middle Kingdom in the ruins of The Sanctuary of the Knife' which formed a part of Raneferef's pyramid complex. Wood with remains of polychrome.

ginning of the 6th Dynasty, in the reign of Teti, the entrance to "the Sanctuary of the Knife" was bricked up and the whole of this part of the temple was permanently taken out of commission. From papyri surviving from Raneferef's temple archive it can be proved that even before this point, in the reign of Djedkare, the appearance and function of the columned courtyard had changed fundamentally. Irregular, sporadic and even bizarre brick constructions of dwellings for the priests who served in the temple appeared in the area between the columns. Raneferef's mortuary cult began to decline, and the tomb complex gradually closed down.

Detail of the inner surface of the wooden box sarcophagus in which the anthropoid coffin of the funerary priest Khuiankh was placed. The so-called 'list of offerings' is recorded on the inner surface of the sarcophagus.

The settlement of priests immediately inside the temple's columned courtyard further reduced the temple's status amd accelerated its decay. From archaeological and written evidence it is clear that the cult in the temple died out at the end of the 6th Dynasty under the long rule of Pepi II. During roughly the following two centuries of the so-called 1st. Intermediate Period, which was characterised by the decay of central state power and by social unrest, Raneferef's mortuary temple and his tomb itself was robbed for the first time.

After the renewal of strong, official state power in the country at the beginning of the Middle Kingdom the cults in the Abusir royal mortuary temples, including Raneferef's, were resuscitated. Unfortunately, however, this new lease of life lasted only a short time. It is from this period that there dates a remarkable interment discovered in a wooden sarcophagus of box type, richly decorated inside with religious texts. The burial pit for the sarcophagus was dug in the floor of a chamber in the, at that time, already long abandoned and ruined "Sanctuary of the Knife." The man buried here was a hunchback, crippled as a result of severe tuberculosis of the bone. He was called Khuiankh and he was very probably one of the last of Raneferef's mortuary priests. Then once again, and this time for ever, Raneferef's tomb complex fell into oblivion.

Under the New Kingdom the temple's destruction as a building began. Particularly in the part of the temple belonging to the first building phase and constructed of high-quality limestone, people began to quarry out the stone for new building works. Simple people from the villages in the nearby Nile valley started to bury the dead here in primitive, anthropoid wooden coffins, in the belief that the best final resting place was in the shadow of the monuments of the mythical rulers and heros of long ago. This common people's cemetery was abandoned as late as beginning of the Roman era, roughly around the divide between BC and AD. In the centuries that followed, the ruin of the Unfinished Pyramid, fallen deep into the desert, apparently repelled rather than attracted the attentions of tomb-robbers. It is partly to this that we today owe the opportunity to study one of the best preserved royal mortuary temple complexes of the Old Kingdom, to plunge into the secrets of the papyri of Raneferef's temple archive, and to admire the pharaoh's superb statues on exhibition at the Egyptian Museum in Cairo.

Abusir shepherd.

The Testimony
of the Papyrus Archives

6

Nobody can precisely identify the day on which a group of men from the village of Abusir set out, as they had often done before, for a nearby pyramid on the raised margin of the desert in order to dig there. It was, it seems, sometime in 1893 and the men were certainly not workers on archaeological excavations. They were called, as they had been long before and still are today, *sabbakhin,* which in translation means "dung men". A peculiar name and a peculiar profession. The whole situation, indeed, was truly curious, with no lack of historical dimension and paradox; the 'sabbakhin' were merely one of its inseperable elements.

In the distant past, four and a half millennia ago when the pyramids were built, unending lines of workmen and bearers travelled up from the Nile valley to the desert. They would not only carry or drag huge stone blocks of dimensions large enough to amaze us even today. They would also carry up to the building-site the most valuable of the Nile's possessions — fertile clay. They would mix it with water and crushed straw and manufacture bricks directly at the building-site. The sun-dried bricks found multiple uses in the building of the pyramid complexes, especially when it was essential to economize or hurry. Sometimes whole temples at the foot of pyramids were built of these mudbricks, and after completion, smoothly plastered, whitewashed and richly decorated with coloured pictures, they looked, to begin with at least, as noble and timeless as the stone monuments beside them. Brick buildings, however, rapidly deteriorated. The mortuary cult and the traffic connected with it, sometimes lasting for a whole series of generations, in some cases slowed the decay and in others accelerated it. Another factor was the no less contradictory

love of order among the mortuary priests; on the one hand they were obsessed with ritual cleanliness but on the other they pushed heaps of refuse into back chambers and corners without scruple. This does not surprise or bother archaeologists who, on the

In Egypt today papyrus grows only in newly established plantations.

The Nile near El-Minya.

contrary, are delighted by the huge layers of rubbish and disintegrated mudbricks which today cover large areas of the pyramid fields. These so-called 'cultural layers', containing in addition to disintegrated clay, rich organic ingredients, attract the attention not only of archaeologists but, long before them, of sabbakhin. For generations these scavengers have been accustomed to set out into the desert for the pyramids with hoes and baskets and to search for and dig out the "clay" from the "cultural levels", bringing it back down to the Nile valley as added fertiliser for their small fields and gardens on the edge of the eternally encroaching desert sands. The thousand-year cycle of the circulation of clay between the Nile valley and the desert by the hands of men is thus once again completed.

On that fateful day in 1893 the Abusir sabbakhin were very successful. They found not only clay to fertilize their fields but also papyri — numerous fragments and larger pieces of scrolls. It is not necessary to emphasize the obvious fact that the dividing line between sabbakhin and tomb-robbers was, to put it mildly, very thin. They rapidly and precisely appraised the rags of papyrus with the black and sometimes red inscriptions that they had turned up with their hoes, and evaluated them from the point of view of possible profits on the illicit market in antiquities. As was shown later, they carefully raked over the site of the discovery and gathered up nearly all the papyrus fragments which they then sold to Cairo receivers of antiquities. Who sold them to whom and for how much is something that nobody will ever find out. It was not long before the papyri turned up on the Egyptian antiquities market. They were very rapidly snapped up by experts who immediately realized their overall value. Some of the papyri ended up in the main Egyptian museum located in the Cairo quarter Giza, whose collections were only at the beginning of the century transferred to the then recently completed and now central Egyptian museum. Others came into the possession of foreign Egyptologists, especially the celebrated expert on Ancient Egyptian religious texts, Henri Edouard Naville, and the no less famous English archaeologist William Matthew Flinders Petrie. The remarkable journeys of the papyri did not, however, end here.

At the end of the 1890s archaeological research commenced on the remains of the great sun temple of the 5th-Dynasty king

Niuserre to the north of Abusir in the locality of Abu Ghurab. It was led by Freiherr Wilhelm von Bissing, and a crucial contribution to the project was to be made by the then young architect and archaeologist Ludwig Borchardt. The latter had already been interested in the Abusir pyramids for some time and, in connexion with the excavations at Abu Ghurab, he had developed a particular interest in the pyramid of Niuserre, which had been identified and briefly described more than sixty years before by the English scholar John Perring. It was very probably the chance discovery of the papyri mentioned above that led Borchardt to decide to start extensive archaeological excavations at Abusir immediately on finishing his work at Abu Ghurab. The excavations took place between 1900 and 1908. Before Borchardt and, indeed, just before excavations

Late Period tombs demolished by *sabbakhin.*

commenced, the German Egyptologist Heinrich Schäfer had attempted to locate the original site of the discovery of the papyri in just seven days of trial digging — without results. Borchardt's first attempt to find other papyri in 1900 was likewise unsuccessful despite his considerable archaeological experience, knowledge of local conditions and rare ability to obtain valuable archaeological information from the native inhabitants. It was only in February 1903 that he managed to find several fragments of papyri, just a few square centimetres in size, in the ruins of Neferirkare's mortuary temple. Borchardt had certainly expected more, but it would be wrong to speak of a complete disappointment. Among the fragments was one which Hugo Ibscher, the celebrated papyri restorer from the Berlin Museum, managed to join together with a piece of papyrus found ten years before by the 'sabbakhin'. The origin of the papyri and even the place in which the 'sabbakhin' had found them was therefore conclusively established.

The Abusir papyri had generated great excitement in specialist circles, and world museums with large collections of Ancient Egyptian antiquities had expressed interest in them. For this reason they did not long remain in the hands of Naville, Petrie and others who had come into contact with them, and they ended up in London, Berlin, Paris and also, of course, in Cairo. In London they were acquired by two institutions — the British Museum and University College. Similarly, in Berlin some of the papyri are today to be found in the Staatliche Museen zu Berlin (the former East Berlin) and some in the Staatliche Museen der Stiftung Preussischer Kulturbesitz (the former West Ber-

Part of a papyrus scroll from Raneferef's temple archive.

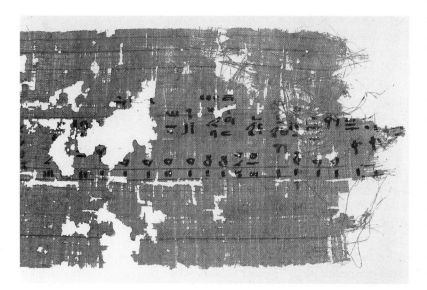

lin). In Cairo they were simply shifted from one bank of the Nile to the other, i.e. from the former museum at Giza to the Egyptian Museum opened in the centre of Cairo in 1900 (the movements of the main state collections of Ancient Egyptian antiquities within the boundaries of modern Cairo were in fact rather more complicated — originally, the collection created in 1858 was located by decision of the Egyptian government on the east bank of the Nile in the Bulaq quarter; it was then transferred to the Giza quarter on the west bank, and finally taken back to the Egyptian Museum on the east bank).

The fragments of papyri which ended up in Paris, in the Museé du Louvre, had made a particularly remarkable journey. Although it sounds unbelievable, and especially odd in view of the excited attention which they attracted from expert circles immediately on their discovery, they only came into the possession of the Louvre in 1956, and it is only from that year that serious research on the Abusir papyri dates. It was also in 1952 that the librarian of the Bibliothèque de la Sorbonne, Louis Bonnerot, randomly opened a journal which had originally belonged to the celebrated French Egyptologist Gaston Camille Charles Maspero, a former director of the Institut Français d'Archéologie Orientale du Caire. From the journal inherited by the library after Maspero's death fell two quite large fragments of papyri. The distinguished Paris expert on papyri, Georges Posener, professor of Egyptology at the Sorbonne, identified them as part of the find made at the end of the previous century by the 'sabbakhin' at Abusir. Only subsequently were the fragments transferred to the Museé du Louvre. This time the interest excited in Parisian Egyptological circles by this small but historically significant discovery did not fade away. At Posener's instigation his student, later his wife, Paule Kriéger began to take a more systematic interest in the Abusir papyri. In 1956 she managed to find further papyrus fragments in the Louvre, in a folio deposited with other books of Maspero's in a trunk which had been transferred from from the Bibliothèque de la Sorbonne four years before. From that moment Paule Posener-Kriéger's career was to be inextricably linked with the fate of the Abusir papyri.

There were reasons behind the apparent contradiction between the attention attracted by the discovery of the Abusir papyri

Mme. Paule Posener-Kriéger was present at the excavations in Raneferef's mortuary temple at Abusir at the moment when the most beautiful of Raneferef's statues was discovered. In this photograph she is accompanied by Usama el-Hamzawi , an inspector of the Egyptian Antiquities Organisation.

and their rapid plunge into obscurity. As has already been mentioned, they consisted in fragments of papyri, altogether numbering a few hundred, from small pieces to the major parts of entire scrolls. In the course of time, at the end of the 1930s and beginning of the 1940s, several small fragments had in fact been published by various scholars in connexion with work on a number of subsidiary questions in Ancient Egyptian history. The first essential condition for scientific cataloguing of the Abusir papyri was, however, to order and classify them and to put together the parts that belonged to each other. This first step, apparently purely mechanical but in fact requiring long-term preparation and a basic grasp of the content of the individual fragments, was so difficult that at the beginning of the century simply nobody was willing to embark on it.

Another serious formal obstacle was represented by the texts themselves, and more precisely by the type of script used to make the records on the papyri. It was the cursive type that today we call Old Hieratic. This was derived from hieroglyphic writing and used particularly on occasions when it was necessary to make a record quickly, simply and without ostentation, for example for the purposes of administration. The record was made with a small brush, most often in black but in special cases red, and most frequently on a small sheet of papyrus but sometimes on a fragment of limestone, a shard of pottery, a wooden tablet or even an animal bone. It was a kind of writing which could turn into a scrawled line when the scribe was in a hurry, and this, of course, further complicates matters for the reader. The difficulties of reading Old Hieratic are increased still more by the fact that only a relatively limited number of examples exist, so reducing the material basis necessary for a thorough understanding of the script and of the mechanism by which individual signs were simplified.

Finally, the actual content of the hieratic records on the papyri in itself constitutes

Panel with a picture of the royal architect and scribe Hesyre from the magnate's tomb in North Saqqara. Hesyre is holding in his hand the emblems of his office: mace, staff and scribe's instruments. Wood, low relief. Egyptian Museum in Cairo (no. 88).

a major barrier. As it at last became clear, they were records of very various kinds, from accounting documents on management of the temple cult to royal decrees. It is therefore no wonder that the Abusir papyri were only to "give utterance" three quarters of a century after they were found. When they did so it was thanks to the lifelong efforts of Paule Posener-Kriéger, formerly Director of the Institut Français d'Archéologie Orientale du Caire and today a renowned expert on hieratic script and especially on what is called Old Hieratic. Her efforts were supported by the encouragement and professional advice not only of her teacher and later her husband Georges Posener but also of the British

Egyptologist Sir Alan Henderson Gardiner and the Czech Egyptologist Jaroslav Černý, both distinguished international experts on hieratic palaeography. After more than twenty years of intensive work Paule Posener-Kriéger, in co-operation with the Museé du Louvre's long-time custodian Jean Louis de Cenival, published the whole set of papyri discovered in Neferirkare's pyramid temple. This work included a list of papyri, photocopies, hieroglyphic transcriptions of the hieratic texts and relevant palaeographical tables. *The Abusir Papyri* was published in the form of an independent volume in the British Museum Series of Hieratic Texts in 1968. Eight years later Mme. Posener-Kriéger added a translation and commentary. Under the title *Les Archives du Temple Funéraire de Néferirkare-Kakaï* the two-volume work came out in 1976 as the 55th volume in the Bibliothèques d'Études series published by the Institut Français d'Archéologie Orientale. With these two volumes the riches of the Abusir pyramid archive were at last made accessible to the expert public.

The edition showed, above all, that the papyri represent only a fragment of the archive of Neferirkare's pyramid temple and that they are all in one way or another related to the pharaoh's mortuary cult. A clear majority of the papyri, however, date from the reign of Djedkare, with a smaller part from the reigns of Unas, Teti and Pepi II. Accurate dating of the papyri has been made possible by the presence, obviously on only a number of papyri, of chronological data including the name of the sovereign and the

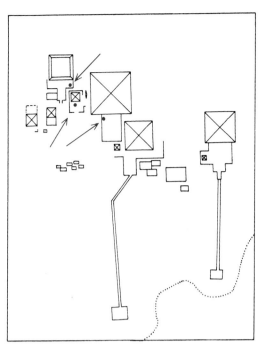

Plan showing the location of discoveries of papyri in the Abusir cemetery.

date in his reign when the document was issued. Time was defined with reference to years in which the cattle were counted (at that period the cattle were counted once every two years and therefore we have to double the number of countings to arrive at the correct number of years of the reign of a particular king), and also the month of one of the three seasons of the Ancient Egyptian year (inundation, emergence and harvest), and the appropriate day. The papyrus have thus been dated to a period between the concluding phase of the 5th Dynasty and the end of the 6th Dynasty, i.e. roughly to a period from the beginning of the 24th to the end of the 23rd century BC. The fact that a large

Fragments of papyri from Raneferef's temple archive with remains of an old hieratic text.

proportion of the papyri have been identified as dating from the reign of Djedkare may be closely linked to the fact that it was this pharaoh who decided not to build his pyramid complex at Abusir, in the cemetery of his immediate royal predecessors, but several kilometres away in South Saqqara. It was a major decision from many points of view, and is also puzzling, the more so because Djedkare founded a cemetery at Abusir for the most immediate members of his family, the princesses, and for his high officials and courtiers. But whatever the reasons, the decision to "abandon" the Abusir necropolis obliged the pharaoh to undertake meticulous regulation both of the running of the mortuary cults in the individual tomb complexes and of the general conditions in the necropolis. This is the background to which the large number of papyri dating from the time of Djedkare is related.

From the point of view of content the papyri can be divided into several categories. One is represented by timetables of priestly duties in Neferirkare's pyramid temple. These were tasks carried out daily, monthly or on the occasion of important festivals, and consisted of the bringing of offerings to the spirit of the deceased, sacrificial rites, and guard duties in various parts of the mortuary temple, among other activities. Particular services would be undertaken on the occasion of religious festivals such as the festival of Sokar, god of the dead, the festival of the night of the god Re, the festival of the goddess Hathor, and that of the god of fertility, Min, etc.. The priesthood was made up of the "servants of god", "the pure", and the *khentyush* (the translation and intepretation of this Egyptian name is still the subject of academic debate). Various officials and workers and others would help them in the performance of their duties. The priesthood was divided into five basic groups, the

so-called *phyles,* designated in terms of the parts of a boat, for example "prow — starboard", "stern — port", etc. This system of organising the workforce, which was still further sub-divided within the groups mentioned, arose in connexion with boat transport, from which the names of the sections were derived. Perhaps 40 priests would make up one group. The lists suggest that the offices and professions represented among the priests and employees of the mortuary temple were extremely diverse; there were, for example, hairdressers, physicians, scribes etc. One of the most curious professions documented in these papyri was undoubtedly the "flute-player of the White Crown", a man who played the flute during the ceremony connected with venerating the crown that symbolically made the pharaoh the ruler of Upper Egypt.

The inventory lists which represented, at the same time, a way of keeping track of the internal furnishings and equipment of the building, are very valuable in giving a better picture of the internal arrangement of the mortuary temple. Figuring in the lists are a whole range of different types of vessels, offering tables, ritual knives, materials, oils, jewellery, boxes etc., precious cult instruments and incidental items. For each object there is a record, in a special column, indicating whether the object is or is not in its correct place, and whether it is damaged. The bureaucratic thoroughness and precision of the priests and officials was so extreme they did not even hesitate to record that a small ball of incense was in its proper place in a box!

Accounting documents make up a large group of the papyri. Records on the supplies of various products and objects and their use or storage, documents on measuring units and financial transactions and suchlike are only superficially dull. Deciphering them offers a unique key to understanding the complex mechanism by which the economic basis of the temple functioned. The wider economic context emerges here with unusual precision and sometimes brings surprises. They record yields from the estates specially allocated to provide the material support for the pharaoh's mortuary cult; these included supplies of grain, fruit, vegetables, milk, wine, beer, fats, poultry, meat etc. Naturally they also mention other provisions such as cloth, staffs and maces, furniture and much else. The volume of individual items allows

Incomplete scroll of papyrus from Raneferef's temple archive.

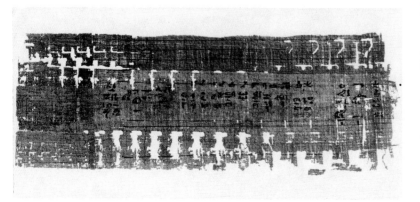

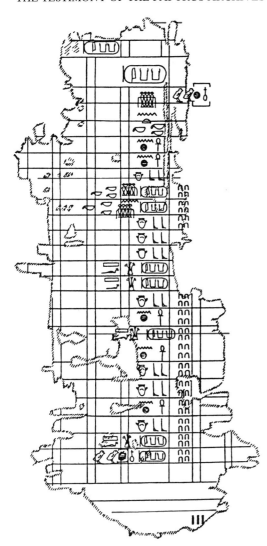

and the position enjoyed within it by the royal mortuary cults.

Of the quite small group of surviving documents not yet mentioned those directly related to the architecture of the temple have a special significance. These contain very heterogeneous and scrappy information connected, for example, with the regular sealing of doors in individual parts of the temple for purposes of inspection, the checking of possible damage to the temple's masonry and other such matters. However fragmentary, this information acquires concrete archaeological importance when set side by side with the temple's real physical remains as uncovered during excavations. For example, in the papyri of Neferirkare's temple archive there is an allusion to damage being sustained to the masonry of the South Bark during a service performed by one of the groups of priests. There is also an even more fragmentary mention of the North Bark. The assumption that two buildings — a South and a North Bark — had existed in the precincts of Neferirkare's pyramid complex became,

Hieroglyphic transcription of a text on a fragment of papyrus from the archive of Neferirkare's mortuary temple. The text contains the names of the people to whom the supplies (not precisely specified) flowing into the mortuary temple must be allocated (by P. Posener-Kriéger).

Seated scribe writing on a papyrus scroll which is supported on his skirt stretched tight between his knees. Polychrome limestone, 51 cm high. Egyptian Museum in Cairo (no. 36).

us to form a more precise picture of life in the temple. From the documents it is clear that supplies to the temple did not only flow in from the funerary estates that the king had already set up during his lifetime to meet the needs of his mortuary cult. They also came from the stores of the royal residence, palace and a number of other important central institutions. Among them a special place was occupied by supplies from Neferirkare's sun temple; these had already been offered up on the altar of the sun god and only then were they taken to be offered on the altar of the deceased king in his pyramid temple. This sun temple, the subject of such abundant mention in the Abusir papyri, has, however, not yet been found, even though it was obviously located not far from Abusir. Although the temple accounting documents are sometimes very fragmentary the information which they provide allows us to reconstruct with surprising precision not only the economic management of the temple but the organisation of economic life in the country, at the end of the 1970s, the starting-point for interesting archaeological research by the Czech expedition at Abusir. With the help of geophysical measuring it proved possible to find and partially uncover the eastern half of a large building shaped like a boat which had stood by the south wing of the enclosure wall of the pyramid, and precisely on its north-south axis. The building had originally been about 30 m. long and had contained a wooden boat in which the dead king could symbolically travel to the other world and join the retinue which accompanied the sun god on his eternal journey across the heavenly ocean. All that had survived of the boat, unfortunately, was mouldering dust. The North Bark has not been uncovered, even though knowledge of the principles of Ancient Egyptian building suggests that it was extremely likely to have been situated — entirely symmetrically in relation to the South Bark — by the north enclosure wall of the pyramid. This small example draws attention to the further, archaeological aspect

of the Abusir archives. It is not an aspect which has so far been much exploited, but the possibilities which it holds out are eloquently attested, for example, by the circumstances leading to the discovery of Raneferef's mortuary temple.

On one extremely tiny piece of papyrus from the Neferirkare temple archive, catalogued in Mme. Posener-Kriéger's publication as fragment 45 C, the name of the pharaoh Raneferef appears not in an oval cartouche but in a rectangular frame. This could not be simply a form of writing the king's name and it was necessary to look for an explanation elsewhere. On the basis of several analogical documents it was very likely that the frame represented a stylised depiction of the rectangular ground plan of a mortuary temple. This hypothetical interpretation of the record on fragment 45 C as "Raneferef's mortuary temple" was to have far-reaching consequences since it presupposed the real existence of such a building and — in the context of Neferirkare's temple archive — placed

Water channel with flowering hyacinths near Saqqara.

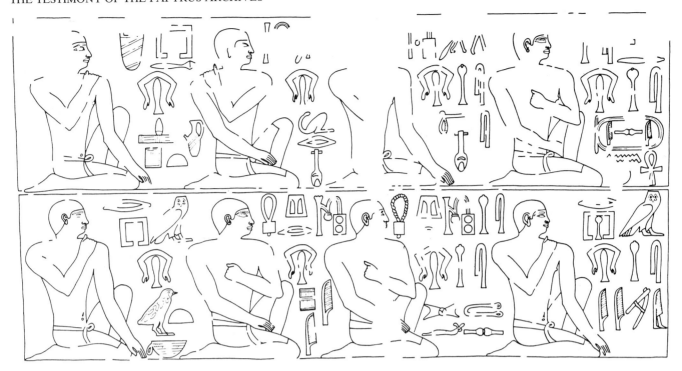

it in the Abusir necropolis. It was this tiny papyrus fragment that became one of the decisive arguments behind the decision to search for Raneferef's temple (see p. 133 ff.), a decision proved correct when the temple was indeed found. What nobody expected, or even allowed himself the smallest hope of, was the discovery of other papyri. But this was to happen in Raneferef's mortuary temple and once again it was a matter of a temple archive.

If the find of the papyri of Neferirkare's temple archive had been shrouded in mystery and the precise archaeological circumstances of the discovery could never be reconstructed, then the find of Raneferef's temple archive was in this respect the complete reverse. The situation had its good and its bad aspects. They were good in that it was possible to make a careful record of all the circumstances surrounding the discovery of the papyri, and so bring together a mass of important supplementary archaeological information. They were bad mainly in that the find aroused almost too much attention and because it consisted of a large number of papyri located all over the relatively large area of the temple. The retrieval and documentation of the papyri required considerable time amounting to several weeks and this meant that there was a grave danger that it would not prove possible to "protect" the find in the open desert and that in an unguarded moment some fragments might be stolen. If this had happened and if, for

example, after a certain time the fragments of papyri from Raneferef's temple archive had been found on the world antiquities market, it would have had very serious negative consequences for further excavations at Abusir. Fortunately the papyri were retrieved without damage being caused, and saved. Major help with the work needed to unearth the papyri, document them and provisionally lodge them in the storage facility of the Czech expedition at Abusir was provided by Mme. Posener-Kriéger. By a lucky coincidence she was at that time working as the director of the Institut Français d'Archéologie Orientale du Caire. Joint efforts were successful in discovering and preserving over 2,000 fragments and entire large sections of papyrus scrolls.

The papyri were found in several different places. The largest number were found in the storage rooms in the north-west part of the temple. There were so many there that their fragments had created an almost continuous layer above the floor of three rooms. The papyrus scrolls had originally been fastened with leather straps and lodged in wooden boxes. It is probable that later, when the temple was ransacked, thieves regarded the ornamented boxes as valuable but ignored the papyri. The contents of the boxes were tipped out onto the ground and in the course of time the papyri had been trampled underfoot, submerged in rubbish and covered over by layers of crumbled collapsing brick masonry from the rooms. Finally everything

Subordinate officials surrounding the Vizier Ptahshepses on a relief decoration in his mastaba at Abusir.

The major part of the papyrus archive was found in three magazines in the furthest north-west corner of Raneferef's mortuary temple.

Experienced workmen carefully uncovering and lifting fragments of the papyrus archive of Raneferef's mortuary temple.

scribe's actitivities — both the method of writing and the writing materials used — in no way damaged the structure of the papyrus. The records were made with a small brush prepared from a thin reed stem, the end softened by chewing and formed into a tip. The scribe dipped the brush either into a black ink made of soot diluted with water or into a red ink prepared from powdered ochre likewise mixed with water. This meant that in case of need text could be removed with water. The scroll could then be used again for making another record. A whole range of such re-used papyri, known as palimpsests, was found among the fragments from Raneferef's archive. Of course, if a papyrus scroll was exposed to the action of water for a longer time or was left in damp conditions it would be entirely destroyed. In the case of Raneferef's archive a number of fortunate accidents had occurred and these had contributed to its preservation, albeit in a fragmentary state. The first of these was the layer of dust and rubbish which had already covered the fragments at the time when the rooms in which the papyri lay were still roofed and therefore did not let in water. Another happy accident was that the brick masonry of the rooms progressively disintegrated and gradually settled on the layer of rubbish covering the papyri. In the end this layer was so thick that it was not damaged by the collapse of the side walls, with their larger volume and weight, as a result of erosion. The huge layer of sand blown onto the ruins of the temple by the desert wind also proved ultimately beneficial.

was engulfed by vast layers of sand which safely preserved the remains of the papyri for four and a half millennia.

It is almost unbelievable that mouldering papyri, fragile as spider's web, should have survived to this day. Originally, of course, they were elastic and robust. This was a result both of the material — the pulp of the papyrus stems — and the technology for producing the scrolls. They were made by laying narrow strips cut from papyrus pulp crosswise over each other. No glue was used to stick the strips together since the papyrus juice squeezed out from the pulp under the pressure of a stone press, and then gradually drying out, was sufficient to bind them. The

The papyri from the archive of Raneferef's mortuary temple are only now being studied, conserved, evaluated and prepared for publication. Mme. Posener-Kriéger is taking the major part of the responsibility for work on the philological section of the publication. In overall volume Raneferef's archive is comparable to that of Neferirkare. The basic content of the surviving documents is also similar, if with certain divergencies. For example, a larger number of royal decrees have been preserved in Raneferef's archive. At this point it would be premature to give a more detailed account of the content of Raneferef's papyrus archive since expert evaluation is still underway. Currently, only partial results are available. The information obtained, for example about the ritual slaughterhouse known as "the Sanctuary of the Knife", in which the sacrificial animals would be killed, has already been mentioned (see p. 152).

What remains to be said? We should perhaps express regret that other papyrus archives are unlikely to be discovered at Abusir. The discovery of the remains of three temple archives — those of Neferirkare, Raneferef and Khentkaus — has been to some extent a matter of chance and the coincidence of a few unique historical circumstances. Under normal conditions the analogous papyrus archives of the royal pyramid complexes were not kept in the storerooms of the mortuary temples but in the administrative buildings which together with the priests' dwellings were concentrated in the immediate vicinity of the valley temples, i.e. in the so-called pyramid towns. They were kept, in other words, not in the tomb complex but still in the "world of the living", although in close proximity to the entry to the "empire of the dead". At Abusir such towns, in which priests, officials and workmen employed in the mortuary cults at the cemetery lived and worked, almost certainly existed in the vicinity of Sahure's and Niuserre's valley temples. Their remains lie at a depth of perhaps 5 metres under the surface of the desert today, under great layers of Nile mud deposits. The current level of ground water in these places is perhaps 70 — 100 cm beneath the surface. This means that the papyrus archives in the administrative buildings of the pyramid towns have long disappeared without trace, dissolving and mouldering. It was sheer accident that Neferirkare did not finish his pyramid complex

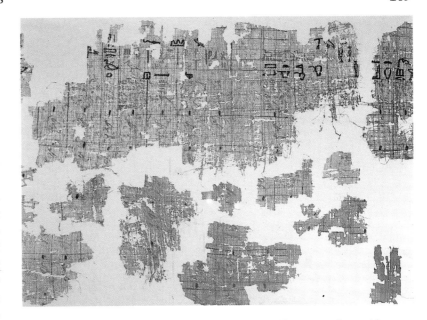

Fragments of papyri from the archive of Raneferef's mortuary temple.

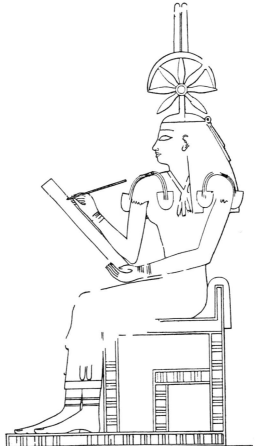

Seshat, the goddess of letters and knowledge, played a significant role in the ceremonies accompanying the founding of important buildings. Detail from the relief decoration of Sahure's mortuary temple at Abusir (by L. Borchardt).

and that this was accomplished for him by his younger son Niuserre who then had the causeway leading from the valley to the mortuary temple of his father diverted and completed as a part of his own pyramid complex. The tombs of the older members of Niuserre's family, all by coincidence unfinished and only completed in his reign, were thus consigned to a somewhat autonomous and isolated position within the cemetery. For that reason their priests did not make their dwellings near valley temples on the edge of the desert but in the immediate neighbourhood of the mortuary temples, and gradually even inside them. The higher site of mortu- ary temples, perhaps 30 metres above the Nile Valley, and the hot and dry conditions of the desert, had then only to interact favourably for the remains of the papyrus archives to be preserved to this day.

In the house of an Abusir
cemetery guard: siesta with
a water pipe.

The Dazzling Career
of the Royal Hairdresser

Richard Lepsius, the celebrated founder of the first German department of Egyptology at Berlin University, and other members of the German expedition who visited Abusir in 1843, were convinced that the remains of a pyramid lay concealed under the huge ruins on the north-east edge of the necropolis. For this reason they assigned the Roman numeral XIX to this antiquity on the maps published subsequently in the first volume of their monumental work, *Denkmaeler aus Aegypten und Aethiopien*. They had earlier decided to use Roman numerals to designate pyramids, starting from the north and proceeding south. The number I was therefore assigned to a large mudbrick building in Abu Rawash, perhaps 7 km south of Giza and regarded by the Lepsius expedition

7

View of the mastaba of Ptahshepses from the top of Niuserre's pyramid.

Head of a statue of the
vizier Ptahshepses. The vizier
wears a wig on his head
and a beard on his chin.
Reddish quartzite, 23 cm
high.

as the northernmost Egyptian pyramid. This was, by the way, a mistake because the mud-brick ruin was not in fact a pyramid. As chance would have it, neither was "pyramid" XIX. This was recognised by the French Egyptologist Jacques de Morgan, who started archaeological excavations in the ruins of "Pyramid no. XIX" in 1893 and instead of a pyramid discovered the entrance to the mastaba of Ptahshepses.

In Abusir alone the Lepsius expedition made several other similar errors, identifying as pyramids remains which were in fact other types of monument, and vice versa. To mention this is not, however, to trivialise the results of the work of the German expedition's work. On the contrary, the scientific value of the documentation produced by the German expedition was not to diminish over the next half-century, and in some cases it actually increased with time. This was because many of the ancient inscriptions which the German expedition had copied and antiquities which the expedition had described were later damaged or entirely destroyed.

The mastaba of Ptahshepses, of which de Morgan had uncovered only a small part, was then forgotten for almost seventy years.

The revial of interest in the monument and completion of research into it was linked to the founding of the Czech (then Czecho-slovak) Institute of Egyptology at Charles University and its branch in Cairo. The Institute

During excavations in the mastaba of Ptahshepses it was necessary to remove layers of rubble up to 8 m thick.

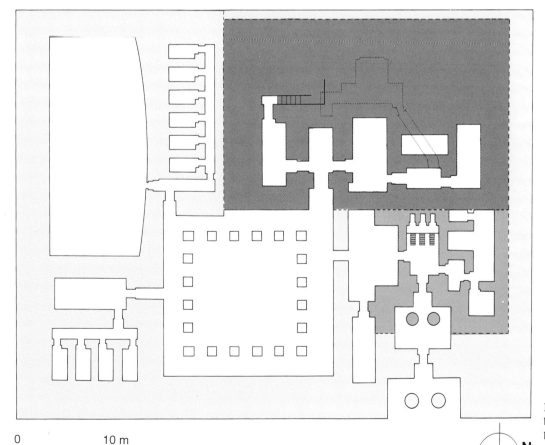

0   10 m

N

Plan of Ptahshepses' mastaba indicating the three building phases of the monument (plan of the mastaba by P. Jánosi with alterations).

acquired the concession permitting completion of the research on the mastaba of Ptahshepses in 1960, at the same time as it committed itself to take part in the UNESCO archaeological rescue operations in Nubia. The excavations in the mastaba of Ptahshepses were initiated in 1960 and up to the mid 1960s they were carried out in intervals between expeditions to Nubia. With the exception of the last season in 1974 they were led by Zbyněk Žába, with the valuable help of Abdu el-Qereti, the experienced foremen of the local workmen.

In the first phase of excavations Žába concentrated on the area where de Morgan had left his work unfinished in the south-east part of the mastaba. Here, seventy years before, de Morgan had unearthed a room containing a pair of six-stemmed lotus columns which, as Žába managed to ascertain, had been converted from the original entrance to the tomb into a vestibule. East of the columned vestibule Žába made a truly unique discovery. He uncovered a new portico with a pair of still larger and even eight-stemmed lotus columns. In the northern part of the north-east corner he excavated four rooms which had once served as magazines for offerings and cult vessels for the ceremonies carried out in a neighbouring large chapel with three niches.

Digging work was then transferred from the north-east part of the mastaba toward the south, and led to the uncovering of a large pillared court. The disintegrated crowns of twenty monolithic limestone pillars had already been measured and marked on a plan by de Morgan but the pillared court had remained as a whole uninvestigated. West of the pillared court de Morgan had

Limestone block from the architrave which originally rested on the pillars in the open court of Ptahshepses' mastaba. On the block Ptahshepses is depicted in sunken relief with his most important titles before him.

uncovered the entrance to what seemed to be another mastaba. Given the very limited extent of his excavations it is not surprising that he judged it to belong to a tomb quite other than that of Ptahshepses. He even believed that a whole group of mastabas were to be found on the site. It was only with Žába's area stripping that it became clear that what was being excavated was not a group of tombs but a single mastaba which had gradually been extended to enormous dimensions in accordance with a very original plan. The entrance discovered by de Morgan west of the pillared court had led to the "original" mastaba of Ptahshepses, in which the burial chamber with the sarcophagus of Ptahshepses had been located. Even just this "original" mastaba, relatively modest in terms of size, contained a number of elements, especially in the underground part, which mean that it far surpasses other contemporary monuments of the same type. For example, the saddle construction of the ceiling out of gigantic limestone monoliths resembled the royal burial chambers in the neighbouring Abusir pyramids. Similarly Ptahshepses' enormous red granite sarcophagus seems in dimensions, material and workmanship to be more appropriate to a royal than to a private tomb. In the place of the "original" mastaba of Ptahshepses, and especially in the *serdab* in the northern part of the monument, a large number of fragments of reliefs were found. They had been stored, or more precisely left to one side here, by Borchardt in the course of his excavations in Sahure's pyramid temple. Borchardt had, in fact published some of these fragments, but the great majority had never been published. A rusty tin, a scrap of a German newspaper and an envelope stamped. January 1904, accompanied and dated Borchardt's deposit.

Two large magazine complexes, one comprising four chambers to the south-east of the pillared court and the other seven chambers to the south-west, both uncovered by Žába in the second half of the 1960s, only strengthened the overall impression of a half-private, half-royal tomb. Magazine complexes similar to those found in the mastaba — the so-called, 'treasury' and 'granary' — are to be met with particularly in contemporary royal pyramid temples.

If these already cited features incorporated into the design of Ptahshepses were more or less inspired by royal architecture, then a room in the south-west corner of the mastaba — the last to be uncovered — was a completely unexpected surprise for the excavators, and also left no one in doubt of the extraordinarily high and truly exceptional social standing of the tomb's owner. This room is the largest in the tomb and in shape resembles a boat. Its northern wall is not only convex but curved in a way that visibly recalls the side of a boat. "The Boat Hall" has no parallel in private tombs, whether of Ptahshepses' time or in the whole period of the Old Kingdom. We meet with the burial of boats, from this period, above all in royal pyramid complexes, because the boat journey in the other world in the entourage of the sun god was exclusively a royal privilege. The famous Barque of Cheops, discovered in 1954 near the south side of the Great Pyramid at Giza and today exhibited in its own "Museum of the Boat of Cheops", close to the site of the find, is an outstanding embodiment of this religious idea.

In 1970 Žába started work on excavating the outer walls of the mastaba of Ptahshepses. He concentrated especially on the east, north and in part the west wall. In several places enormous blocks of fine white limestone, which had originally been a part of the outer casing of the mastaba, were found *in situ*. A number of these blocks, for example by the north wall, had originally been destined for the roofing of Niuserre's pyramid temple.

East of the entrance to the mastaba of Ptahshepses, and already outside the limits

East-west cross-section of the sarcophagus chamber and the eastern part of the superstructure of the first building phase of Ptahshepses' mastaba (V. Fiala).

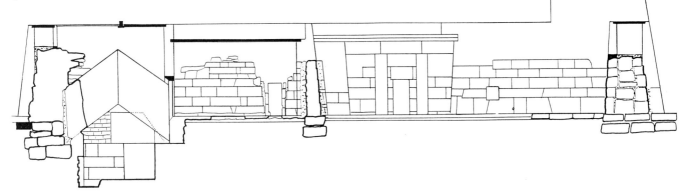

of the Czech concession, Žába discovered another mastaba. Research into this much more modest tomb was undertaken by an Egyptian expedition led by Mohammad Zurayar. It became clear that it belonged to a man who was also named Ptahshepses. It is even possible that this individual was one of the two sons of Ptahshepses, both of whom had the same name as their father. Also, on the other side of the mastaba, west of the north-west corner, Žába partially uncovered the entrance to another large tomb. This entrance, originally adorned by a pair of lotus columns made of limestone, was recovered because this site as well was outside Žába's concession.

A large quantity of fragments of the reliefs which once decorated the walls of individual rooms were found in the thick layers of rubble concealing the mastaba's extant enclosure walls — walls which in places reached 6 m. The fragments had accumulated around the mastaba at the time when it be-

came an easily accessible quarry and its systematic demolition was underway.

Excavations in the mastaba of Ptahshepses were undertaken over seven archaeological seasons between 1960 and 1974. They resulted in the unearthing of what is as yet the most extensive and architecturally the most articulated non-royal tomb known from the period of the Old Kingdom. The tomb had been constructed in three major building phases, i.e. its design had twice been modified in the interests of creating a larger and architectonically more demanding structure. What ultimately emerged was a building which had no parallel in its time. Viewed from the Nile valley the mastaba of Ptahshepses would have towered majestically on the edge of the raised desert plateau and alongside the royal pyramids it undoubtedly represented one of the dominating features of the necropolis. The smooth, rectangular, white limestone walls of the mastaba would have shone brightly in the intense rays of the sun and would have harmoniously complemented the similarly shining immense triangular surfaces of the neighbouring pyramids. The site for Ptahshepses' mastaba was not chosen at random. On the contrary, its position in front of the pyramids of Sahure and Niuserre, and almost precisely equidistant from both, was chosen very deliberately. It was as if the owner and builder of the mastaba had wanted to round off the monumental architectonic composition of the tombs of the kings and magnates — a composition of which he had himself been to a considerable extent the author. From Ptahshepses' titles it is clear that he was overseer of all the building works in the royal necropolis by what is today Abusir.

The entrance to the tomb, situated in the eastern wall near the north-east corner, was adorned with a pair of six-metre-high eight-stemmed columns shaped like lotus sheaves with closed buds and tied under the capitals with cord wound several times around them. Each column was made from a single piece of the fine white limestone which Arabs today call *batn el-baqara*, "Cow's Belly", perhaps because this is what the smoothness of the stone brings to mind. The columns supported a heavy architrave on which rested the enormous slabs of the roof terrace. Both architrave and slabs were of the same high-quality limestone as the columns. Originally the portico reached a height of eight metres. The eight-stemmed lotus columns are up to

The entrance to Ptahshepses' mastaba was decorated by a pair of eight-stem lotus columns of fine white limestone. These 6-metre high columns represent the oldest known examples of the type from ancient Egypt.

The pair of eight-stem lotus columns after the partial reconstruction of the entrance to Ptahshepses' mastaba.

Fragment of a relief from Ptahshepses' mastaba with the remains of a text, and a part of the portico which formed the architrave decorated with a concave cornice and supported by an eight-stem lotus column.

Seshseshet, the "Lotus Flower", daughter of the Vizier Mereruka. Low relief with remains of polychrome. 6th Dynasty. Mastaba of Mereruka, Saqqara.

now the oldest known examples of their type from Ancient Egypt. It is no accident that this unique example of the technical im-

agination of the Ancient Egyptians — the eight-stem geometrically and aesthetically allowed the most harmonious transition between the circular base on which the column stood and the square abacus on the lotus capital, on which rested the rectangular architrave — first appears in Abusir and here in the Mastaba of Ptahshepses. Nor was the choice of plant motif, that of the lotus, a matter of mere chance. The lotus, whose flower closes at night and sinks into the water and then at morning opens again, was a symbol of resurrection and rebirth in Ancient Egypt. This was not really a columned entrance to a tomb; it was rather the gate where the way opened up to resurrection and a new life, eternal and blissful.

Lotus columns, but this time of course only six-stemmed, also adorned the room into which the monumental entrance immediately opened. This columned vestibule was also originally the main entrance but lost its function during the second reconstruction, becoming a closed room. Its walls are decorated with scenes of boats and bearers bringing from the funerary estates and workshops Ptahshepses's burial equipment and everything else necessary for setting up the mortuary cult: furniture, jewellery, cloth, grain, fruit and suchlike. Probably what is known as the 'biographical inscription' was first placed in this columned vestibule. Only a few fragments of this inscription have been found, and this is a great pity. It means that Ptahshepses' origins and the circumstances of his dizzy social ascent remain shrouded in mystery.

Flowering lotuses.

The Vizier Ptahshepses with his wife the princess Khamerernebty kneeling at his feet. Detail from the relief decoration of Ptahshepses' mastaba.

Scenes of the slaughter of sacrificial animals and pictures of Ptahshepses fill up the walls of a narrow passage leading from the columned vestibule to one of the most important cult rooms in the tomb — the chapel with the three niches. Inscriptions accompanying the pictures contain a range of titles which attest Ptahshepses' high social status: "Local Prince, Only Friend (of the pharaoh), Ruler of Nekheb, Guardian of the (royal) Diadem, Privy to the Secret of the House of Morning, Beloved One of his Lord, Chief Justice, Vizier, Overseer of all the Royal Works, Servant of the Throne, Lector-Priest, Privy to the Secret Sacred Writings of the God's Words...".

The chapel with the three niches in its western wall had an important cult function. Originally, slightly larger than life-size

Detail of a man pouring water across the deck of a boat. Low relief with remains of polychrome. Mastaba of Ptahshepses, Abusir.

Ptahshepses with his wife (fascimile, see the photograph on the foregoing page).

statues of the standing Ptahshepses, made out of reddish quartzite, stood in these niches behind narrow two-leaf doors. Only fragments of these have been found. Judging from the inscriptions on the facing wall of the niches, the statues represented Ptahshepses in three different forms or functions: as an official, a priest, and a private individual. Offerings were placed on altars at the foot of the statues during funerary ceremonies accompanied by the recitation of religious formulae by the lector-priest. The pictures carved in the stone on the walls of the chapel revived and created the intimate world of blissful eternity enjoyed by the divinely

transfigured Ptahshepses in the other world.

The greater part of the low polychrome relief decorating the chapel walls has survived to this day. The scenes depicted here are thematically linked by a single basic idea: the owner of the tomb overseeing work in the fields, pastures, gardens and workshops where all that is necessary for his mortuary cult is grown, manufactured and collected. On the chapel's northern wall there are scenes in which gardeners are working in the grain fields and vegetable plots, and bearers, entrusted with carrying the fruits of the fields and gardens, are bringing them on offering tables and in baskets to the feet of

Ptahshepses. On the south wall there are fishermen, herdsmen milking cows and the overseer of a poultry farm driving flocks of duck, geese and crane in front of him. And there are also, of course, scribes who are carefully recording everything on papyrus scrolls.

On the northern part of the east wall of the chapel there are superb scenes of a sculptor's atelier where two of Ptahshepses' statues — one in red granite and seated and the other in wood and standing — are being finished. Metal founders and chisellers are also depicted at their work and carpenters making a staff.

Opposite the scenes of crafts and near the entrance from the columned vestibule is an apparently simple but in fact very mysterious scene depicting the six sons of Ptahshepses walking. The figure and name of the first-born have been carefully chiselled off and almost entirely removed. Two of the sons bore the same name as their father, Ptahshepses, the others being called Kahotep, Hemakhty and Khenu. By the use of appropriate lighting it has also proved possible to decipher the name of the first-born son — Khafini. The form of this name is of no small significance for the reconstruction of the chronology both of the tomb and of Ptahshepses' family relationships. This is because the name Khafini is basiliform, containing *Ini* — one of the names of the king Niuserre — in a cartouche. This name also represents an important date recording *post quem* that Ptahshepses was approximately Niuserre's contemporary. The chiselling off of the name — and there is a similar example elsewhere in the tomb — points to a deliberate action which according to the religious ideas of the Ancient Egyptians would have dire consequences. For them a "name" was one of the enduring spiritual elements of a person and lasted beyond his earthly lifetime. The explanation for the action probably lay in family disputes triggered by Ptahshepses' marriage

to the pharaoh Niuserre's daughter Khamererebty. Ptahshepses, a man of non-royal origin, gained the extraordinary honour only at an advanced age when he was at the peak of his official career. It is almost unimaginable that at that time he would not already have had a family for many years and that this family would not have had to give place to the new family, immediately related to the pharaoh. It was perhaps for this reason that the first-born son of the non-royal family had to yield to the first-born in whose veins ran royal blood. The circumstances surrounding these events can only be guessed at.

Ptahshepses "double-portrait". The sculptor who carved the figure of the tomb's owner in low relief in the chapel with the three niches wrongly estimated the space for the figure and then had to correct his error.

Metal founders and metal chisellers. Detail from the relief decoration of the mastaba of Ptahshepses.

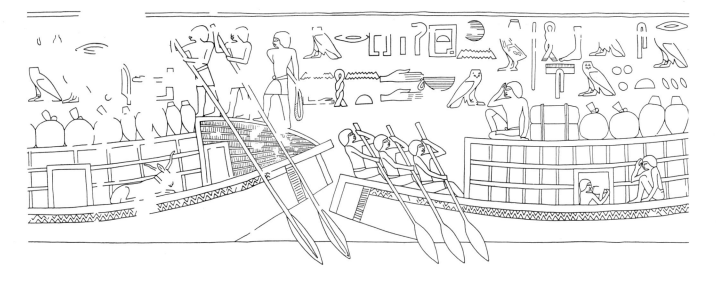

Boats bringing products
destined for the mortuary
cult from Ptahshepses' funerary estates. Detail from
the relief decoration of the
mastaba of Ptahshepses.

The young sons of Ptah-
shepses carrying hoopoes.
One of them is holding his
father's staff, another is
sniffing at a lotus flower.
Low relief with remains of
polychrome. Mastaba of
Ptahshepses, Abusir.

Detail from a scene depicting sculptors at work. The sculptors are working on a granite seated statue and a wooden standing statue of Ptahshepses. Low relief with remains of polychrome. Mastaba of Ptahshepses, Abusir.

Ropemakers from Mit Rahina.

Butchers at work. Detail
from the relief decoration of
the mastaba of Ptahshepses.

Detail from a scene depicting the slaughter of sacrificial animals. Low relief with
remains of polychrome.
Mastaba of Ptahshepses,
Abusir.

The area between the chapel with the
three niches and the pillared court, unfortunately seriously damaged, had already
been partially uncovered by de Morgan in
the last century. De Morgan believed that
a pillared portico had existed here and this is
what he recorded on his plan; but even the
most thorough examination revealed no
trace of pillars. The walls of the supposed
portico are decorated with a series of remarkable scenes in low relief, and in places
there are even remains of the original co-
lours.

On the eastern wall of the "portico" Ptahshepses is depicted surrounded by his subordinate officials. On the eastern half of the
northern wall of the "portico" he is being
carried on a litter for a walk. An interesting
inscription has survived above the line of
men carrying Ptahshepses. It contains a dia-
logue between the first and the last, the man
leading and supervising and the man at the
end of the row of bearers. The bearer at the
rear is being reprimanded and asked to settle
down and fulfill his bearer's duties well. But
the subject of the reprimand is holding his
ground and ironically commenting that the
chief, called the "privileged one", would do
better to mind his own business and follow
his nose. From this sneering remark it is

Detail from a scene depicting the administrator of a poultry farm bringing cranes. Low relief with remains of polychrome. Mastaba of Ptahshepses, Abusir.

apparent that the man selected as the leader and supervisor of the bearers was probably one of them and enjoyed no great respect among his fellows.

The western part of the "portico" is decorated with scenes depicting the transport of Ptahshepses' statues and the storage of the offerings. The statues were dragged in a way characteristic of Ancient Egyptians. i.e. on wooden sleds over a pre-levelled route which, during transport, would also be smoothed with water mixed with soft Nile mud. This would create a slippery surface making transport easier. From the inscriptions accompanying these scenes it is clear that some of the statues were of red granite

and measured seven cubits, i.e. approximately 3.5 m. Discovered during excavations in the mastaba of Ptahshepses was a large number of fragments of alabaster, red granite, limestone and red quartzite which came from several dozen statues, mostly of Ptahshepses. The question of where these statues had been positioned in the tomb and which cult function they fulfilled is complex and has still not been satisfactorily answered.

The pillared court came into existence only with the third, concluding building phase of the mastaba. Originally offerings were made here under the open sky on a huge altar, the upper face of which was decorated with the large hieroglyphic sign

Pillar with picture of the
magnate Ptahshepses in
sunken relief. Mastaba of
Ptahshepses, Abusir.

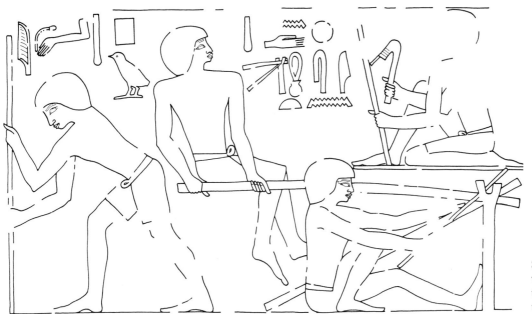

Straightening and polishing wooden staffs. Detail from the relief decoration of the tomb of Ptahshepses.

hetep, "offering". The side walls of the pillared court were once richly decorated with reliefs, of which only a tiny fragment has survived *in situ.* The flat roof of limestone slabs which protected the reliefs was supported by twenty monolithic pillars. The faces of the pillars that were turned inward to the court bore life-size pictures of Ptahshepses in sunken relief. The figures of Ptahshepses were arranged on the pillars in such a way as to lead the visitor from the south, on a north-south axis, into the court and in the direction of the altar, thence to the north-western corner of the court towards the entrance to the "original mastaba" and therefore towards Ptahshepses' burial chamber. Above the figures and likewise in sunken relief — a type of relief particularly suitable for open space accessible to sunlight allowing the aesthetic effect of pictures and inscriptions to be deepened by the play of light and shadow — Ptahshepses' titles and name were carved. None of the crowns of the pillars has been preserved in its entirety and they have all been damaged by natural erosion. Nonetheless some of their fragments have survived. It is clear from the inscriptions on several of these fragments that Ptahshepses' titulary began with the title "King's Son". At the time when the final extension of the mastaba was underway, then, Ptashepses had already become a prince, undoubtedly as a result of his marriage with Khamerernebty, daughter of the pharaoh Niuserre. At that time it was unheard of that a private person should not only become a member of the immediate royal family but also should be allowed to use

a royal title, the title of prince. Ptahshepses had reached the height of his dazzling career and the royal hairdresser and manicurist had become the king's son. It is, of course, necessary to bear in mind that a royal hairdresser and manicurist was not so lowly a personage as it might seem today. The fact that in the course of his duties he was allowed to touch the body of the one god living among men on earth — the pharaoh — gained him, to a certain extent for religious reasons, an important status and thus would have smoothed his path to other still higher offices at the royal court.

The "original mastaba" had once been a complete tomb with enclosure walls. The decision to reconstruct and extend it on a grand scale must have been taken at the time when Ptahshepses had already gained an important social position and had already built a tomb that was itself by no means small. Unfortunately, of the once rich relief decoration and many inscriptions which decorated the walls of the "original mastaba" only a tiny fragment has been preserved *in situ;* this fragment has a surface of a few square centimetres with only the lower part of the figure of an offering bearer.

It is both remarkable and mysterious that the burial chamber even in the "original mastaba" had already been constructed on the model of royal burial chambers, i.e. a saddle ceiling had been built by bracing huge monolithic limestone slabs against each other in the form of a reversed "V". Two red granite sarcophagi had also already been placed in this burial chamber — the larger for

View into the burial chamber in the mastaba of Ptahshepses. The larger sarcophagus made of Aswan red granite belonged to Ptahshepses and the smaller, made of the same material, to his wife the princess Khamerernebty.

Incomplete statuette of a steatopygic woman found during excavations in the mastaba of Ptahshepses. Baked clay, 16.5 cm high. Roman period.

Mason's inscription found in the mastaba of Ptahshepses reads: "4th month of summer, 4th day. Khnumhotep."

Ptahshpepses and the smaller for Khamerernebty. The princess's sarcophagus, however, could not possibly have been transported there by the narrow descending passage. In the original plan of the chamber only Ptahshepses' sarcophagus had been taken into account. In any case Khamerernebty had at that time an already completed burial chamber of her own in the neighbouring Mastaba of the Princesses, discovered by Borchardt near the north-east corner of Niuserre's pyramid. The terms of the original plan of Ptahshepses' mastaba were therefore disregarded; Khamerernebty's sarcophagus was placed in Ptahshepses' burial chamber, although this must have happened at a time

Detail from a scene of the bringing of offering gifts. Low relief with remains of polychrome. Mastaba of Ptahshepses, Abusir.

when the "original mastaba" was still only half-built, the burial chamber was still open, and Khamerernebty's sarcophagus could still be lowered into it from above. In this context it is not insignificant that the name of the princess Khamerernebty has been found among the inscriptions recorded by the builders in red directly on the rough limestone blocks which were used to construct the core of the "original mastaba". These so-called "masons' inscriptions" with the princess's name, were discovered on blocks from the northern outer wall, just beneath the level of the mastaba's foundation.

All this information indicates that the princess Kamerernebty apparently began to play an ever more significant role in the life of Ptahshepses (or he in hers) relatively soon after the start of work on the building of the "original mastaba". What could have been happening at the royal court, inside the royal family and at the top of the country's pyramid of power if the royal hairdresser and high official could begin to concentrate in his own hands power and wealth so great that he could be on the way to equal status with those who were the direct issue of the pharaoh, the living god on earth? We can only guess at the answer, and put it together from the fragments of information that have gradually been found during archaeological excavations at other places in the Abusir necropolis, for example at the so-called Unfinished Pyramid. Niuserre obviously had

Bearers of offerings — produce from the fields and gardens of Ptahshepses funerary estates. Detail from the relief decoration of the tomb of Ptahshepses.

compelling reasons for being exceedingly personally obliged to Ptahshepses for services rendered in his highest state capacities. The unravelled mystery of the Unfinished Pyramid and the tomb of the celebrated queen, the "Mother of the Dynasty" (see p. 115 ff.) are throwing further light on these reasons.

Like the royal pyramids and rich tombs which surround it, the exquisite mastaba of Ptashepses was ravaged by looters, probably during the 1st Intermediate Period. Ptahshepses mummy too was destroyed. This, according to Ancient Egyptian conceptions, was the most terrible fate that might befall a person. The soul of Ptahshepses could no longer visit his body and his image, and could no longer receive offerings and live "forever in ctcrnity". One of the fundamental aims behind Ptashepses' striving and vertiginous ascent — the longing to build, in his tomb, a "palace of the spirit" which would endure through the ages — was not to be fulfilled. Of the magnate and near equal of the pharaoh there have remained only a few fragments of bone, and of the once undoubtedly rich funerary equipment in his tomb only a few

insignificant scraps. The abandoned mastaba of Ptahshepses, gradually disintegrating and vanishing under the sand dunes, still defied merciless fate for several centuries. Under the New Kingdom, in the 19th Dynasty and in the reign of Ramesses the Great and his successors, it was, like many other burial monuments in the area, gradually dismantled and some of its parts were re-used for the construction of other buildings. At this period a stone-masonry workshop was set up inside the mastaba, and here the stone broken away from its walls was prepared as if in a quarry. Nomads even camped with their herds of goats and sheep in the Boat Hall. It is possible that the decay of Ptahshepses's wonderful monument was also hastened by the development of the cult of the lion goddess Sakhmet in the neighbouring pyramid temple of the pharaoh Sahure under the 18th Dynasty, and by the creation of a cemetery for the common people in the vicinity of the mastaba. This work of destruction then continued with intervals up to the Roman era and, in the end, the ruins vanished under a six-metre layer of sand and rubble. One tomb had lived out its destiny.

Palm grove by Abusir.

The Traitor's Tomb?

The Memphite necropolis has been a centre of Egyptological and archaeological interest from as early as the start of the last century. It has been criss-crossed by the paths of dozens of scientific expeditions, and hundreds of researchers, and archaeological, geodetic and geological surveys, epigraphic surveys, excavations and major reconstruction projects are always underway here. The mass of published information and the detailed archaeological maps of individual localities suggest, at first sight, that everything here has long ago been discovered, and studied and described several times over; the casual observer might easily believe that there is now no scope left for a new and revolutionary find. But this would be very superficial and inaccurate impression. On the archaeological map of the necropolis there are "white" areas: places about which we know little or nothing. These are, in fact, extensive, and

they exist at Abusir as well. One could almost say that they represent the greater part of this particular royal necropolis. The Abusir cemetery was not, after all, composed only of pyramids and the tombs lying in their immediate neighbourhood.

Until recently Egyptologists and archaeologists looked at Abusir in a distinctly one-sided way. Thanks to the pyramids which the pharaohs of the 5th Dynasty built here, Abusir was considered to be a royal cemetery belonging exclusively to that period. Moreover the belief prevailed that all that was historically significant and interesting here had already been discovered and studied, particularly during the excavations by the German Oriental Society's expedition at the beginning of this century. In recent years there has been widespread change in this view and one of the major reasons has been the surprising discovery of a cemetery with shaft

Detail of the face mask of Udjahorresnet from the basalt inner sarcophagus.

Work on uncovering a shaft
during excavations at Abusir
today proceeds much as it
did centuries ago.

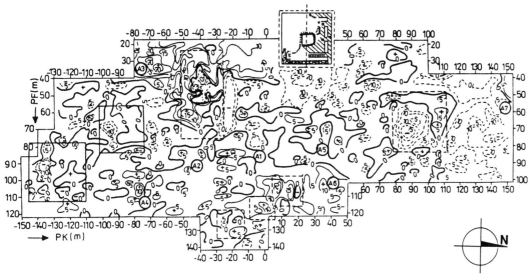

A map drawn up on the basis of geophysical measuring in the south-west sector of the Abusir cemetery shows, the approximate location of the shaft tombs from the Saite-Persian period. (V. Hašek).

tombs dating from the end of the 26th and the beginning of the 27th Dynasty, i.e. from the end of what is known as the Saite Period and the beginning of Persian Domination over Egypt. Deep in the desert and perhaps 1 kilometre west of the edge of the Nile valley, in an area already apparently far back from the Abusir pyramid field, a group of large square-shaped structures was found at the end of the 1970s and beginning of the 1980s. It was found partly as a result of a hint on an old map of Abusir drawn up in 1843 by the Lepsius expedition but largely through the extensive geophysical survey carried out by the Czech Egyptological expedition at the turn of the 1970s and 1980s. The survey indicated the existence of perhaps half a dozen large and several smaller structures, all square in ground plan, on an area of approximately 1/2 km². This discovery was interesting but also confusing. The existence of so many previously unknown monuments in this remote corner of the Memphite necropolis was almost incredible. The square ground plan of the structures was anyway mysterious since it ruled out the possibility that they were mastabas, the most common type of tomb at Abusir with a rectangular, north-south oriented ground plan. Yet the shallow relief drawn on the desert surface by the remains of these structures made it clear that they were not pyramids, as Lepsius had perhaps supposed. An answer to the riddle was expected from excavations undertaken on the site of the structure which seemed to be the largest, highest, most advantageously located and probably the oldest of the whole group.

The excavations were initiated in 1980 and the monument under investigation was

Archaeological work in the huge and deep shafts filled with fine sand is exceedingly difficult and dangerous.

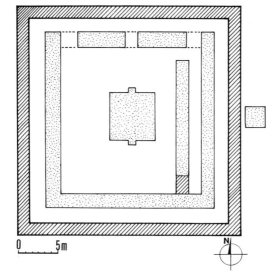

Horizontal cross-section at the foundation level of the superstructure of Udjahor-resnet's shaft tomb. The plan shows the arrangement of shafts inside and outside the sqare stone enclosure wall of the tomb.

and found to be arranged according to a very original plan. The largest, 5 × 5 m calibre shaft, which has already been mentioned, was in the middle and on all four sides it was surrounded by shafts, rectangular in horizontal cross-section, which were arranged at regular intervals to form a square pattern.

Work on uncovering the site continued and brought further surprising discoveries: all the shafts had been filled up with very fine sand from which the coarser pebbles and small boulders had been removed by sieving. The peripheral shafts arranged in the square design were linked together at various levels by large apertures and so the fine sand could flow freely through them. The bottom of the peripheral shafts had still not been reached when excavation work in them was stopped in several places at a depth of approximatcly 15 m. This decision was dictated by the fact that further excavation of the shafts could have endangered the stability of the whole tomb complex. This was because the system of shafts had not been dug in a homogeneous rock base but in a thick layer of the hardened clay which in Arabic is called *tafla*, interwoven with narrow layers of petrified salt,.

The problem just described in relation to the peripheral shafts did not apply to the central shaft. Since it was expected that there would be a burial chamber at the bottom the whole shaft had to be cleared. As the sand was removed the shaft had to be reinforced

allocated the identification mark "H" on the map of the Czech archaeological concession at Abusir. The first days brought further puzzles rather than immediate explanations. What was found was a sizeable enclosure wall constructed of limestone blocks and defining a square area of ground containing flat irregular stones laid on a layer of sand, and the remains of mudbrick buildings. In the middle of this area was the mouth of a large shaft with a calibre of perhaps 5 × 5 m above which rose the remains of a false vault of limestone blocks. It was only when the layer of sand and the stones, which had been laid without mortar, had been removed that the mouths of several long shafts were revealed

Carpenter's assistant.

with beams and boards because the circulation of warm air was beginning to damage the structure of the side walls. At a depth of perhaps 14 m the vaulted ceiling of the burial chamber was discovered.

The chamber, including the ceiling, had been constructed of well crafted blocks of fine white limestone. Thieves had once tunnelled a hole in the massive vaulted ceiling. When they had broken into the burial chamber they too must undoubtedly have had to clear away the sand filling of the shaft from the greater part of it. This thieves' route was clearly not the original way of access to the burial chamber. This had been allowed by a smaller, so-called 'side shaft' discovered in front of the eastern face of the stone enclosure wall of the tomb.

The central and the sideshaft, both located on the east-west axis of the whole tomb complex, were of roughly the same depth and were linked at the bottom by a short passage. This passage was not completely carved out of the clay base but had at one point to cross the eastern peripheral shaft which had been placed like a "screen" between the side shaft and central shaft. The "screen" effect is apparent from the fact that the bottom of the eastern peripheral shaft is much lower than the floor of the horizontal passage that crosses it. The place where the shaft and the passage cut across each other represented the critical point of an entire security system. For this reason it was here that the tomb's architect installed a sophisticated "drawbridge", or "safety valve" preventing entry to the burial chamber. He created it in the following way. He had the part of the horizontal passage that crossed the vertical eastern shaft constructed at the time when the shaft was already being filled with the fine sand. First the limestone slabs of paving were laid on the sand and then, likewise on the shaft's sand filling, the side walls of the perhaps two-metre section of the passage were constructed out of mudbricks. Finally an arch, also of mudbrick and perhaps 70 cm thick, was erected over the section. When the arch was completed the whole eastern periphery shaft could be filled with sand up to the very top. This complicated construction had, as has been shown, a well-calculated function in the ingenious system for protecting the burial chamber.

The burial chamber at the bottom of the central shaft contained other features making up part of the "sand" undergound security sealing system. These were funnelled apertures in the vault of the chamber's ceiling, which in the course of building had been sealed with "plugs" of conically-shaped pottery vessels. Only the bottoms of these relatively thin-sided vessels protruded into the chamber. With the plugs installed it was possible to start filling the central shaft above the vault of the burial chamber with sand. This, however, would have been one of the very last phases in the construction of the tomb. Before this came the minutely thought-out construction of the burial chamber and the no less ingenious stage of lowering the giant sarcophagus into it.

First, at the bottom of the central shaft and a depth of perhaps 23 m, foundations were laid for the side walls of the burial chamber, which had a rectangular groundplan with an east-west orientation. The walls, made of ashlars of fine white limestone, were built up to a point roughly just under the level at which construction of the vaulted roof of the chamber was to begin. This further stage of building was, however, deliberately delayed and instead the whole of the shaft, including the half-built chamber which was still open at the top, was filled right up to its mouth with sand. Then a giant limestone sarcophagus of box type was hauled onto the filled shaft. Its lower part had been carved out of a limestone monolith. The lid too was made from a single huge block of fine white limestone 510 cm long, 290 cm wide and 110 cm thick. A horizontal row of hieroglyphic inscriptions with the name and titles of its owner ran around the lower part of the sarcophagus just under its upper edge.

Inside the limestone sarcophagus another was placed, this time anthropoid in form and made of basalt. This anthropoid, or mummiform, sarcophagus was also huge in dimensions and consisted of two parts, a lower part and a lid, the smoothed outer surfaces of which were covered by hieroglyphic inscriptions carved in sunken relief and similar in character to those on the limestone sarcophagus.

When the sarcophagus had been dragged onto the mouth of the shaft, work commenced on removing sand from below — from the half-built burial chamber — and carrying it back up through the short horizontal passage and the so-called side shaft. The sand then began to diminish and the huge double sarcophagus little by little sank lower and lower until it finally reached

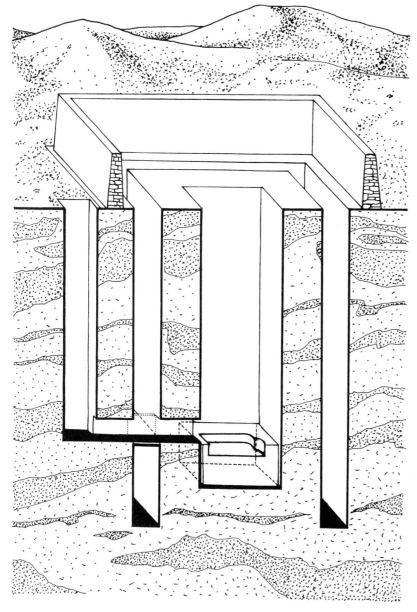

into the chamber. The last operation carried out before the retreat from the sarcophagus chamber to the side shaft, from which the escape route led upwards, was to break down the mudbrick vault above the "sand sealing"; sand from the eastern peripheral shaft would then begin to pour down into the passage. In a few minutes the whole underground section with the sarcophagus would be buried. Any subsequent attempt to get through to the sarcophagus was foredoomed to failure, since the sand that would have to be removed to make an entry would immediately be replaced by more sand falling from the upper parts of the shafts. The only possible way of overcoming this brilliantly cunning system blocking access to the sarcophagus was to clear the sand filling from both the central and the peripheral shafts. This was the method which thieves finally hit on when they carried out the first break-in, which, to judge by the remains of pottery, occurred in the Roman era. At first they tried to get through to the underground section by clearing the eastern peripheral shaft and beginning to dig an access tunnel downwards, toward the burial chamber, in its exposed western wall. Where this route led, i.e. where it ended, we do not know. It certainly did not reach the burial chamber. They finally decided on clearing the greater part of the central shaft and reached the sarcophagus after breaking through the thick vault of the burial chamber. But were the efforts of the tomb robbers really crowned with success?

During excavation of the underground section of the tomb, the approach of the Czech archaeologists was distinctly similar to that ultimately taken by the tomb robbers, i.e. the removal of the sand filling from the central shaft. It is necessary to add that this was not the original filling but sand that had blown into the shaft over the long centuries after it had been cleared by the robbers, and had mounted right up to the level of the surrounding desert. The greater part of the burial chamber, to which the expedition gained access via a hole left in the ceiling by the thieves, was choked with sand and rubble. The chamber bore the unmistakable signs of the robbers' activities, including large soot marks left on the vaulted ceiling by torches. The hieroglyphic inscriptions on the chamber's side walls were not carved in relief but only lightly drawn in black ink. They contained passages from religious texts and the name and titles of the owner of the tomb.

Schematic plan of Udjahorresnet's shaft tomb (east-west cross-section). The dotted line indicates the mudbrick wall in the place where the eastern shaft cuts across the horizontal access corridor and the "drawbridge" was located.

the level of the burial chamber. At this point there was probably some mechanical intervention to slow the descent of the lid and to insert stopmotions in the gap between the lower part of the sarcophagus and the lid. The lid of the inner anthropoid sarcophagus had evidently already been slightly raised before the lowering operation began. Finally the giant double sarcophagus settled on the bottom of the shaft, i.e. on the floor of the burial chamber, and both inner and outer lids left slightly raised to just the level that would later allow the mummy of the tomb's owner to be slid inside. Only after all this would the ceiling vault be completed.

Finally, after the burial ceremony, the last of the priests leaving the burial chamber would give the order to break the pottery plugs in the funnelled openings in the arched ceiling. Sand would have started to cascade

What at first seemed to be the floor of the burial chamber in fact turned out to be the enormous limestone monolith of the lid of the outer limestone sarcophagus. A large hole had been made in the eastern side of the outer sarcophagus, by which the thieves had got through to the inner, anthropoid sarcophagus. Another hole, this time much smaller and about 30 × 40 cm in size, had been made in the lower part of the lid of the inner sarcophagus. The anthropoid sarcophagus, the lid and lower section sealed with red plaster, was empty and its inner surfaces were perfectly clean; there was no trace of physical remains. To break a hole in the basalt sarcophagus the thieves had used a fire which they had kindled at the chosen spot. By repeatedly heating this spot and pouring water over it they weakened the structure of the hard stone so much that they could then easily break a hole in it. This method of breaking hard stone was one that the Ancient Egyptians had been using from the time of the pyramid-builders. It is hardly likely that the resins and oils used in mummification would have left no traces on the inner surface of the sarcophagus. Furthermore, the hole was not large and it would have been very difficult to pull out the mummy, wrapped as it would have been in linen bandages, without damaging it. Yet not the smallest fragment of the mummy or its linen bandages was found either in the sarcophagus or in the burial chamber. As investigation of the tomb continued, the mysteries increased rather than diminished.

As soon as it proved possible to decipher them the inscriptions on the outer and inner sarcophagi and on the walls of the burial chamber caused amazement. These left not the shadow of a doubt that the tomb belonged to Udjahorresnet, one of the most important and at the same time one of the most controversial figures in Egypt at the end of the Saite Period and the beginning of the Ist Persian Domination, i.e. in the second half of the 6th century BC. Udjahorresnet had been known to Egyptologists for many years before the discovery of his tomb at Abusir. He was known primarily thanks to the inscriptions on a naophorous statue of dark-green slate preserved in the Vatican Museum (inv. no. 196). This statue was probably once a part of the Emperor Hadrian's Egyptian collection. The inscriptions with which it is densely covered are biographical in character and provide very important historical testi-

The celebrated naophorous statue of Udjahorresnet made of black-green slate and preserved in the Vatican Museum collections (no. 196) has even found a place on postage stamps.

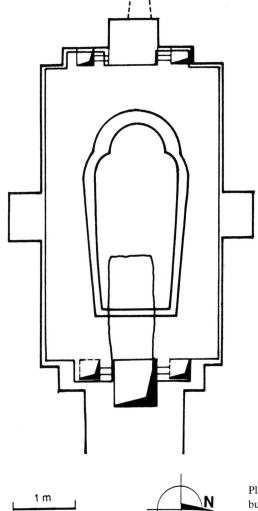

Plan of Udjahorresnet's burial chamber with the box limestone and anthropoid basalt sarcophagus.

mony concerning the beginning of Persian rule over Egypt. They were first translated and published with a commentary in the 1930s by the celebrated French Egyptologist of Russian origin, Georges Posener, in a work entitled *La Première Domination Perse en Egypte* (Cairo, 1936).

The uncovering of the intact
'foundation deposit' laid
when work on the building
commenced at the north-
west corner of the stone
enclosure wall of Udjahorresnet's shaft tomb at Abusir.

Miniature faience and wooden tablets forming part of the foundation deposit at Udjahorresnet's shaft tomb. On several of the tablets there is a cartouche with the name of Ahmose II (Gr. Amasis), the penultimate ruler of the 26th Dynasty.

Miniature symbolic bowls and goblets made of reddish and white-grey baked clay were also part of the foundation deposit at Udjahorresnet's shaft tomb.

From the texts on the statue it appeared that Udjahorresnet, commander of the Greek soldiery in Egypt, commander of the Egyptian fleet, and the bearer of many other titles in the reigns of Amasis and Psammetichus III, the last kings of the Saite Dynasty, surprisingly became a high state official in the administration of the Persian Occupation after the Persian defeat of the Egyptians at the Battle of Pelium. At this time, in the reigns of Cambyses and Darius I, he even occupied one of the highest offices in the land — the office of Head Physician of Upper and Lower Egypt. This office was far from having the professional connotations that the name suggests at first glance, but roughly corresponded to the position of chancellor. This evidence has led some Egyptologists to regard Udjahorresnet as a traitor to Egypt, a man who as one of the highest-ranking of military commanders forsook his country and went over to the Persians, ultimately becoming their devoted ally. Other Egyptologists reject the theory that Udjahorresnet's was simply a traitor and collaborator and view his career in a more positive light. This they base on the interpretation of a fragment of an inscription on a piece of a statue of Udjahorresnet discovered during American excavations at Memphis in the mid 1950s. The evidence of the inscription appears to suggest that Udjahorresnet enjoyed an extraordinary reputation as a great sage, and that his cult flourished at Memphis

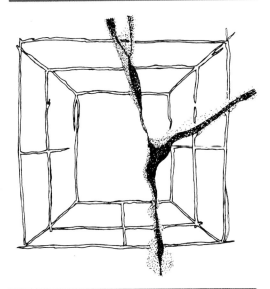

Gaming board chiselled into a piece of stone found in Udjahorresnet's shaft complex. The engraving dates from the time at which the tomb was robbed.

A fragment of pottery with a picture of a sphinx was found at the mouth of the so-called working shaft' of Udjahorresnet's tomb. Red baked clay with remains of polychrome. 8.5 x 6.5 cm. Import from the Aegean area, beginning of the 6th century BC.

Transporting archaeological finds from Udjahorresnet's shaft tomb to the on-site storage facility of the Czech Egyptological expedition at Abusir.

during the 4th century BC. In the inscription there is an allusion to "177 years" and this is believed to refer to the time that had passed since Udjahorresnet's death. It is likewise suggested that the statue of Udjahorresnet from which the fragment came had originally stood in one of the Memphite temples where it had been placed at the beginning of the 2nd Persian Domination over Egypt in order to remind the Egyptians, after more than one and three-quarter centuries, of the memory and services of this important sage and loyal Persian ally. If this belief is correct, then Udjahorresnet died in approximately 517 BC. The discovery of fragments of two other naophorous statues coming from Memphis indicate that the cult of Udjahorresnet did indeed exist there. The statues were similar to the one preserved in the Vatican Museum, which quite possibly itself came originally from Memphis.

There is, however, a certain element of contradiction here. This is because while the discovery of the statues points to Memphis, Udjahorresnet's high-ranking titles and functions, referred to in the inscriptions on the statues, are for the main part linked not to Memphis but to Sais. This was a town in the

western Delta which at the time, in the 26th Dynasty, was the royal seat of the Egyptian kings. For this reason it was long believed that any search for Udjahorresnet's tomb should be conducted in Sais. Some Egyptologists even thought that he might be buried as far away as Persepolis. They based this theory on an allusion at the end of the biographical inscription on the Vatican Museum's statue from which it is apparent that Udjahorresent was summoned to Persia by the Persian king Darius I to help suppress a rebellion in the very heart of the empire with the Egyptian army. The next part of the inscription is damaged or absent, but it has been argued that Udjahorresent died in that campaign and was buried outside Egypt.

Whatever the fate of Udjahorresnet, neither the inscriptions on his statues nor any other contemporary antiquities provide the least explanation of why this high-ranking dignitary should have chosen the southwestern edge of the pyramid field at Abusir, this remote corner of the Memphite necropolis, for his final resting-place. Did he feel politically and socially isolated in view of his close links with the Persian occupiers, and therefore have his tomb built apart from the others, albeit in the Memphite necropolis? Or was the site chosen, on the contrary, so that Udjahorresnet's tomb might in the future become the centre of another large cemetery where other high-ranking dignitaries might ultimately be buried near the great sage? It is possible that the choice of the site was influenced by its proximity to the Serapeum, the cemetery of the sacred bulls in north-west Saqqara, which at the time was an important religious and cult centre not only for the Memphite necropolis but for the whole of Egypt. In the vicinity of the Serapeum were catacombs where ibises, baboons, lions and other sacred animals were interred, cult temples and many other significant religious buildings. The Serapeum is no more than fifteen hundred metres south-east of Udjahorresnet's tomb. But on the other hand it is possible that the choice of site was primarily a matter of quite practical considerations. In this case the determining factor might have been the fact that here the geological base was not composed of rock but of thick layers of hardened clay in which the daring and architecturally very original plan for the system of shafts surrounding and protecting the tomb's sarcophagus chamber could be carried out. The questions and conjectures surrounding Udjahorresnet's tomb are legion. One almost cardinal question, however, stands out from all the rest: was the tomb found at Abusir really Udjahorresnet's?

Neither in the burial chamber nor elsewhere in the underground parts of the tomb that have as yet been excavated have any of Udjahorresnet's physical remains, or any other evidence proving beyond doubt the existence of a genuine burial, been discovered. On the contrary, archaeological research has so far brought to light several facts that suggest the opposite, or at the least provide grounds for caution and reflection.

1. The inner anthropoid basalt sarcophagus in which Udjahorresnet should have lain was found sealed, partly damaged by thieves and empty. The hole which the thieves had broken in it is so small that the bandage-swathed mummy, if it could have been pulled out at all, would have had to have been torn into pieces. After any such violent tearing, however, the mummy would certainly have left traces inside the sarcophagus or near it, for example pieces of bandage or one of the small amulets wound into the bandages. Not a single fragment of bandage from a mummified body has been found either in the sarcophagus or in the whole burial chamber.

2. The inscriptions on the walls of the burial chamber remained only at the stage of preliminary drawing and were never carved in the relief (sunken rather than low) as must surely have been the original intention and requirement given the standing of the owner. This fact is in striking contrast to the size of the tomb and the originality of its design.

3. Neither in the sarcophagus chamber nor anywhere else in the excavated part of the undergound section of the tomb have canopic jars been discovered. If a genuine burial had taken place in the burial chamber then not only would the mummy in the sarcophagus have been placed there, but also four canopic jars. These were massive stone vessels containing the sealed remains of the internal organs of the deceased which were removed during the mummifying ceremonies. It is very difficult to imagine that thieves would laboriously, and leaving no trace, carry up to the surface heavy stone vessels which

Ushebti found in the substructure of Udjahorresnet's shaft tomb. Faience, light green glaze. 12.7 cm high.

Shard with demotic text dicovered in the area of Udjahorresnet's tomb. 19 x 17 cm. Beginning of the 27th Dynasty.

their experience would certainly have told them contained nothing of value.

4. Five faience statuettes known as *ushebtis* and two miniature models of votive offering trays were found in the underground section of the tomb. Surprisingly little even for the remnants of funeral equipment! A magnate and political functionary of Udjahorresnet's importance should have been buried with much richer funeral equipment. For example, for religious cult reasons 365 of the 'ushebti' statuettes would usually have been deposited in a tomb, one for every day of the year and, in addition, statuettes of foremen, one for every ten of these statuette servants in the other world. It should be added in this context that three of the five 'ushebti' statuettes found were discovered in the sand filling which had slid down into the undergound section from the eastern peripheral shaft in a direction leading from the mouth of the thieves tunnel, today sand clogged, in the southern wall of that shaft. Unfortunately it is not possible to clean out and investigate the thieves' tunnel today. But as has already been noted, it certainly does not lead to the sarcophagus chamber.

5. In the rubble and sand which choked the horizontal passage linking the bottom of the side shaft and the burial chamber two fragments of limestone were found which fitted together. These came from a curved vaulted ceiling. On the fragments were remains of hieroglyphic inscriptions in sunken relief. Yet nowhere in the underground parts of the tomb so far excavated is there a hieroglyphically inscribed limestone ceiling arch or arched portal from which both these fragments could have come. At the same time it is very unlikely that these were intruded objects deposited as a result of some strange set of chances and hauled into the undergound part of Udjahorresnet's tomb from some other neighbouring tomb.

6. The peripheral shafts, arranged in a square around the central shaft, have not yet been cleaned out. This, as has been described, is because of the great volume of sand filling which they contain and the danger that clearing them completely could pose for the stability of the whole tomb. The deepest places reached are all at a depth of more or less 15 m, and sounding probes using a strong steel rod have indicated that the shafts continue down to a depth of at least 20 m. The shafts were linked to each other by large apertures which allowed the free flow of the sand filling and there seems to be a progressive clockwise increase in their dimensions from the eastern edge of the southern peripheral shaft to the southern edge of the eastern peripheral shaft. It is not

Cemetery of the sacred animals from the Late Period. North Saqqara.

In the catacombs of the Serapeum at Saqqara.

yet known how the floors of the peripheral shafts are constructed. It is possible that the architect's aim was not only to ensure the circulation of sand in the shafts but also at the same time to focus the final phase of the sand's movement toward the eastern peripheral shaft, and the place of the "sand seal" of the horizontal passage leading to the sarcophagus chamber.

But the system of shafts could have had yet another purpose. It is worth considering the fact that the peripheral shafts were filled up, like the central shaft, with fine sand from which the coarser pebbles had been removed. It is possible to grasp the reason for this in the case of the central shaft: the fine sand was the guarantee of the smooth flow of the sand through the filling funnels in the ceiling of the burial chamber and therefore of the complete submergence of the chamber in sand. Given that the periphery shafts too are filled with laboriously sifted sand with a volume of several thousand m³, could one expect that at the bottom of these shafts the same mechanism functions as in the case of the central shaft? Are there then yet further undiscovered chambers under the peripheral shafts?

7. It is rather puzzling that no convincing evidence of a mortuary cult has been found in the above-ground part of the tomb and its immediate surroundings. Egyptian history was full of reverses, periods of advance and decline, victories and defeats. New religious ideas developed and some of the old customs would be abandoned. In fundamental principles, however, continuity remained unbroken, and one of those principles was belief in a life after death and the duty of ensuring that the dead were provided with a mortuary cult. Yet no mortuary cult site has been found either in the above-ground area of the shaft tomb which is defined by the massive stone wall (there is no entrance aperture in the wall, but a ramp or staircase could have provided access) or outside this enclosure wall. Such a site might be indicated, for example, by a simple offering table on which offerings would have been placed, but nothing of the kind has been discovered. Does the absence of a mortuary cult reflect the fact that no one was buried in the tomb ?

Composite capital of a limestone column. Late Period. Cemetery of the sacred animals, Saqqara.

well. It has already been mentioned, for example, that they dug a tunnel in the dense *tafla* between the eastern and central shafts, the mouth of which is to be found perhaps 6 m under the upper edge of the western wall of the eastern shaft. Immediately behind the entrance aperture the tunnel divides, one branch leading horizontally to the north and the other turning straight down at right angles. The tunnels, however, have collapsed and are full of rubble and sand, and for reasons of safety they cannot be explored. It is nevertheless surprising that nowhere in the part of the underground section yet excavated have their exits been found.

We can now summarise the archaeological discoveries and observations here, although they could in fact be further elaborated and augmented, in terms of two conclusions or questions which only appear to contradict one another. First, is the ingenious shaft tomb complex constructed for Udjahorresnet on the south-east edge of the Abusir cemetery genuine or only symbolic in character? Second, is there, in addition to the excavated underground section of the tomb, yet another part that has so far not been discovered ?

Finding answers to these questions will not be easy. Further excavations in the shafts would be not only very expensive but also, and above all, very unsafe and liable to have serious effects on the stability of the whole tomb. In practical terms the only possibility left open is that of completing research on the underground part of the shaft complex by geophysical measuring. Even the employment of this method, however, will not be easy in the conditions involved. Will it prove possible to unravel the mystery of Udjahorresnet's tomb ?

8. Robbers, as has been mentioned several times, got through to the underground part of the tomb in the face of the entire cunning security system of its builders. Robbers even managed to break in several times, probably first in the Roman Period, then during the Coptic Period and also sometime in the Arab Middle Ages. The central shaft and, in part, the eastern shaft were even cleared out by the tomb robbers. The thieves repeatedly tried to get down to the underground part not only via the shafts but in other places as

The sarcophagus of
a sacred bull of Apis in the
Serapeum was broken by
thieves long ago.

In Search of Time Lost

Like so many of Ancient Egypt's illustrious places Abusir sank into an oblivion from which, it seemed, there would be no recall. It was an oblivion only confirmed by the activities of generations of tomb robbers, 'sabbachini' and stone thieves, whose work of destruction started as early as the end of the 2nd millennium BC and gradually turned the once noble pyramids into heaps of unlovely ruins. Desert and sand have done no more than mercifully conceal the damage inflicted by man. Nevertheless, it seems that at least the pyramids of Abusir were still standing in the fullness of their beauty and majesty as late as the 1st century AD. One of the rare written pieces of information about Abusir to come down to us from the ancient world is Pliny's allusion (*Hist.* 36,16) to the village of Busiris, whose inhabitants used to climb up the pyramids despite their smooth walls.

There is scarcely room for error in the identification of Pliny's Busiris with modern Abusir. Even if we put on one side the etymology of the word Abusir, itself convincing enough, Pliny could not have been referring to any other place with pyramids on the route from Memphis to Giza that he described. The Abusir pyramids did not, indeed, pass entirely unnoticed even in the Arab Middle Ages, but interest in them did not go further than mere mentions of their existence in the works of contemporary historians such as Abd el-Latif and Abu Djaafar el-Idrisi.

Interest in the cemetery at Abusir, as in the other antiquities of Ancient Egypt, was to be aroused only with Napoleon's campaign at the turn of the 18th and 19th century. It was only from that time, and hand in hand with the emergence and gradual development of

The Great Sphinx saw the beginning and end of Napoleon's Egyptian campaign.

Gamaal's family.

Egyptology, that efforts were increasingly made to investigate and study Abusir. Scholars from the scientific commission of Napoleon's campaign, unfortunately without much precision, recorded three "ruined pyramids" near the village of "Abusyr". What especially interested them were the visible remains of the causeways leading to the pyramids from the east and up from the Nile valley. One remark in their monumental work, *"Description de l'Egypte"* (vol. 10, p. 455) is, however, very confused. It suggests that one of the Abusir pyramids was made of brick, and this clearly does not correspond to the facts. The error can only be explained by some accidental mistake in the documentation or faulty interpretation of the field records during compilation and editing of the work.

"Soldiers, forty centuries are watching you!"

The Englishman John Shae Perring was originally an engineer by profession but Egyptian antiquities, especially pyramids, so captivated him that he devoted the greater part of life to investigating them. It is to him that we owe the first archaeological survey of the Abusir pyramids, which was carried out in 1838. Perring even set himself the dangerous task of unblocking the access routes to the underground sections of the pyramids, and his explorations were not without their dramatic moments. He was given invaluable assistance by the experienced native foreman Abd el-Ardi. Perring was unable to identify the owners of the pyramids with any certainty and so he used "substitute terms" to designate the monuments. The Northern (Sahure's), the Central (Niuserre's) and the Great Pyramid (Neferirkare's). The so-called, 'Small Pyramid' represented an error on Perring's part. As was later to be shown, it was not a pyramid but a large mastaba. The plan of the Abusir cemetery which Perring drew up was already much better than the map produced by the scholars of Napoleon's campaign. His first plan of the Abusir pyramids, including basic survey data, was particularly valuable.

Perring's pioneering researches became a solid basis on which the next expedition to arrive in Abusir, not long after his own and in 1842, was able to build. This was a German, Prussian expedition led by Richard Lepsius, the founder of German Egyptology. Although the Lepsius expedition only stayed at Abusir for a very short period it nevertheless managed to obtain remarkable results. The archaeological map of the locality prepared

Richard Lepsius.

by the expedition's surveyors and drafted by O. Erbkam became a very valuable and relatively precise aid for subsequent work at Abusir. It contains some inaccuracies, especially in the identification of some ruins as pyramids when in fact they were not and vice versa, but on the other hand it records some features that have since vanished for ever, such as the Lake of Abusir. The expedition's observations and conclusions relating to the largest of the Abusir pyramids — that of Neferirkare — were to exert a long-term influence on Egyptologists and their ideas of how these monuments, still in many respects mysterious, were constructed. The Lepsius

The Lepsius expedition on the top of the pyramid of Cheops: Lepsius' birthday celebration (Staatliche Museen zu Berlin. Preussischer Kulturbesitz — picture reproduced by kind permission of Dietrich Wildung).

Map of Abusir and Zawiyat el-Aryan drawn up by the Lepsius expedition.

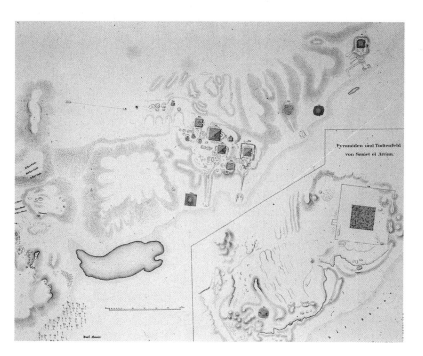

expedition did not carry out large-scale excavations at Abusir although even the little that its members uncovered here became an important part of Egyptological source material, for example Fetekta's tomb with its wonderful wall paintings.

The British MP Henry Windsor Villiers Stuart, British parliamentary special envoy to Egypt and enthusiastic admirer of Egyptian antiquities, conducted work in the Abusir area — in Abu Ghurab — for a short time during the winter of 1882/83. It is to him that we are indebted for such discoveries as the alabaster altar and alabaster basins in Niuserre's sun temple at Abu Ghurab.

After the departure of the Lepsius expedition archaeological interest in Abusir waned once again, and this time for a long half-century. Only in 1893 — by coincidence at the same time that tomb robbers in the Abusir cemetery made the priceless discovery of the papyri from the archive of Neferirkare's mortuary temple — were excavations started again here, this time by Jacques de Morgan. French in origin, de Morgan was at that time employed as the head of the Antiquities Inspectorate at Saqqara. He wanted to excavate the pyramid designated no. XIX on the Lepsius expedition's map although later, finding that this was "only" the mastaba of the vizier Ptahshepses, he curtailed his excavations after a few weeks. He also devoted attention to survey of the whole cemetery and brought together his observations, measurements and conclusions in his *"Carte de la Nécropole Memphite. Dahchour, Sakkarah, Abou-Sir"* (Caire, 1897), an archaeological map of the Memphite necropolis which naturally included Abusir. One is obliged to add that the older archaeological map drawn up by the Lepsius expedition, which at that time had been available for a half-century and which de Morgan undoubtedly used, is more complete and precise that de Morgan's own.

There are very few archaeologists whose work has won them a name written deep in the history of archaeological excavations in Egypt, who early and accurately anticipated the priorities of archaeological research in their time, and who pushed through new methods of fieldwork, and of studying, cataloguing and making public the knowledge gathered. Ludwig Borchardt is indisputably one of them. In a way it was a piece of "archaeological luck" that nobody except Perring with his short-term research had shown any interest in the Abusir pyramids. This meant that an expert of Borchardt's stature could, at the very beginning of this century, embark on investigation of pyramids that were relatively untouched by modern excavations. He chose outstanding contemporary German Egyptologists as his colleagues both for fieldwork and for the study, cataloguing and publicization of the archaeological finds and information. They included, for example, George Möller, Heinrich Schäfer and Kurth Sethe. The organisational arrangements for the excavations were also on a very generous scale. The Deutsche Orientgesellschaft provided financial resources at a level that no previous German excavations in Egypt had enjoyed. Moreover, in Abusir and the surrounding villages adequate labour resources were at that time easily available and very cheap. Borchardt could therefore hire what is by today's standards an unbelievably large number of workmen — in several seasons more than 500 people. The experienced foreman *reis* Mohammed Ahmad el-Senoussi was employed at the head of the workforce.

Borchardt started excavations immediately on finishing his archaeological work in Niuserre's sun temple at Abu Ghurab in September 1901. Information obtained from the research at Abu Ghurab led him to regard excavations in Niuserre's mortuary temple at Abusir as the most urgent priority. His decision was influenced by his "Christmas" visits to Abusir in 1896 and 1898 and the architectonically and archaeologically unique surface finds that he had made on the site of Niuserre's temple. Another factor was, of course, the discovery of the papyri at the Abusir pyramids, since 1893 the subject

Ludwig Borchardt.

Ludwig Borchardt in his Cairo study (reproduction of a photograph sent out as a new year greeting in 1988 by the Swiss Institute in Cairo on the occasion of the 125th anniversary of Borchardt's birthday).

of very lively debate in Egyptological circles and one which strongly attracted Borchardt's attention. His excavations in Niuserre's pyramid complex took place over a period from the beginning of January 1902 to roughly the middle of April 1904, always in the winter and spring months. Then Borchardt transferred his attentions to the immediately neighbouring pyramid complex of Neferirkare. Here, if we leave aside the two small trial diggings of 1900 and 1903 which were

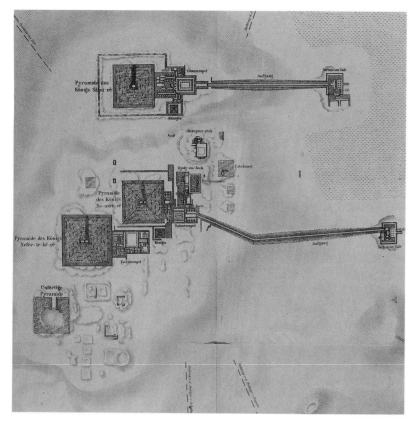

Plan of the pyramid cemetery drawn up at the end of Borchardt's archaeological excavations at Abusir.

cemetery such as at the Unfinished Pyramid (Raneferef's) and on the edge of the desert south of Niuserre's valley temple.

Borchardt would give immediate reports on his excavations in provisional form in *Mitteilungen der Deutschen Orientgesellschaft*. He also did not put off, as is unfortunately so often the case in Egyptian archaeology, overall evaluation of his archaeological discoveries and publication of the final excavation reports. These he published in the *Wissenschaftliche Veröffentlichungen der Deutschen Orient-gesellschaft* series, in a series of monographs devoted to the three largest Abusir pyramid complexes. One of the volumes in this series, entitled *Priestergräber und andere Grabfunde vom Ende des Alten Reiches bis zur Griechischen Zeit vom Totentempel des Ne-user-re* and devoted to the non-royal, later monuments uncovered during the excavations, was prepared by Heinrich Schäfer.

The overall contribution of Borchardt's work at Abusir cannot be expressed in a few sentences. One can only, perhaps, emphasize the aspects of his achievement which far transcended the limits of his period and today still represent a standard which many excavations at the end of the twentieth century are a long way from reaching. Borchardt's fieldwork and archaeological publications are pervaded by his ability, so rare yet so essential in an Egyptologist, to orient himself quickly and surely in the face of a large number of the most diverse archaeological finds and to distinguish between the significant and the inessential in the tangled web of their wider historical contexts. To this day the imaginative powers which enabled Borchardt to reconstruct the original form of a column, wall or even the plan of a whole pyramid complex from a few fragments, arouse admiration. It is no wonder that Ludwig Borchardt, founder of the Deutsches Archaologisches Institut — Abteilung Kairo, and later also of the Schweizerisches Institut für Ägyptische Bauforschung und Altertumskunde in Kairo, represents a model for the next generations of Egyptologists and field archaeologists, and not only for those from Germany.

influenced by his efforts to identify the place where the 'sabbachin' had found the papyri in 1893, he carried out excavations in the winter and spring months of 1904 and 1907. Borchardt concluded his researches at Abusir with unbroken work in Sahure's pyramid complex from the end of March 1907 to the end of March 1908. Particularly during these concluding phases he also undertook several smaller trial diggings in other places in the

After Borchardt's excavations Abusir again found itself on the periphery of Egyptological interest. It was almost fifty years before archaeologists returned there once more. Between 1954 and 1957 a joint German-Swiss expedition spent three ar-

Georg Möller.

chaeological seasons in the ruins of Userkaf's sun temple on the northern edge of the Abusir cemetery. This monument had already been known for a long time and had even been entered on the Lepsius expedition's archaeological map of Abusir. The excavations were headed by Hanns Stock, the then director of the German Archaeological Institute in Cairo and by Herbert Ricke, the then director of the Swiss Institute for Research into Egyptian Architecture and Antiquities. They worked alongside several other outstanding Egyptologists: Elmar Edel, Gerhard Haeny, Werner Kaiser, Peter Kaplony, Wolfgang Helck and Siegfried Schott. The results of the excavations were something of a disappointment for the German-Swiss expedition since the whole great building complex of Userkaf's sun temple had been almost completely destroyed in the course of the centuries. Nevertheless, thanks to the outstanding professional qualities of all its members, the joint expedition managed to reconstruct from the scanty remains both the original plan of the sun temple and the plans of its later reconstructions.

Behind the arrival of a Czech expedition in Abusir at the very beginning of the 1960s lay an interesting and somewhat tangled story that had really begun twenty years earlier. The outbreak of the Second World War had caught the Czech Egyptologist Jaroslav Černý in Egypt, where he was taking part in French excavations at Deir el-Medina. He could not return to his occupied homeland and so he lived out the war in Egypt. There was one very important bright side to Černý's involuntary years of exile. They allowed him to devote himself, in the relative calm of the Institut Français d'Archéologie Orientale du Caire and of Egypt at that time, to a thorough sudy of Ancient Egyptian antiquities both in museums and depositaries and at famous and lesser-known archaeological sites. Černý visited Abusir among other sites and in Ptashepses's mastaba he copied down the inscriptions that he considered interesting and important. During his work he realised how historically significant a person Ptahshepses had been, and saw that de Morgan had only uncovered a small part of a monument that must originally have been much larger. Two decades later he remembered this information in connexion with the launch of the activities of the Cairo branch of the Czech (then Czechoslovak) Institute of Egyptology at Charles University.

Hanns Stock.

Herbert Ricke.

In the first years of its existence the main task of the newly-founded institute was to make a scientific contribution to the international UNESCO rescue projects in Nubia. Although this was urgent and important work, however, it represented only a short-term episode in the institute's planned activity in Egypt. The basic aim was to conduct long-term Egyptological research on chosen archaeological locations in Egypt. On

A postage stamp issued in 1976 on the occasion of the 100th anniversary of the birth of František Lexa. This date was included in the UNESCO list of important anniversaries.

Jaroslav Černý and Zbyněk Žába by a portrait of the founder of Czech Egyptology František Lexa (Prague, April 1967).

Jaroslav Černý on a visit to the mastaba of Ptahshepses.

easy. This was because the work of the Czech Egyptological expedition in Egypt began in two places at once, i.e. at Abusir and in Nubia. Each of the two research projects was very demanding in organisational terms, had its own specific scientific character and required a completely different methodological approach. Yet another complication arose from the fact that the team of co-workers that Žába had assembled was distinctly heterogeneous and he was the only Egyptologist among them. It should be added that he was an Egyptologist with a philological orientation linked to his original schooling in the field of classical philology. Although these circumstances could not but leave their mark on the beginning of the work of the Czech expedition in Egypt, Žába in fact managed in the course of the 1960s to consolidate the position of the Institute in Egypt, to fulfill the scientific tasks allocated to it in the framework of the UNESCO international rescue project in Nubia and to develop systematic Egyptological research in the mastaba of Ptahshepses at Abusir.

Žába finished the 1970 excavation season on June 18th, earlier than he had originally planned. This was because on May 29th 1970 Jaroslav Černý, Žába's teacher and great academic model, had died in Oxford. Only a short time before, Černý and his wife had been in Egypt where they had visited the excavations in the mastaba of Ptahshepses. His death shook Žába severely. Žába's health was also seriously at risk at the time, following a heart attack which he had suffered one year earlier. A question mark began to appear over the future of the

Černý's recommendation, the choice ultimately fell on Abusir. Zbyněk Žába, who had taken on the leadership of research as the deputy of the then already elderly director of the Institute František Lexa, had taken various additional circumstances into account. Above all there was the fact that Abusir was part of the great and historically immeasurably valuable necropolis of ancient Memphis. It was also not unimportant that Abusir was near Cairo since economic considerations were further factors in the decision.

The circumstances in which Žába started excavations in Ptahshepses' tomb were not excavations in Ptahshepses' mastaba and the doubts multiplied with the oppressive political situation in the wake of the military occupation of Czechoslovakia on August 21st, 1968. In February 1971 Žába left for Oxford in order formally to take charge of Jaroslav Černý's celebrated Egyptological library and prepare for its transportation to Prague. Černý had started to build up his library before the Second World War when there had been plans for his nomination as

professor of Egyptology at Masaryk University in Brno and for the founding of a second Czech university Egyptological centre in addition to Charles University in Prague. On his departure for London in 1947 Černý had taken his library with him and had continued to add to it in Great Britain. In the end it came to be regarded as the greatest private Egyptological library in the world. It had been Jaroslav Černý's wish, however, that after his death the library should be returned to Prague and contribute to the further development of Czech Egyptology. Zbyněk Žába arranged for transport of the library to Prague but did not live to see its arrival and installation at Charles University. After his return from a holiday in the Slovak Tatras on August 15th, 1971 he died suddenly in Prague. The excavation season in the first half of 1970 had been his last in the mastaba of Ptashepses.

After Žába's death the position of the Czech Institute of Egyptology became ever

more complex and difficult, both in Prague and in Cairo. The excavations at Abusir were suspended for several years. Žába had enjoyed a range of personal contacts with important Egyptian archaeologists and representatives of the Egyptian Antiquities Organisation and these contacts naturally ceased with his death. In the political situation in Czechoslovakia at the beginning of the 1970s there was even serious talk of the administrative liquidation of the Institute. Further problems appeared. During the Czech expedition's several-year absence from Abusir after Žába's death the storage facility with the archaeological finds was broken into and some of the antiquities kept there were stolen. It was only in the first half of 1974 that excavations in the mastaba of Ptahshepses could be restarted.

The man appointed to lead the work was František Váhala, a scholar who had studied Egyptology with František Lexa before the war and had entered the Institute at the

Zbyněk Žába during work in the mastaba of Ptahshepses.

Žába's diary.

František Váhala.

beginning of the 1960s as a distinguished linguist — a specialist in Czech. The team completed the uncovering of the mastaba's outer walls, prepared photogrammetric documentation and drew up a building plan of the mastaba to a scale of 1 : 25. Epigraphic documentation was added and large sets of pottery and anthropological material were catalogued. Only after the end of this archaeological season did it prove possible to prepare for publication the first preliminary report on what was then already fourteen years of excavations in the mastaba (*Preliminary Report on Czechoslovak Excavations in the Mastaba of Ptahshepses*).

Unfortunately sudden death had caught Zbyněk Žába just as he was putting together the great stacks of documentation from the excavations and preparing them for publication. It may seem surprising that he did not publish interim, running reports on his excavations in Czech or international archaeological and Egyptological journals. To those who knew Žába even slightly, however, it is not so difficult to understand. His passion for detail, precision, exhaustive analysis of problems and as far as possible incontestable conclusions were at odds with the requirements

Reis Muhammad Talal al-Qereti.

of a preliminary archaeological report. Even František Váhala, however, was not to live to see the publication of the *Preliminary Report...* He died shortly after his return from Egypt in 1974.

In the mid 1970s and with the end of excavations in the mastaba of Ptahshepses the Czech Institute managed to obtain the consent of the authorities of the Egyptian Antiquities Organisation to the transfer of research to the southern, archaeologically under-investigated area of the Abusir cemetery. This new archaeological concession is geographically defined in the north up to a line linking Neferirkare's pyramid with Niuserre's valley temple, and in the south by the shallow valley of *Wadi Abusiri* which divides South Abusir from North Saqqara.

So far work has been carried out over ten excavation seasons in the new concession in South Abusir. The excavations have been led by the author of this book with the long-term

Reis Abdu al-Qereti.

Reis Ahmad al-Qereti.

Archaeological work ends. It only remains for the Czech archaeological expedition at Abusir to build a protective stone wall in front of the sealed iron gates of the storage facility.

Václav Havel, President of the Czech (in December 1991 still Czechoslovak) Republic on a visit to the Czech archaeological excavations at Abusir.

The archaeological season in
Abusir is over. Only
a guard remains at the
cemetery.

The Egyptian Museum in Cairo is the destination of the antiquities discovered during excavations at Abusir.

participation of Czech Egyptologists Ladislav Bareš and Břetislav Vachala. Experts in other fields, such as geophysics, anthropology, geodetics, restoration, have joined in the expedition alternately according to need and the specific tasks involved. Students of Egyptology from Charles University have also participated. In recent years the Czech expedition has also enjoyed close co-operation during excavations with a number of foreign Egyptologists, in first place among them Mme Paule Posener-Kriéger. The foreman of the workmen at the excavations is the son of *reis* Abdu al-Qereti, the experienced and energetic *reis* Muhammad Talal al-Qereti. Another of *reis* Abdu's sons, Ahmad al-Qereti, is helping the expedition with its work of restoration and conservation. The Czech expedition's archaeological concession in South Abusir, so remarkable in its location and extent, is enabling us to develop broadly conceived and long-term research aimed at providing knowledge and understanding of a number of key questions in Egyptian history. It is for the reader to judge how far we are succeeding in this aim. This book is offered as one account which may help the reader to form an opinion.

The Great Sphinx at Giza.

List of Czech Archaeological Expeditions to the Arab Republic of Egypt

1st Expedition
May — 11th October 1960

Zbyněk Žába (Egyptologist, Expedition Leader), Jaroslav Novotný (photographer, conservation specialist), Rudolf Veselý (Specialist in Arabic), Muhammad Mohsen (Inspector of the Egyptian Antiquities Organisation, hereafter EAO).
Launch of the activities of the Cairo centre of the Institute and beginning of archaeological research in the area of the mastaba of Ptahshepses at Abusir.

2nd Expedition
4th April — 18th December 1961

Zbyněk Žába (Egyptologist, Expedition Leader), Milan Fiedler (Specialist in Arabic), Milan Hlinomaz (Captain of the expedition's boat), Evžen Hnátek (secretary), Miroslav Korecký (architect), Jaroslav Novotný (photographer, conservation specialist), Eugen Strouhal (anthropologist), Zdeněk Uherek (historian), Kamal Fahmi (EAO inspector), *reis* Husain Ibrahim Ibrahim (foreman of the workmen), *reis* Sa'id Mahmud Husain (foreman of the workmen).
Continuation of the archaeological research in the area of the mastaba of Ptahshepses at Abusir. Beginning of Egyptological rescue work, within the framework of the UNESCO international project in Nubia, in the Czechoslovak concession at Tafa (the site of the South Temple) and in Kertaasi (architectonic and archaeological documentation of a Roman fortress).

3rd Expedition
16th June 1962 — 10th September 1962

Zbyněk Žába (Egyptologist, Expedition Leader), Milan Hlinomaz (Captain of the expedition's boat), Jaroslav Novotný (photographer, conservation specialist), Jaromír Tlustý (surveyor), Faruq Guma (EAO inspector), Mahmud Abd al-Raziq (EAO inspector), *reis* Abdu al-Qereti (foreman).
Surveying, photographic and epigraphic work in the mastaba of Ptashepses at Abusir. Discovery of the South Temple at

Tafa and putting it on the map. Completion of photogrammetric and architectonic documentation work in the Roman fortress in Kertaasi.

4th Expedition
26th March 1963 — 11th September 1963

Zbyněk Žába (Egyptologist, Expedition Leader), Milan Hlinomaz (Captain of the expedition's boat), Jaromír Málek (student of Egyptology), Ján Midžiak (student of Egyptology), Jaroslav Novotný (photographer, conservation specialist), Abd al-Aziz Sadeq (EAO inspector), *reis* Abdu al-Qereti (foreman).
Epigraphic documentation work in the Southern Czechoslovak concession in Nubia. Comparative study of materials in ancient quarries in the Egyptian Eastern Desert with a view to throwing light on the Tafa-Kertaasi complex of buildings.

5th Expedition
22nd March 1964 — 15th June 1964

Zbyněk Žába (Egyptologist, Expedition Leader), Pavel Červíček (student of Egyptology), Evžen Hnátek (secretary, captain of the expedition's boat), Jaromír Málek (student of Egyptology), Ján Midžiak (student of Egyptology), Jaroslav Novotný (photographer, conservation specialist), Eugen Strouhal (anthropologist), František Váhala (Egyptologist), Miroslav Verner (student of Egyptology), Faruq Guma (EAO inspector), *reis* Abdu al-Qereti (foreman).
Epigraphic documentation work in the Northern Czechoslovak Concession in Nubia.

6th Expedition
24th February 1965 — 16th July 1965

Zbyněk Žába (Egyptologist, Expedition Leader), Evžen Hnátek (secretary, captain of the expedition's boat), Eugen Strouhal (anthropologist), Milan Stuchlík (ethnographer), František Váhala (Egyptologist), Fathi Melek (EAO inspector), *reis* Abdu al-Qereti (foreman).
Excavations in the Late Roman to Early Byzantine tumulus cemeteries in Wadi Qitna and Kalabsha-South. Ethno-

graphical surveys in several Nubian villages. Division of the finds from the Nubian projects between the Czech Institute of Egyptology at Charles University and the Egyptian Antiquities Organisation.

7th Expedition
2nd April 1966 — 12th December 1966

Zbyněk Žába (Egyptologist, Expedition Leader), Ján Midžiak (student of Egyptology), Karel Petráček (specialist in Arabic), Milan Zemina (photographer), Mamduh Abd al-Zahir (EAO inspector), *reis* Abdu al-Qereti (foreman).
Documentation of the rock inscriptions along the desert route between Edfu and Marsa Alam in the Egyptian Eastern Desert. Renewal of archaeological research in the area of the mastaba of Ptahshepses at Abusir.

8th Expedition
20th January 1968 — 19th December 1968

Zbyněk Žába (Egyptologist, Expedition Leader), Miroslav Raab (secretary, documentation specialist), Eugen Strouhal (anthropologist), František Váhala (Egyptologist), Milan Zemina (photographer), Ragab Abd al-Haqq (EAO inspector), Muhammad al-Sarit (EAO inspector), *reis* Abdu al-Qereti (foreman).
Completion of archaeological research in the interior areas of the mastaba of Ptahshepses at Abusir.

9th Expedition
12th December 1969 — 18th June 1970

Zbyněk Žába (Egyptologist, Expedition Leader), Jaromír Málek (Egyptologist), Miroslav Raab (secretary, documentation specialist), František Váhala (Egyptologist), Miroslav Verner (Egyptologist), Milan Zemina (photographer), Muhammad al-Sarit (EAO inspector), Girgis Daud (EAO inspector), *reis* Abdu al-Qereti (foreman).
Research outside of the eastern, northern and part of the western enclosure wall of the mastaba of Ptahshepses in the Czechoslovak archaeological concession at Abusir.

10th Expedition
16th January 1974 — 13th June 1974

František Váhala (Egyptologist, Expedition Leader), Ladislav Bareš (student of Egyptology), Vladimír Fiala (architect), Petr Charvát (archaeologist), Vladimír Martinák (documentation specialist for photogrammetry, Eugen Strouhal (anthropologist), Zdeněk Uherek (secretary), Miroslav Verner (Egyptologist), Milan Zemina (photographer), Lutfi Farid (EAO inspector), *reis* Abdu al-Qereti (foreman).

Completion of excavations outside the mastaba of Ptahshepses (in the southern and part of the western sector). Completion of documentation work in the mastaba of Ptashepses. Division of the finds from the excavations in Ptahshepses' mastaba between the Institute and the Egyptian Antiquities Organisation.

11th Expedition
12th September 1976 — 8th January 1977

Miroslav Verner (Egyptologist, Expedition Leader), Vladimír Fiala (architect), Milan Fiedler (specialist in Arabic), Milan Zemina (photographer), *reis* Abdu al-Qereti (foreman).

Negotiation of the conditions for the signing of a Czechoslovak-Egyptian agreement on co-operation in Egyptology, start of research on the newly allocated archaeological concession of Abusir — South Field (trial diggings in the pyramid complex of the queen Khentkaus, uncovering of the mastaba of the princess Khekeretnebty). Beginning of reconstruction work in the mastaba of Ptahshepses, Division of the finds between the Institute and the Egyptian Antiquities Organisation. Participation in the 1st International Egyptological Congress in Cairo.

12th Expedition
11th September 1978 — 5th March 1979

Miroslav Verner (Egyptologist, Expedition Leader), Ladislav Bareš (Egyptologist), Vladimír Fiala (architect), Vladimír Hašek (geophysicist), Tomáš Kraus (documentation specialist), Josef Menšík (technician), Zdeněk Uherek (secretary), Břetislav Vachala (Egyptologist), Milan Zemina (photographer), Muhammad al-Ashari (EAO inspector), *reis* Mutaal al-Qereti (foreman), *reis* Muhammad Talal al-Qereti (foreman), *reis* Ahmad al-Qereti (foreman).

Area stripping at the pyramid complex of the queen Khentkaus, area strippping in the western part of the mastaba field south of Niuserre's causeway, trial diggings carried out following preliminary geophysical survey results, architectural reconstruction and conservation work, continuation of architectural reconstruction work in the mastaba of Ptahshepses.

13th Expedition
17th September 1980 — 4th March 1981

Miroslav Verner (Egyptologist, Expedition Leader), Vladimír Fiala (architect), Tomáš Kraus (documentation specialist), Josef Menšík (technician), Eugen Strouhal (anthropologist), Josef Šulc (photographer), Břetislav Vachala (Egyptologist), Muhammad al-Ashari (EAO inspector), *reis* Muta'al al-Qereti (foreman), *reis* Muhammad Talal al-Qereti (foreman), *reis* Ahmad al-Qereti (foreman).

Completion of area stripping of the mortuary temple of the pyramid complex of the queen Khentkaus, trial diggings in Raneferef's mortuary temple, trial diggings and measurements in the area of pyramid complex no. XXIV (by Lepsius's numerical system of identification), area stripping of the shaft tomb complex in the western sector of the Southern Field, continuation of architectural reconstruction work in the mastaba of Ptahshepses and in the pyramid complex of the queen Khentkaus, anthropological study of skeleton material.

14th Expedition
20th January 1982 — 10th June 1982

Miroslav Verner (Egyptologist, Expedition Leader), Ladislav Bareš (Egyptologist), Vladimír Fiala (architect), Karel Preuss (archaeologist), Petr Milde (photographer), Zdeněk Uherek (secretary), Usama al-Hamzawi (EAO inspector), *reis* Muta'al al-Qereti (foreman), *reis* Muhammad Talal al-Qereti (foreman), *reis* Ahmad al-Qereti (foreman).

Area stripping of the south-east and south-west sector of Raneferef's mortuary temple, trial digging at the south-eastern corner of pyramid no. XXIV (Lepsius' numbering), architectonic survey of the shaft tomb complex, continuation of architectural reconstruction work in the mastaba of Ptahshepses. Division of finds between the Institute and the Egyptian Antiquities Organisation.

15th Expedition
19th September 1984 — 24th January 1985

Miroslav Verner (Egyptologist, Expedition Leader), Ladislav Bareš (Egyptologist), Josef Grabmüller (photographer), Tomáš Kraus (documentation specialist), Wolf B. Oerter (Egyptologist, specialist in Coptic studies), Karel Preuss (archaeologist), Usama al-Hamzawi (EAO inspector), *reis* Muta'al al-Qereti (foreman), *reis* Muhammad Talal al-Qereti (foreman), *reis* Ahmad al-Qereti (foreman).

Area stripping at Raneferef's mortuary temple, excavation of the shaft tomb complex in the western sector of the South Field, continuation of architectural reconstruction work in the mastaba of Ptahshepses.

16th Expedition
15th September 1985 — 6th February 1986

Miroslav Verner (Egyptologist, Expedition Leader), Mojmír Švec (surveyor), Břetislav Vachala (Egyptologist), Otakar Vosika (surveyor), Usama el-Hamzawi (EAO inspector), *reis* Muhammad Talal al-Qereti (foreman), *reis* Ahmad al-Qereti (foreman), Muhammad Abdallah (photographer).

Excavation in the area of „the Sanctuary of the Knife", trial diggings in Raneferef's pyramid, in the central part of Raneferef's mortuary temple, in front of the foundation platform of his pyramid, in the area between the pyramid complexes of Raneferef and Khentkaus, architectural historical research into Raneferef's pyramid complex, geodetic mapping of the Czechoslovak archaeological concession of Abusir — South Field, detailed survey of Raneferef's pyramid complex, architectural reconstruction work in the mastaba of Ptahshepses and on a smaller scale at other sites. Division of the finds between the Institute and the Egyptian Antiquities Organisation.

17th Expedition
1st January 1987 — 29th April 1987

Miroslav Verner (Egyptologist, Expedition Leader), Michael Balík (architect), Darina Bialeková (archaeologist), Jan Brodský (architect), Eugen Strouhal (anthropologist), Jiří Svoboda (archaeologist), Stanislav Šiška (archaeologist), Mojmír Švec (surveyor), Břetislav

Vachala (Egyptologist), Otakar Vosika (surveyor), Usama al-Hamzawi (EAO inspector), *reis* Muhammad Talal al-Qereti (foreman), *reis* Ahmad al-Qereti (foreman).

Area stripping east of pyramid no. 25 (Lepsius' numbering), excavations of the mastabas of the court lady Nebtyemneferes, the princess Hedjetnebu and the nameless mastaba ("L"), smaller scale diggings in the vicinity of Raneferef's mortuary temple, survey of prehistoric Abusir, archaeological survey in the area of pyramid no. XXVIII (Lepsius' numbering), geodetic measurement in the eastern and Western sector of the South Field, architectural reconstruction work in the mastaba of Ptahshepses, anthropological research.

18th Expedition
19th October 1988 — 2nd February 1989

Miroslav Verner (Egyptologist, Expedition Leader), Ladislav Bareš (Egyptologist, Expedition Deputy Leader), Tomáš Kraus (draughtsman), Jiřina Růžová (documentation specialist), Eugen Strouhal (anthropologist), Abdallah Mahmud (EAO inspector), *reis* Muhammad Talal al-Qereti (foreman), *reis* Ahmad al-Qereti (foreman).

Conservation and reconstruction work in Udjahorresnet's shaft tomb, cataloguing of anthropological material from the preceding archaeological season at Abusir, audit of finds from excavations 1960 — 1974 in the storage facility of the Czech archaeological expedition at Abusir.

19th Expedition
3rd February — 3rd May 1989

Miroslav Verner (Egyptologist, Expedition Leader), Břetislav Vachala (Egyptologist, Expedition Deputy Leader), Wolf P. Oerter (Egyptologist, specialist in Coptic Studies), Jan Brodský (photographer), Eduard Gombár (specialist in Arabic), Michael Balík (architect), Ludvík Losos (restorer, conservation specialist), Milan Zemina (photographer), Abdullah Mahmud (EAO inspector), *reis* Muta'al al-Qereti (foreman supervising building and reconstruction work), *reis* Muhammad al-Qereti (foreman).

Conservation and reconstruction work in Raneferef's mortuary temple, Khentkaus's mortuary temple and Ptahshepses' mastaba. Documentation work in the Egyptian Museum and the Coptic Museum. Research on Arabic sources related to questions of Egyptian culture and Islamic tradition.

20th Expedition
2nd October 1990 — 7th February 1991

Miroslav Verner (Egyptologist, Expedition Leader), Ladislav Bareš (Egyptologist, Expedition Deputy Leader), Peter Jánosi (Egyptologist), Tomáš Kraus (draughtsman), Mojmír Švec (surveyor), Otakar Vosika (surveyor), Usama Fahmi al-Hamzawi (EAO inspector), Muhammad Talaal al-Qereti (foreman), Abd al-Muta'al al-Qereti (foreman supervising building and reconstruction work), Ahmad al-Qereti (foreman).

Continuation of research on Udjahorresnet's shaft tomb. Archaeological survey and geodetic-cartographic work on the whole Abusir necropolis.

21st Expedition
2nd October 1991 — 15th January 1992

Miroslav Verner (Egyptologist, Expedition Leader), Břetislav Vachala (Egyptologist, Expedition Deputy Leader) Ivan Vaněček (restorer), Kamil Voděra (photographer), Milan Zemina (photographer), Miroslav Bárta (student of Egyptology), Jaromír Krejčí (student of Egyptology), Issam Labib Awad (EAO inspector), Usama Fahmi al-Hamzawi (EAO inspector), Muhammad al-Qereti (foreman), Abd al-Muta'al al-Qereti (foreman), Ahmad al-Qereti (foreman).

Rescue excavation in Kaaper's mastaba in South Abusir. Discovery and investigation of the tomb of Fetekta and the cemetery from the end of the 5th and beginning of the 6th Dynasty in South Abusir. Building work to ensure the stability of the newly excavated archaeological monuments. Photo-documentation of the monuments of the pyramid zone. Reconstruction of the Northern Magazines of the mastaba of Ptahshepses. Adaptation of the Czech expedition's excavation house at Abusir.

Visit of the President of the Czech (in December 1991 still Czechoslovak) Republic, Václav Havel to the excavations of the Czech Institute of Egyptology, Charles University, at Abusir.

22nd Expedition
6th January — 10th May 1993

Miroslav Verner (Egyptologist, Expedition Leader), Ladislav Bareš (Egyptologist), Tomáš Kraus (draughtsman), Milan Zemina (photographer), Miroslav Bárta (student of Egyptology), Issam Labib Awad (EAO inspector), Ramadan Hashim al-Saud (EAO inspector), Muhammad al-Qereti (foreman), Abd al-Muta'al al-Qereti (foreman supervising building work), Ahmad al-Qereti (foreman).

Research in the area of Udjahorresnet's shaft tomb and the filling up of a section of the peripheral shafts threatened as a result of an earthquake in October 1992. The discovery of cemeteries from the early Old Kingdom and the beginning of research in the Mastaba of Ity from the 3rd Dynasty and in the nameless mastaba from the period at the end of the 3rd and beginning of the 4th Dynasty. Study in the Egyptian Museum. Photo-documentation of the monuments in the pyramid zone and in Luxor.

Select Bibliography of Books and Articles concerning Archaeological Excavations in the Pyramid Cemetery at Abusir

F.W. VON BISSING, *Das Re-Heiligtum des Königs Ne-woser-re (Rathures). I. Der Bau* (Berlin 1905). *II. Die kleine Festdarstellung* (Leipzig 1923). *III. Die grosse Festdarstellung* (Leipzig 1928)

H. BONNET, *Ein frühgeschichtliches Gräberfeld bei Abusir* (Leipzig 1928)

L. BORCHARDT, *Das Grabdenkmal des Königs Ne-user-re^c* (Leipzig 1907)

L. BORCHARDT, *Das Grabdenkmal des Königs Nefer-ir-ke3-re^c* (Leipzig 1909)

L. BORCHARDT, *Das Grabdenkmal des Königs Sa3hu-re^c I. Der Bau* (Leipzig 1910). *II. Die Wand bilder* (Leipzig 1913)

E. EDEL, S. WENIG, *Die Jahreszeitenreliefs aus dem Sonnenheiligtum des Königs Ne-user-re* (Berlin 1974)

R. LEPSIUS, *Denkmaeler aus Aegypten und Aethiopien. Abth. 1—6, Bd. 1—12* (Berlin 1849—1856)

R. LEPSIUS, *Denkmäler aus Aegypten und Aethiopien — Text I—V* (Leipzig 1897—1913)

J. DE MORGAN, *Découverte du Mastaba de Ptah-chepsés dans la nécropole d'Abou-sir*, in: *Revue archéologique 3 éme série — t. XXIV (Janvier-Juin 1894)*, (Paris 1984), 18—33

J. S. PERRING, *The Pyramids of Gizeh, from actual survey and measurement*, Part III (London 1842), pp. 5—9

H. RICKE, *Das Sonnenheiligtum des Königs Userkaf. I. Der Bau* (Kairo 1965), *II. Die Funde* (Wiesbaden 1969)

H. SCHÄFER, *Priestergräber und andere Grabfunde vom Ende des Alten Reiches bis zur Griechischen Zeit von Totentempel des Ne-user-re* (Leipzig 1908)

M. VERNER, *Abusir. I. The Mastaba of Ptahshepses. Reliefs. I/1* (Prague 1977)

M. VERNER, *Abusir. II. Baugraffiti der Ptahschepses-Mastaba* (Praha 1992)

H. VYSE, *Operations carried at the pyramids of Gizeh in 1837, with an account of a voyage into Upper Egypt, and an appendix. III* (London 1842), pp. 12—37

* * *

For the detailed Egyptological and archaeological bibliography relating to Abusir (up to 1974), see B. Porter, R. L. B. Moss, J. Málek, *Topographical Bibliography of Ancient Egyptian Hieroglyphic Texts, Reliefs, and Paintings. III. Memphis. Pt. 1* (2nd ed., Oxford 1974). The recent bibliography relating to Abusir (up to 1988) was published by M. Verner et al., *Unearthing Ancient Egypt 1958—1988 (Activities of the Czechoslovak Institute of Egyptology in Egypt)* (Praha 1990).

Chronological Table

EARLY DYNASTIC
PERIOD
(cca. 3,100 − 2,635 BC)

Dynasty 0
"Scorpion"
Ka
Narmer

1st Dynasty
Aha
Djer
Djet (Uadji)
Den (Udimu)
Anedjib
Semerkhet
Qa'a

2nd Dynasty
Hotepsekhemui
Nebre
Ninetjer
Peribsen
Khasekhemui

OLD KINGDOM
(cca. 2,635 − 2,130 BC)

3rd Dynasty
Nebka
Djoser
Sekhemkhet
Khaba
Huni

4th Dynasty
Sneferu
Cheops
Radjedef
Chephren
Mycerinus
Shepseskaf

5th Dynasty
Userkaf
Sahure
Neferirkare Kakai
Raneferef
Shepseskare
Niuserre
Menkauhor
Djedkare Isesi
Unas

6th Dynasty
Teti
Pepi I
Merenre I
Pepi II
Marenre II
Nitocris

7th/8th Dynasty
Ibi I
Iti
Imhotep

1ST INTERMEDIATE PERIOD
AND BEGINNING OF MIDDLE
KINGDOM
(cca. 2,134 − 1,991 BC)

9th/10th Dynasty
Cheti III. Nebkaure (?)
Merikare

11th Dynasty
Mentuhotep I
Antef I
Antef II
Antef III
Mentuhotep II
Mentuhotep III
Mentuhotep IV

MIDDLE KINGDOM AND 2ND
INTERMEDIATE PERIOD UP TO
HYKSOS DOMINATION OVER
EGYPT
(1,991 − cca. 1,650 BC)

12th Dynasty
Amenemhet I
Sesostris I
Amenemhet II
Sesostris II
Sesostris III
Amenemhet III
Amenemhet IV
Sobekneferu

13th Dynasty

14th Dynasty

2ND INTERMEDIATE PERIOD:
HYKSOS DOMINATION
(cca. 1,650 − 1,551 BC)

15th Dynasty
Khyan
Apophis

16th Dynasty

17th Dynasty
Intef V (?)
Tao I
Tao II
Kamose

NEW KINGDOM
(cca. 1,551 − 1,080 BC)

18th Dynasty
Ahmose
Amenophis I
Tuthmosis I
Tuthmosis II
Hatshepsut
Tuthmosis III
Amenophis II
Tuthmosis IV
Amenophis III
Amenophis IV − Akhenaten
Semenkhare
Tutankhamen
Ay
Horemhab

19th Dynasty
Ramesses I
Seti I
Ramesses II
Merenptah
Seti II
Amenmesse
Siptah
Twosret

20th Dynasty
Sethnakhte
Ramesses III
Ramesses IV
Ramesses V
Ramesses VI
Ramesses VII

Ramesses VIII
Ramesses IX
Ramesses X
Ramesses XI

3RD INTERMEDIATE PERIOD
(cca. 1,180 − 712 BC)

21st Dynasty
Smendes
Psusennes I
Amenemope
Siamun
Psusennes II
Herihor

22nd Dynasty
Sheshonq I
Osorkon I
Sheshonq II
Takelot I (?)
Osorkon II
Takelot II
Sheshonq III
Sheshonq V
Osorkon IV

23rd Dynasty
Pedubast
Sheshonq IV
Osorkon III
Takelot III
Rudamen

24th Dynasty
Tefnakht
Bekenrenef

LATE PERIOD
(cca. 712 − 332 BC)

25th Dynasty
Kashta
Piankhy
Shabaka
Shebitku
Taharqa
Tanutamun
Necho I

26th Dynasty
Psammetichus I
Necho II
Psammetichus II

Apries
Amasis
Psammetichus III

27th Dynasty
Cambyses
Darius I
Xerxes
Artaxerxes I
Darius II

28th Dynasty
Amyrtaios

29th Dynasty
Nepherites I
Psammuthis
Achoris

30th Dynasty
Nectanebes
Teos
Nectanebos

31st Dynasty
Artaxerxes III
Arses
Darius III

Index

GEOGRAPHICAL NAMES

MISCELLANEOUS

INSTITUTIONS & EXPEDITIONS

List of Illustrations

The author and photographer would like to offer their thanks to the Egyptian Museum in Cairo for allowing exhibit some of which are represented in this book, to be photographed.

Photographs in the book which were not taken by Milan Zemina are accompanied by the name of the photographer in brackets.

p. 111   Jean-Philippe Lauer by the red granite pyramidion of an obelisk discovered in April 1974 near the south-western corner of the mastaba of Ptahshepses.

p. 113   The Step Pyramid on the boundary of day and night.

p. 115   View of the pyramid cemetery at Giza from the south-east. The "bridge" in the foreground was in fact the great gate of a stone ceremonial wall which protected the royal cemetery from the south.

p. 116   The stepped tomb of the royal mother Khentkaus at Giza. (Archive of the Czech Institute of Egyptology, Kamil Voděra).

p. 117   Plan of the tomb complex of Khentkaus at Giza (by Salim Hassan).

p. 119   Detail from a relief depicting the goddess Nekhbet, protectress of the crown of Upper Egypt, with the vulture diadem on her head (by L. Borchardt).

p. 120   Fragment of a relief from the tomb of Mersetjefptah at Abusir, with the reamins of in inscription mentioning the mortuary temple of the royal mother (by H. Schäfer).

p. 120   View of the pyramid complex of the royal mother Khentkaus at Abusir (bottom right and in the background are the two small pyramid complexes L no. XXIV and L no. XXV, likewise just before excavations were started).

p. 121   View of the pyramid complex of the royal mother Khentkaus at Abusir during archaeological excavations.

p. 122   Plan of the royal mother Khentkaus's pyramid complex at Abusir.

p. 123   This inscription on a clay sealing from the reign of Djedkare mentions the unique title "Mother of the King of Upper and Lower Egypt (exercising office as) King of Upper and Lower Egypt".

p. 123   Found 15 cm beneath this sand drift was the disintegrated head of the only pillar still standing in the court of the mortuary temple of the royal mother Khentkaus at Abusir.

p. 123   Limestone pillars, one standing, one fallen with remains of hieroglyphic inscriptions containing the name and titles of the queen Khentkaus. Khentkaus's pyramid complex at Abusir.

p. 124   View of the entrance section of the extended mortuary temple of the queen Khentkaus at Abusir. In the background rises Neferirkare's pyramid.

p. 124   This small limestone column capital in the form of a lotus flower in full blossom was found in the mortuary temple of the queen Khentkaus at Abusir.

p. 124   Detail of a relief from Sahure's mortuary temple with the subsequently altered picture of the pharaoh Neferirkare (by L. Borchardt).

p. 125   Detail from an inscription on a standing pillar in the mortuary temple of the queen Khentkaus at Abusir: the queen Khentkaus is sitting on the throne, holding the *wadj* sceptre in her right hand and with the uraeus on her forehead.

p. 126   Detail of a picture of Khentkaus on a pillar at the original entrance to the queen's mortuary temple at Abusir.

p. 126   Detail of a picture of the queen Khentkaus with the uraeus on her forehead. Mortuary temple of the queen, Abusir.

p. 126   This limestone cylindrical seal belonging to the administrator of the granaries was discovered in the magazines of the mortuary temple of Khentkaus at Abusir.

p. 127   Clay sealing with hieroglyphic inscription and cartouche of the pharaoh Djedkare.

p. 127   Facsimile of inscription on the clay sealing.

p. 127   Amulet in the shape of a so-called 'sacred eye' found during excavations in Khentkaus's pyramid complex. Faience with coloured glaze. Late Period.

p. 128   Reconstruction of a potter's wheel, from a surviving turning plate found during excavations in Khentkaus's mortuary temple at Abusir.

p. 129   Detail of inscription on a fragment of the granite gate in front of the south-east corner of the tomb of the royal mother Khentkaus at Giza: additional features were added to the picture of the queen sitting on the throne.

p. 128   Fragments of a large storage vessel decorated with geometrical *motifs* and a small bird. These come from the Coptic stratum in Khentkaus's mortuary temple at Abusir. Red baked clay, remains of polychrome.

p. 128   Detail from inscription on the granite gate of Khentkaus's tomb at Giza. The picture of the royal mother has been augmented with the vulture diadem, beard and mace.

p. 130   Anthropoid wooden coffin from a burial of the Late Period found during excavations in Khentkaus's pyramid complex at Abusir.

p. 133   View of the Unfinished Pyramid from the summit of Neferirkare's pyramid just before excavations were started.

p. 134   Plan of Raneferef's pyramid complex (by M. Švec and O. Vosika).

p. 135   View of the largely uncovered pyramid complex of Raneferef from the top of Neferirkare's pyramid.

p. 136   View of Raneferef's pyramid complex from the south-east, from the ruins of pyramid L no. XXIV.

p. 137   Projection of Raneferef's mortuary temple on a map drawn up on the basis of geophysical measurements in front of the eastern wall of the Unfinished Pyramid. The projection confirms the accuracy of the geophysical measurements which enabled the expedition to locate the thick mudbrick enclosure walls of the temple (by V. Hašek).

p. 139   The gravel roof terrace of the Unfinished Pyramid. (Archive of the Czech Institute of Egyptology, Jan Brodský).

p. 139   Fragment of a faience tablet with cartouche of Raneferef from the pharaoh's mortuary temple at Abusir. (Archive of the Czech Institute of Egyptology, Jan Brodský).

p. 140   Horizontal cross-section at the foundation level and north-west cross-section of the Meidum pyramid showing how the stepped core of the monument was constructed with masonry arranged in slanted layers.

p. 141   Plan showing a horizontal cross-section across the crown of the Unfinished Pyramid. The broken line indicates the direction in which a trench was dug in the masonry of the monument. The trench confirmed that the core of the Unfinished Pyramid (and probably those of the other Abusir pyramids as well) was not constructed in inner slanted layers. Instead it was built out of irregular pieces of lower-quality limestone. Only on the outside were large precisely fitted blocks of limestone used.

p. 141   In several places the mudbrick masonry of Raneferef's mortuary temple has survived to a surprising height.

p. 142   The hypostyle hall in the south-western part of Raneferef's mortuary temple represents the earliest example of its type in ancient Egypt yet discovered.

p. 143   Limestone six-stemmed papyrus column from Niuserre's mortuary temple at Abusir (according to L. Borchardt). Similar columns, although made of wood and smaller in size, originally adorned the column hall of Raneferef's mortuary temple.

p. 143   The extraordinary artistic and historical value of Raneferef's statue, its head shielded by the falcon god Horus, has been recognized by its reproduction on a postage stamp.

p. 144   Raneferef sitting on the throne. In his right hand, placed on his breast, he holds the ruler's mace. The pharaoh is dressed in a short skirt. A uraeus, probably made of gold, originally adorned his forehead. The statue, originally approximately 35 cm in height, has a low base. Rose limestone. Today Raneferef's statue is stored in the

Egyptian Museum in Cairo. (Archive of the Czech Institute of Egyptology, Jan Brodský)

p. 145   The head of Raneferef's statue is shielded from the back by the outspread wings of the falcon god Horus, whose earthly incarnations the pharaoh was considered to be. The statue thus very eloquently expresses the pharaoh's exceptional position and universal power. (Archive of the Czech Institute of Egyptology, Jan Brodský)

p. 146   Detail of the head and chest of the statue of Raneferef striding. The ruler wears the crown of Upper Egypt on his head. In his right hand, which is placed on his breast, he holds the ruler's mace. Basalt. Originally the whole statue, which now lacks several pieces, was approximately 80 cm. high. The statue is today in the Egyptian Museum in Cairo (JE 98181). (Archive of the Czech Institute of Egyptology, Jan Brodský)

p. 147   *Reis* Ahmad al-Qereti with the find of the first two fragments of the basalt statue of the pharaoh Raneferef striding.(Archive of the Czech Institute of Egyptology, Josef Grabmüller)

p. 147   Head of a statue of the pharaoh Raneferef. He is wearing the head-covering *nemes* and a long ritual beard is tied to his chin. Diorite. The head with the beard is 13.2 cm high. The statues is now in the Egyptian Museum in Cairo (JE 98180). (Archive of the Czech Institute of Egyptology, Jan Brodský)

p. 148   Head of a young man with hair cut short and a moustache. Alabaster. The head is 9.8. cm high. It was found together with fragments of a sculpture of the pharaoh Raneferef but shows none of the symbols of royal office. The identity of the man represented is therefore debatable. Egyptian Museum in Cairo (JE 98179). (Archive of the Czech Institute of Egyptology, Jan Brodský)

p. 148   Detail of the upper half of a statuette of a captive Asian chieftain discovered in Raneferef's mortuary temple. The chieftain was represented kneeling and with hands bound behind his back. His shoulder-length hair is tied with a headband and he has a pointed beard. The statuette was originally inserted in a larger object, perhaps a throne or a *naos*. Wood, 15.5 cm high. Egyptian Museum in Cairo (JE 98182). (Archive of the Czech Institute of Egyptology, Jan Brodský)

p. 149   Statuette of kneeling Libyan (?) captive found in Raneferef's mortuary temple. The man has his hands bound behind his back and long hair reaching to his shoulders. He is dressed in a short skirt. Wood, 14.1 cm high. Egyptian Museum in Cairo (JE 98182). (Archive of the Czech Institute of Egyptology, Jan Brodský)

p. 149   Statuette of a kneeling Nubian captive found in Raneferef's mortuary

temple. He is dressed in a short skirt and wears a wig. Wood., 14.1 cm high. Egyptian Museum in Cairo. (Archive of the Czech Institute of Egyptology, Jan Brodský)

p. 149   Relief decoration of the captive enemies of Egypt from Sahure's mortuary temple at Abusir (by L. Borchardt).

p. 150   Bust of the pharaoh Raneferef, his head adorned by the *nemes*. The bust is a fragment of a statue which originally represented the ruler sitting on his throne. Basalt. The bust is 23.8 cm high and is now in the Egyptian Museum in Cairo (JE 98177). (Archive of the Czech Institute of Egyptology, Jan Brodský)

p. 151   Fragment of a fritt tablet with pictures of deities. The raised figures of the deities were modelled with paste and then covered by thin gold leaf. The fragment (8 x 5.5 cm), found in Raneferef's mortuary temple at Abusir, is now in the Egyptian Museum in Cairo. (Archive of the Czech Institute of Egyptology, Jan Brodský)

p. 151   *Peseshkef* knife in the shape of a swallow-tail, conical limestone bowl and conical basalt bowl. These were cult objects used in the ceremony of the Opening of the Mouth. The knife, made of grey-black slate, is 16.7 cm long, the limestone bowl if 4 cm high and the basalt bowl is 3 cm high. They were all found in Raneferef's mortuary tomb and are now in the Egyptian Museum in Cairo (JE 97340). (Archive of the Czech Institute of Egyptology, Jan Brodský)

p. 152   The hieratic sign *nmt* (butcher's block with knife sticking into it), used in writing the name 'Sanctuary of the Knife', appears several times on the potsherds of grease vessels discovered during excavation of Raneferef's mortuary temple.

p. 152   Flint knife and blades found in Raneferef's mortuary temple.

p. 153   Diorite bowls at the moment when they were discovered in Raneferef's mortuary temple. (Archive of the Czech Institute of Egyptology, Jan Brodský)

p. 153   On the inner surface of two of the three diorite bowls from Raneferef's mortuary temple are visible traces of red ochre. (Archive of the Czech Institute of Egyptology, Jan Brodský)

p. 153   On the edge of the inner surface of one of the diorite bowls the inscription, "Sneferu, King of Upper and Lower Egypt" is lightly incised. (Archive of the Institute of Egyptology, Jan Brodský)

p. 153   Wooden implements used in the era of the pyramid builders: a hoe, mallet and drag-sleds (H. Schäfer and L. Borchardt).

p. 154   Fragment of the anthropoid coffin of the funerary priest Khuiankh. The priest was buried at the beginning of the Middle Kingdom in the ruins of 'The Sanctuary of

the Knife' which formed a part of Raneferef's pyramid complex. Wood with remains of polychrome. (Archive of the Czech Institute of Egyptology, Josef Grabmüller)

p. 154   Detail of the inner surface of the wooden box sarcophagus in which the anthropoid coffin of the funerary priest Khuiankh was placed. The so-called 'list of offerings' is recorded on the inner surface of the sarcophagus. (Archive of the Czech Institute of Egyptology, Josef Grabmüller)

p. 155   Abusir shepherd. VI

p. 157   In Egypt today papyrus grows only in newly established plantations. (Dale Osborn)

p. 158   The Nile near el-Minya.

p. 159   Late Period tombs demolished by "sabbakhin".

p. 160   Part of a papyrus scroll from Raneferef's temple archive.

p. 161   Mme. Paule Posener-Kriéger was present at the excavations in Raneferef's mortuary temple at Abusir at the moment when the most beautiful of Raneferef's statues was discovered. In this photograph she is accompanied by Usama el-Hamzawi , an inspector of the Egyptian Antiquities Organisation. (Archive of the Czech Institute of Egyptology, Josef Grabmüller)

p. 162   Panel with a picture of the royal architect and scribe Hesyre from the magnate's tomb in North Saqqara. Hesyre is holding in his hand the emblems of his office: mace, staff and scribe's instruments. Wood, low relief. Egyptian Museum in Cairo (no.88).

p. 163   Plan showing the location of discoveries of papyri in the Abusir cemetery.

p. 163   Fragments of papyri from Raneferef's temple archive with remains of an old hieratic text.

p. 164   Incomplete scroll of papyrus from Raneferef's temple archive.

p. 163   Hieroglyphic transcription of a text on a fragment of papyrus from the archive of Neferirkare's mortuary temple. The text contains the names of the people to whom the supplies (not precisely specified) flowing into the mortuary temple must be allocated (by P. Posener-Kriéger).

p. 165   Seated scribe writing on a papyrus scroll which is supported on his skirt stretched tight between his knees. Polychrome limestone, 51 cm high. Egyptian Museum in Cairo (no. 36).

p. 166   Water channel with flowering hyacinths near Saqqara.

p. 167   Subordinate officials surrounding the vizier Ptahshepses on a relief decoration in his mastaba at Abusir.

Contents

Forgotten Pharaohs,
Lost Pyramids.
ABUSIR

by Prof. PhDr. Miroslav Verner, DrSc.
Photographs by Milan Zemina

Vydala Academia,
nakladatelství Akademie věd České republiky,
a
Škodaexport,
Praha 1994

Přebal, vazba a grafická úprava Ivan Urbánek
Redaktorka publikace Jolana Malátková
Technický redaktor Antonín Bartoušek

Vydání 1.
Ediční číslo 6875
Vytiskla Polygrafia, a. s., Svobodova 1, Praha 2

ISBN 80-200-0022-4